The Cat Owner's

VETERINARY HANDBOOK

The Cat Owner's
VETERINARY HANDBOOK

John Bower

THE CROWOOD PRESS

First published in 2009 by
The Crowood Press Ltd
Ramsbury, Marlborough
Wiltshire SN8 2HR

www.crowood.com

British Library Cataloguing-in-Publication Data
A catalogue record for this book is available from the British
Library.

ISBN 978 1 84797 128 9

Dedication
To Boony, Becky, Tom and Jack.
Sophie and Rachel.
All in The Veterinary Hospital Group, Estover, Plymouth

Disclaimer
The author and the publisher do not accept any responsibility in
any manner whatsoever for any error or omission, nor any loss,
damage, injury, or liability of any kind incurred as a result of the
use of any of the information contained in this book, or reliance
upon it. This book is not in any way intended to replace, or
sidestep, the veterinary surgeon and, if in doubt about any aspect
of their cat's health, readers should seek professional advice from
a qualified veterinarian.

Designed and typeset by Focus Publishing, Sevenoaks, Kent

Printed and bound in Singapore by Craft Print International Ltd

Contents

Foreword

In 1994 my father, Alf Wight – better known as James Herriot – released his final publication; it was called *James Herriot's Cat Stories*. This book, as with many other Herriot titles, was an immediate best-seller. Not only was James Herriot such an accomplished and popular author, but the public's love and fascination for the feline race ensured that copies of the book would fly off the shelves within weeks of publication. Within its pages the tremendous variation in character to be found among cats was amply illustrated. He loved cats, from the rough tabby to the sleekly groomed show cat, and in his many years of treating them, they never failed to fascinate him.

I too, when working in my father's practice, was intrigued by the feline character. Compared to dogs, cats seemed to possess a peculiar independence. One day, many years ago, my ample and extremely well-spoken neighbour shouted over the garden wall from her adjoining field with a warning. 'Jim', she cried, 'my friend's dog Pockets is coming to stay for a day or two. She is a big dog with a reputation as a cat killer, and I am worried about your cat! If she comes into my field when Pockets is there, it may well be the end of her!'

My cat, Crumpet, a hairy, slit-eyed, inscrutable feline was around nine years old at the time. I had acquired her from one of my farming clients, and from the day I bought her home, she had displayed an effortless ability to deal with any hazard that life as a hunting, foraging cat could throw in her way. 'Thanks for the warning, Mrs Withycombe!' I replied, 'but Crumpet has always done exactly as she wished. If she intends to visit your field as usual, I have little doubt that she will!'

'Well I hope she will be alright, Jim. You have been warned!'

As my neighbour stepped serenely back into her cottage, I began to have doubts. I was most certainly not going to confine my cat to the house for an indefinite period of time, but nevertheless I was worried.

A day or two later, I was astonished to hear a commotion coming from the field. I could see a large black dog, barking excitedly and jumping up and down in the long grass. Tufts of hair, clumps of grass, dirt and assorted debris flew into the air. Suddenly there was a distressed series of high-pitched howls, followed by the sight of the dog fleeing at high speed towards the sanctuary of Mrs Withycombe's cottage. Moments later, my cat stalked imperiously out of the field, before sitting impassively on the lawn where she began to delicately groom her coat. Another of life's irritating little obstacles had been brushed aside. Within a minute or two, the languidly upper-class tones of Mrs Withycombe drifted in from the field, 'Round one to Crumpet, I believe!'.

Crumpet survived until the stately age of twenty-two years, but especially in her later years, she grew gradually more dependent upon us. Visits to our surgery became more common as she underwent several operations, including repair to a broken leg, hospitalization for a shattered pelvis and, in the last two years of her life, enucleation of a badly damaged eye.

Cats seem such resilient creatures that it is easy to forget that they can suffer from a wide variety of ailments, many of them peculiar to cats; and it is part of our responsibility as owners to be able to recognize when our cats need some support, and when they need expert attention from the veterinary surgeon.

The Cat Owner's Veterinary Handbook has been especially written to help those who love their cats. The author is a highly experienced veterinary surgeon, heading a large veterinary hospital, with many years of dealing with countless different problems in his feline patients. It is always an added bonus for the busy veterinary surgeon when the owner of the cat has a true understanding of their pet and some knowledge of the problem that it is experiencing. The importance of cooperation between the veterinary surgeon and an intelligent, well-informed owner cannot be over-emphasized.

This book deals, in clear and concise text, with diseases and conditions that a cat owner could face. Psychological and behavioural problems are not forgotten, and there is an excellent chapter on the old cat, including the subject of euthanasia, one of the most difficult and emotive procedures for both the veterinary surgeon and the owner.

Clear illustrations throughout add to the pleasure of reading this book. I have been retired from veterinary practice for more than seven years, but reading it has brought back many memories, as well as reminding me of the significance of that unique human–animal bond, and the equally important understanding between cat owners and their veterinary surgeons.

The Cat Owner's Veterinary Handbook is to be recommended to all those who love cats and who understand that, for the continuance of their well-being, these wonderfully adequate and independent animals do depend upon us – the great, cat-loving British Public.

James A. Wight BVMS MRCVS

Acknowledgements

I am indebted to the following who have helped with the book in one way or another, either checking my facts, making suggestions or providing photographs: Adam Coulson, Bayer plc Animal Health Division; Professor Danielle Gunn-Moore, The Feline Advisory Bureau; Gill Harris; Graham Campbell; Jasmin Malm; Joan Simmons; Joanne Hewitson; Karen Sargent; Dr Kate Chandler; Kate Salmon; Katie Lenton; Nicola Ackerman; Professor Peter Bedford, Petplan; Dr Philippe Moreau; Sanjaya Kanagasundaram; Sally Colledge; Sarah Heath; Sarah Mitchell; Derek Colligan; Stephen O'Shea; many of the staff in The Veterinary Hospital Group in Plymouth, and especially Mel Lean for the front cover photo of Pebbles, Louise Sumner for the back cover photos (www.louisesumnerphotography.co.uk) and Alex Hedger for his photograph of the Scottish Wild Cat (www.flickr.com/photos/alexhedger). As I am no artist, the input of David Youngs, Katherine Whiteley and Keith Field, who between them provided all of the diagrams, has been invaluable. I must especially thank my wife, Caroline Bower, who is both a veterinary surgeon and animal behaviourist for writing Chapters 2 and 19, and for her general help with the book. Finally, I am delighted that Jim Wight MRCVS, the son of 'James Herriot' and a good friend agreed to read the book and write the foreword, as his father did for the companion volume *The Dog Owner's Veterinary Handbook*.

Introduction

As a veterinary surgeon and cat owner myself, having bred and shown Siamese in the past, and currently as the proud owner of a fine sixteen-year-old Moggie, Millie, I know how important cats are to their people. They are certainly more independent than dogs, which are pack animals, and therefore cats fit into family life in a more mysterious fashion. It has been said that we don't own cats but rather that they choose to live with us, and this seems very true. Nevertheless, having a cat as company, whether on our lap when watching TV or when carrying out domestic chores in the house or garden, is somehow a very gratifying experience.

It is the very fact that cats are individuals rather than pack members that makes a book like this more interesting. It is easy to tell when a dog is ill – he comes and tells you because he feels safe revealing this with his pack around to protect him. If a cat shows he is ill or in pain, it makes him feel more vulnerable to attack, so he may hide his illnesses to a great extent. I hope this book explains some of the mysteries of how cats function, what can go wrong with their physiology and how to recognize it.

The Cat Owner's Veterinary Manual is aimed at the responsible cat owner who is keen to learn more about the cat, how his body functions and his special disease problems. It is, in reality, a text book on the cat but written in a more readable form than the usual reference books. Accepting that the cat is invariably 'one of the family', I have not referred to a cat as 'it' but rather as 'he' to avoid the clumsy 'he or she' and hope the reader will forgive me. Where the problem or reference is specifically that of a female cat or queen, I have of course referred to her as 'she'. In a similar vein, I have mostly referred to the vet as 'she', again to avoid the clumsy alternative and not necessarily because some 80 per cent of new veterinary graduates are female!

The manual begins by explaining the cat in his healthy state and gives guidelines on how to recognize if he is indeed healthy. Normal behaviour of cats is explained and why they are so individualistic and different from dogs, as well as how to acquire, settle in, feed and care for your new kitten or kittens. After a section about the prevention and treatment of the common infectious diseases of cats, and of their parasites, both internal and external, the bulk of this manual examines the cat system by system. Firstly I describe the normal structure and function of each system and then the more common disease problems of that system with their symptoms and treatments. Chapters then follow on breeding cats and the potential associated problems, behavioural problems and how to handle them, accidents and emergencies and useful first-aid advice. The final chapter is about the special problems of the older cat, including a section on the emotive subject of euthanasia.

The Cat Owner's Veterinary Manual is written in practical, easily understood terms and explains the cat and his problems as seen in a busy small-animal veterinary hospital practice with a team of some twelve vets and over twenty veterinary nurses. It will not replace the veterinary surgeon but it is hoped it will become a readable reference book for the interested cat owner.

Chapter 1
The Healthy Cat

To understand your cat and how he behaves, it is necessary to consider both the instinctive behaviour of his ancestors and wild counterparts, and his adaptation to living with man for centuries.

ORIGINS

The European or African wild cats are almost certainly the ancestors of the domestic cat, which explains some of the behaviours of our modern-day cats. These wild cats are not pack animals like their larger cousins, the lions, but live individual lives and hold territories of about 3km² each. They have to defend themselves and hunt alone without a pack around to help them. They were probably originally attracted to rodents around grain stores as man became less nomadic and started to farm, and were gradually welcomed by humans for this purpose. Gradually, their close association with man grew until today when they either serve a purpose killing vermin or, more usually, are close companions within the family unit.

Due to the various habitats in which the wild cats are found, there is a wide range of coat colour and markings, which vary from a pale sandy colour in the semi-desert and grassland areas to a darker grey/brown in the more afforested areas. Markings vary from tabby stripes to spots, and all these variations are to be seen in our domestic cats to this day.

Our domestic cats usually hunt at night, as do the wild cats, and the various rodent species also form the main part of the African wildcat's diet, although other prey species include hare, rabbits, insects, birds and small reptiles. Feral cats (domestic cats turned semi-wild) in the UK may live happily in small, related colonies or family groups, but they still hunt alone. These colonies are healthier if caught, neutered, vaccinated, ear-tipped for recognition and re-released. In a domestic environment, a cat is also most likely to be compatible with a relative, particularly a sibling. In the UK, most cats are mixed breed, usually called domestic cats or Moggies, either domestic shorthaired or domestic longhaired, but of course there is also a large variety of individual breeds of cat from which to choose.

RELATIONSHIP WITH HUMANS

The relationship that develops between people and their cats is very strong indeed. Until one has owned a cat it is difficult to realize how much pleasure a cat can bring. Research shows that nowadays, the cat is regarded as a member of the family, but not a child substitute, or surrogate, rather an equivalent member. We talk to the cat, play games with it, discipline it, feed it, spoil it, cuddle it and chastise it using the same level of conversation that we would with a child. Furthermore, when we lose the cat, whether unexpectedly or with age, we can suffer enormous grief. The relationship is powerful and can be two-way, as the cat can derive as much pleasure and security out of it as the owner. Unlike a dog though, he is rarely unquestioningly faithful and loving, and in my experience, if he doesn't like the set-up in the home, he will move home and adopt someone else!

This characteristic of being regarded as a family member has led to their successful involvement in certain forms of medical therapy – especially of mentally ill patients who find they can communicate with cats but may not be able to relate to humans. Pet cats are marvellous therapy for the elderly and lonely, and the cat in the nursing or residential home is an eagerly anticipated resident or visitor.

HEALTH SIGNS

In general, a healthy cat *looks* healthy. It does not take a vet to recognize a healthy cat. Most owners, in fact, can tell their cat is unwell before their vet, because they are attuned to all the small behaviour patterns and characteristics that their cat shows every day. If these change, then something may be wrong.

A healthy cat's eyes are bright and alert. They glisten slightly due to their healthy tear film and, apart from the small amount of 'sleep' in the inner corners, there should be no discharge. His nose is usually cold and wet, although a warm nose does not necessarily indicate illness. There should be no discharge from healthy nostrils, although a little clear fluid can be normal. His ears are also alert, he has excellent hearing and is responsive to sounds around him, whether it be the food bowl, the fridge door, or a small rodent moving in the undergrowth. The inside of his ear flap is silky in texture and there will be no wax visible, nor will there be any unpleasant smell. He will only occasionally scratch his ear.

A healthy cat's coat, which you should groom regularly, especially if the coat is long or thick, will be glossy and feel pleasant to the touch. He will not itch excessively, there will be no scurf or matts, no bald areas or scabs, and his coat will not have an unpleasant smell. He may, however, continuously shed hairs (moult) because most cats live indoors where it is warm most of the day, and their bodies becomes confused as to which season of the year it is.

The teeth of a healthy cat should be white and smooth. If they are yellow and dull there may be plaque formation – a deposit on the teeth formed by chemical change of leftover food particles. Where the tooth meets the gum there

This cat is obviously one of the family!

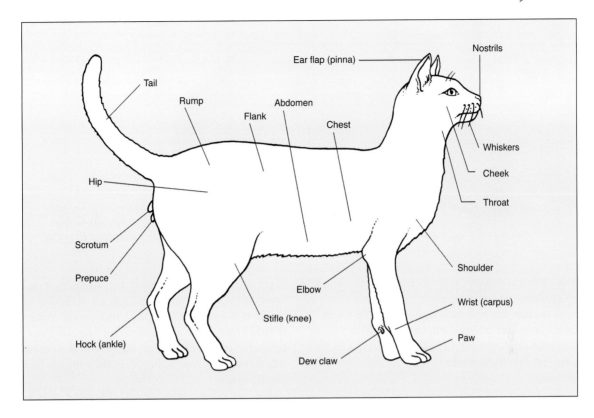

Fig 1 *Points of a cat (male).*

may be inflammation, as the plaque problem leads to gum disease, which, again, results in a foul smell to his breath (halitosis). The answer, of course, is dentistry, which is covered in a later section.

A cat's claws should not be broken or too long, but they are very sharp to allow him to catch his prey! Just like human nails, there is a short non-sensitive tip. Cats continually need to be sharpening their claws by using a scratching post, or in the wild, a tree trunk or similar. If the claws are too long, the claw will break off, exposing the sensitive nail-bed area, which is the equivalent of the pink part of human nails. The front feet normally have four toes each, plus a fifth (dew claw), which is equivalent to our thumb. Most cats are born with just four toes on the hind feet, although a few are also born with dew claws, and sometimes extra toes on both front and hind feet. These cats are generally known as polydactyl. These extra claws invariably require clipping from time to time.

A healthy cat will pass stools (faeces) once or twice daily depending on diet (more roughage, more stools), his individual digestive system, temperament, breed and opportunity. It is important to realize this normal variation and not worry if your cat is very different in his habits to the neighbour's cat.

Apart from normal cleaning, a cat will pay little attention to his anus. Excess licking or scooting usually indicates that something is wrong.

An un-neutered male tom cat will urinate several times a day, but will very often also spray small amounts of urine around his territory to let other cats know it is his domain. In fact, all cats are likely to spray to some extent – it is a normal part of their behavioural repertoire, but un-neutered cats spray more frequently. This can cause problems if it is in the house! Female cats or queens, will also do this, especially when calling (in season). Cats neutered early, before maturity, spray much less often. An increase in the number of times a cat of either sex urinates

A healthy British shorthair Blue Cat.

may indicate disease, especially if accompanied by straining or haemorrhage.

A healthy cat will look in good bodily condition – not too fat and not too thin. Many cats nowadays are overweight, so be careful not to let your cat join these ranks!

DIET

Cats are obligate carnivores, i.e. they must eat meat and cannot be fed a vegetarian diet. A cat will usually be ready for his meal and (surprise, surprise) research has shown that cats like a mouse-sized meal several times a day! So once adult, he should be fed both wet and dry food as several meals a day. The complete dried food can be left down for him to nibble on and off throughout the day. The food should be a balanced meal of protein, fat and carbohydrates, vitamins, minerals and trace elements, which are all found in the better quality dried and wet foods. Water should be available all the time for him, and, surprisingly, cats prefer large water bowls so their whiskers don't touch the sides; they do not like plastic bowls.

For an overweight cat, a slimming diet is needed where the calorie intake is restricted so that his fat deposits are reconverted into energy, resulting in weight loss. It is important to appreciate that feeding recommendations are only guidelines – all cats vary and the important thing is to correlate food with weight and activity. If your cat is overweight, seek advice from your veterinary practice.

Good-quality, dried, prepared foods are a perfectly acceptable diet for cats, provided attention is paid to water intake. Many cats fed only wet food drink very little water, as they obtain their requirements from the water in the food, but a bowl of water should always be available regardless of his diet. They often prefer the taste of rain water to tap water.

In my experience, there are two main nutritional problems: obesity and diarrhoea. Both of these problems are usually caused because the owner humanizes the cat, i.e. feeds the cat the type and sometimes the quantity of food he or she would like to eat. Cats do not need much food in comparison with a human. Never overfeed your cat.

Suitable bowls for food and water.

Chapter 2
Normal Cat Behaviour

Caroline Bower

As a proud cat owner, one of the most important things for you to learn is how to keep your cat contented. In order to do this you must 'think cat', in other words understand how the cat likes to live, how he thinks and what his needs are. Failure to do this can lead to behaviour problems and, in some cases, stress-related health problems.

Many people interpret cats' behaviour as though they were small dogs. They are not, so unfortunately this leads to misreading of cat behaviour, and often the wrong decisions and actions follow, particularly when a behaviour problem exists. So to begin with I will examine the most important points about normal, natural cat behaviour and how this may be used to keep our domestic cat happy.

UNDERSTANDING YOUR CAT

Social Behaviour

Cats are not pack animals. In the wild they are solitary predators who co-exist in certain situations as colonies or affiliated family groups, and the size of the group is likely to be determined by the food supply. This also occurs in the UK and most countries, where groups of domestic cats live wild in feral cat groups. However, cats do not have the sophisticated group communication systems that dogs have to help avoid injury in conflict, i.e. appeasement, submission, and so on, so if cats argue it usually ends in injury and even when one cat runs away, it still gets bitten by the aggressor, usually on the tail! Dogs posture and vocalize but usually avoid injury within their own pack. Dogs also join forces when the pack is threatened by an impostor and hunt in a co-operative way, whereas cats act alone in both these situations.

In a domestic context, cats in a multi-cat household may form a social bond, or they may tolerate each other, or there may be active dislike between them. It can be difficult to interpret the difference between basic tolerance and dislike unless owners are very observant and understand feline body language, which is often subtle. There does not have to be hissing and fur flying to prove mutual dislike. Think of it as a group of people living together in a house or flat who don't actually enjoy each others' company, who may actually dislike each other, but are forced to co-exist. What happens in such a situation is that there tends to be avoidance and minimal communication. The same is true of cats that are not socially bonded in a multi-cat household. Where social unrest or unease exists, the cats are often stressed and this can lead to

A cat is not a small dog.

behaviour problems or stress-related illnesses, such as cystitis, inflammatory bowel disease or skin disease. Stress-related diseases tend to increase in relation to the number of cats in the home and the number of hours spent indoors.

Cats that are bonded tend to cuddle up to sleep together, groom and rub against each other. If they all sit separately, tend to turn their backs, and particularly if they avoid eye contact, that means they are just tolerating each other. If there is veiled aggression, such as staring and barring access to food resources, this is potentially very stressful, particularly for the intimidated cat.

Cats in a multi-cat household may remain as individuals or form sub-groups within the home. Careful observation of their postures and behaviours will help to identify what pattern you have amongst your own cats.

It is important that cats have the option to get away from other cats, other pets and people in the household should they wish to. Being forced into close contact all the time is a common source of stress for cats. Too much attention from other pets and humans can also be stressful. If you remember that the cat is by nature solitary, this is not surprising. Ensure that your cat can choose a variety of places to go: indoors, outdoors, upstairs downstairs, with or without company.

Hiding in a high piece of furniture.

If you intend to keep more than one cat you would be well advised to get two cats or kittens at the same time, who have been raised together, and the best bet is a sibling pair, i.e. litter mates. Introduction of a new cat or kitten to a household where the original cat or cats are well-established can be disastrous, or at best, disappointing. There is absolutely no guarantee that they will enjoy each other's company.

Feeding and Drinking Habits

Cats are solitary hunters and in the wild where they have to fend for themselves, they eat prey species such as rodents and birds. Insects and invertebrates may also be eaten and the exact composition of the diet varies according to which country, climate and season they are in. They are also carnivorous, unlike dogs who are omnivorous, and for preference will eat ten to twenty small meals per day.

In the wild, cats tend to kill their prey and eat it and they need to do this to survive. However,

Cats in tension. These cats are tolerating each other but note they avoid eye contact.

Cats are natural hunters.

the motivation to hunt is strong in many domestic cats, even when they are very well fed by their owners. It is known that predatory and feeding behaviour are motivated by different parts of the brain; this explains why cats will hunt and kill their prey but may not eat it, and why they tend to enjoy toys and games that mimic the hunting sequence, i.e. stalking, chasing, pouncing and grabbing.

Feeding cats large meals twice daily is not suitable and can also actually encourage obesity. Because the cat is an obligate carnivore, the diet should contain high levels of protein and fat and low levels of carbohydrate. The cat's metabolism is adapted to utilize fat and protein as the main energy sources. Feeding cheaper brands that contain a higher proportion of carbohydrate will encourage obesity and other related diseases such as diabetes. Feeding good-quality, dry food and leaving it available all day allows the cat to help himself to frequent small meals.

Cats tend to have individual preferences for food and many enjoy a bit of variety. Always offer a good quality brand of food but consider varying the flavour. Also ensure you give all the cats separate bowls and do not force cats that are not in the same socially bonded group to eat alongside each other.

A word about water; it is important to encourage regular intake of fresh water, particularly if the cat is fed an all dry diet. Many cats prefer the taste of rain water to tap water. Leaving tap water to de-fluorinate by standing it in a jug before placing in the bowl can improve palatability. Also ensure there are several water bowls around the house, especially if there are

Cats prefer to eat ten to twenty small meals a day.

Cat greeting and scent marking the owner.

several cats living there. Consider collecting rain water, or filter your water. Running water in a cat drinker fountain appeals to some, as does a dripping tap. Offer several different types of containers, and try flavoured ice cubes (fish or meat stock) in the water.

Territorial Instincts

Cats like to have a territory of about 100m² within which they have a secure core where they sleep, eat and toilet in safety. In the wider territory the cat will explore and hunt. Cats use various means of marking to provide signals to other cats around their territory, and also to enhance their own feeling of safety and security. Most of the signals are scent marks but they may also be visual. Scent is particularly important in the cat's world for giving and receiving information. The cat has scent glands in various parts of the body, in particular the chin and cheeks, the flanks and the anus. Pheromones are produced in these scent glands. Hence, when a relaxed cat wishes to leave a scent mark somewhere, he will often rub his chin or flanks against an upright surface, depositing a smell there containing a pheromone signal. Chin and flank marking are often used in greeting behaviour between friendly cats and when a cat greets their owner. Anal sac scents are deposited when a cat defecates.

Stronger scent marks are produced by urine and faeces deposits. Toileting in specific areas around the territory is normal for the cat. Urine spraying is also normal behaviour in the wider territory of the cat and is used as a means of marking boundaries. Persistent spraying within the *core* of the territory can be a sign of behavioural disturbance and is dealt with later in this section.

Scratching on posts, trees and other upright surfaces is also quite normal behaviour and serves several functions: it leaves a visual mark for other cats to see, and it helps to maintain good health of the claws. As the claws grow they suffer wear and tear, especially in an active outdoor, hunting and tree-climbing cat, and the outer layer of the claws must be shed to allow exposure of the fresh layer growing underneath. Scratching furniture and carpets in the home is practised by many cats, especially those not given the opportunity to scratch elsewhere, but an increase in frequency can be related to anxiety or changes in the environment that the cat finds stressful. Many cats will find their own scratching surfaces outdoors but some, particularly indoor cats, must have a scratching surface provided in order to allow this normal behaviour. Scratch posts and boards are widely manufactured; the most attractive to the cat will have vertical striations, which allow the cat to run his claws down the ridges in the fabric.

A word about perfumed, plug-in diffusers, which are used to keep the home smelling pleasant; most cats do not like those with a citrus smell and many will find it stressful to have such a product in their core environment.

Cats are happiest when they have a variety of options as to where to spend their time. A timid cat is likely to avoid crowds of visitors and noisy situations, and may choose to disappear outside, upstairs or on to the highest piece of furniture he can find until peace is restored.

Toileting

Cats need a safe, undisturbed place to toilet. Outdoor cats will often toilet entirely outside, although they need access to a litter tray if shut in overnight, when they are ill or when the weather is bad. Indoor cats need access to a litter tray at all times. Cats with access to outdoors will tend to choose their own places to go, such as areas of soft soil, gravel or sand (children's sand-pits are a favourite!). Cats usually try to bury their deposits, especially the faeces.

The type of litter to use in a tray should be that which the cat finds most appealing and preferably the same litter on which it was trained as a kitten. In general, cats tend to prefer soft, scratchable litters like sand and fine gravel, whereas woodchip and odorized litters are less popular.

There should always be more litter trays than the number of cats so that they can choose to pass urine and faeces in different trays if they wish to, and can avoid toileting in the same tray as another cat if they want to. In addition, each tray should have clumps and solids lifted out on a daily basis, with the whole tray cleaned thoroughly two to three times a week.

It is essential that litter trays, if used, are situated in areas where the cat can toilet in private, where there is minimal disturbance or noise, and well away from food and water bowls, entry and exit points. Some cats, and owners, prefer covered litter trays. Litter trays must obviously be accessible, so when the older cat becomes less active and possibly has difficulty climbing up or over certain obstacles, such a stairs, it is important that they are placed in suitable positions.

Use of Space

This is important with reference to sleeping and resting behaviour, but also for enrichment of the cat's environment, particularly in the case of the indoor cats whose options are limited and are completely controlled by humans.

Sleeping and resting spaces can consist of various beds, boxes, cat igloos, cushions, radiator hammocks and furniture. Timid cats often choose higher resting surfaces, where they can survey their surroundings in safety. Obviously these spaces should be warm, draught free and secure for the cat, i.e. safe from boisterous dogs and over-attentive young children. Some cats like to hide under furniture, covers or bedding. Choice is important, particularly when there are several cats in the home. In some situations, even if cats don't like each other, they may co-exist without stress problems if they are able to avoid each other and are not forced to eat, sleep or toilet in the same areas.

Owners should help their cats to make the best use of vertical space, particularly if they have a relatively small house, and even more so

Litter tray containing litter in area of minimal disturbance.

if the cat is kept indoors. Ropes, ladders, ramps and climbing areas can greatly enhance the cat's environment, helping to relieve boredom, offering a variety of choices and giving the cat the option to escape from situations it finds unpleasant, such as the arrival of a noisy dog in the house.

AVOIDING PITFALLS WITH A NEW KITTEN

Give your kitten a few days to adjust to his new environment, don't over-face him with too many visitors and allow him plenty of time to rest; like human babies, young animals grow most when they are asleep!

Early Handling

An enlightened breeder or stray home worker should already have handled your kitten every day, got him used to being lifted off the ground, being gently stroked and groomed, and turned over to have his tummy stroked. In addition, more than one person should have handled him, preferably both sexes and a variety of ages. This type of upbringing from two to seven weeks is really important if you want a 'bomb-proof' family pet. The timing of this handling is related to the primary socialization phase of the kitten, when he is able to take new stimuli in his stride. Kittens that have been brought up in an isolated environment, such as a farm shed or a breeder's kennels where handling is not encouraged, tend to be timid and may remain less friendly throughout life. Friendliness and relaxed attitude are also related to genetic make-up, but the early environment and human handling plays an important part too, so when you visit the litter, check the temperament of the mother (and father if available to see), as well as the way they have been brought up. If you have a family with young children who will want to pick up and cuddle the cat, it is very important that you look into this. Many cat breeders are well aware of the importance of selecting their breeding cats for temperament as well as health and looks, and are also good at early handling. Make sure you find one of them! Then be careful to supervise small children holding the kitten to avoid accidents, and make sure the kitten is allowed plenty of time to rest in a quiet, warm and peaceful place. A kitten pen or box can be helpful and if you have a very busy household, find a room away from all the action for him to sleep.

A breeder handling kittens to socialize them.

Kitten playing with fishing toy.

Litter Training

Most kittens know how to use a litter tray when they arrive, so all you have to do is use the same type of litter tray and litter that the breeder has been using and follow the rules for where the litter tray should be situated. If he is not fully litter trained yet, start him off with some fine gravel litter or sand to encourage him, as this is nice and soft on the paws. Restrict him to one room with the litter tray at one side and food, water and bed at the other. Avoid giving him the run of the house, as he may find somewhere to toilet that he likes better than his litter tray! Reward him by praising and giving a little food treat when he has 'performed'. He will soon get the idea.

Grooming

It is a good idea to start grooming while the kitten is young, especially if he is going to have long hair, which needs attention to stop it becoming matted. Start by ensuring he is happy to be stroked in all parts of the body, and then get him used to a soft brush or flannel, being very gentle. In due course he will accept a metal comb but do be careful not to hurt him.

Play

All normal kittens are playful and should be encouraged to play with toys, which provide exercise and an outlet for their energy and allow them to develop hunting behaviour. Avoid encouraging him to chase your feet or hands as this can inadvertently lead to play-related aggression later. It is best to encourage object play, which means throwing toys for him or dangling toys on strings. He will also enjoy playing with moving objects himself, such as plastic balls and rolled up balls of paper. Use your imagination; you can create cheap and entertaining toys out of cardboard boxes with holes cut in the sides, ropes hung in doorways, paper bags and corks swinging on strings, and so on. Pet shops, the internet and some vets' surgeries also sell good-quality toys for cats and kittens.

INDOORS VERSUS OUTDOORS

In the UK, a relatively small percentage of cats are kept indoors, and the usual reasons why owners do not allow their cats to roam freely are to prevent road accidents, attack from other cats or dogs, and loss through theft or wandering. These are all laudable reasons but if one is to restrict the cat to an indoor environment it is most important to consider the situation from the cat's point of view. You now know that cats need variety and stimulation in their environment, as well as options and ability to escape from adverse conditions. The owner of an indoor cat must be particularly aware of these needs and ensure the cat is not bored, stressed, overcrowded, or lacking stimulation and exercise. My usual advice, if planning to get a kitten that is to be kept indoors, is to get two, preferably litter mates. That way they will both have company, stimulation and exercise through play. If you keep one indoor cat on his own, you must work hard to ensure you provide an interesting

A sunny outdoor pen.

which he can climb.

Indoor cats can be more prone to behaviour problems caused by lack of stimulation or stress, particularly if there is any social unrest in a multi-cat household. Given the natural behaviour of the cat, we are asking a lot when we expect the cat to cope with a tiny territory, using a litter tray only, and being confined with other cats, dogs and humans. However, careful planning, extra effort and an understanding of the cat's needs can help to overcome the difficulties.

INTRODUCING A NEW CAT OR KITTEN

If you wish to introduce an additional cat or kitten to a resident cat you must be most careful; there is no guarantee of success. As stated previously, the best combination of cats are sibling pairs. If you have had a pair of cats and you lose one of them, you will not necessarily be doing the remaining cat a favour by getting him a companion. He may be missing the cat that has gone, and cats can pine for months, but that does not mean he wants a stranger to take the place of his lost friend. Any new cat is likely to be in a separate 'group', therefore not bring companionship or comfort to the resident, and may bring stress.

In such a situation it is essential to consider the life-style and temperament of the resident cat, whether he has ever enjoyed the company of other cats in the past, whether he is actually more sociable with people, in which case extra attention and input from you may be more appropriate. If he is a cat who does not respond well to changes of company or environment, or he is very nervous with strangers and strange cats, he will probably be happier left alone. Look at ways of giving him more human companionship, make his meals interesting, and play actively with him, if he enjoys that.

If you are going to introduce a new cat or kitten you must ensure that they meet in a very controlled way over the first few weeks and, if possible, keep them apart until they have been introduced to each others' scent. This may be done by stroking the flank or cheeks of each cat with a soft cloth and exchanging cloths on to

environment with climbing and hiding places, choices of resting places, and you must be sure to play and interact frequently with him. Provide a scratch post or board, more than one litter tray, more than one food and water bowl, and vary the toys provided.

It can help the indoor cat if he is harness trained, so that the owner can safely take him outside for a change of scene. Introduce a light-weight cat harness, allow him time to get used to wearing it around the house, then attach a lightweight lead and start by wandering around the garden with him, letting *him* take *you* for a walk. If this works well you may consider going further afield, provided you avoid busy traffic areas or places where there may be loose dogs. Another possibility is to construct a large, outdoor cat pen of wood and wire netting where he may spend part of the day. He will still be restricted but he can watch the garden birds and insects and it is a change of scene for him. Provide shelter, ledges and boards or branches the resting place of the other cat. If the cats investigate the new scent and show no adverse reaction that is a good start.

Next, place a partially covered basket or pen in a room where the cats are to be introduced and put the new cat in for short, frequent periods, allowing the resident kitten to investigate. If there is no hissing or growling after meeting on a few occasions, allow them together but supervise closely. If you get a kitten, be sure not to let him chase and irritate the older cat, especially if this cat is not particularly playful. Let the kitten have an active play session and then have time to calm down before meeting the adult cat.

For the first few weeks there should be no unsupervised mixing and both cats should be kept apart unless you are there. The use of synthetic pheromone sprays or diffusers seems to help in some cases and these may be acquired from your vet. The pheromone in *Felifriend* can be wiped on to each cat to encourage direct mutual acceptance, whilst *Feliway*, in the form of a plug-in diffuser, tends to reduce stress in the environment once they are beginning to accept each other.

Feeding strange cats together is not helpful in developing acceptance or friendship. This is like making two people who have nothing in common, or dislike each other, sit down at the same table for every meal. Generally speaking, if this care is taken and the cats have not accepted each other after two to three weeks, the outlook is poor.

In a multi-cat household it is usual for groups of cats to develop, as described in section one. Alternatively, several individuals who do not gel together will just tolerate each other, and there may be stress issues in some or all of these cats. Do not force cats or groups of cats who do not get on well to feed together in the same area. Ideally use separate areas for all their resources, i.e. water and food bowls, litter trays and resting places. Also make good use of vertical space so that the cats can move away from each other if they want to.

Think carefully before adding a new cat to a household. The resident cat is not guaranteed to accept the new addition and may be happier with just human company.

Cat and kitten getting on well.

Chapter 3
You and Your Vet

THE VETERINARY SURGEON

There are seven universities in the UK that award a veterinary degree and all veterinary surgeons will have studied at one of these, or another European or foreign university, for at least five years for a veterinary degree, before being accepted as Members of the Royal College of Veterinary Surgeons (MRCVS). They are then entitled to place the relevant qualification after their name. For example, BVSc (Bachelor of Veterinary Science) is this author's qualification from Liverpool University, while another may be BVM+S, (Bachelor of Veterinary Medicine and Surgery) from Edinburgh University. All veterinary universities award their own degree but there is no difference between them – all recipients are equally qualified. Once a degree is awarded, Membership of the Royal College of Veterinary Surgeons follows and the letters MRCVS are added to the title on payment of an annual retention fee to the Royal College. Only then is the vet able to begin his or her professional life.

Increasingly now, vets from all over Europe and further afield, are coming to Britain to work here. To do so they are required to pass exams set by the Royal College of Veterinary Surgeons to the same standard as UK graduates and are not allowed to practise until they have received their MRCVS.

The university veterinary training course covers all animals from horses, farm animals and poultry, to dogs, cats and smaller children's pets and exotic animals. There is a tremendous amount to learn and to remember, so many vets in practice now tend to treat only certain species, or groups of species, such as horses, farm animals, or small animals (pets). There are

also many alternatives to working in general practice for a veterinary surgeon. Once qualified he or she may decide to enter the teaching side of the profession, or research, or work for the Department of the Environment, Food and Rural Affairs (DEFRA), a pharmaceutical or nutrition company or one of the animal charities. Another interesting fact is that, nowadays, over 70 per cent of the vets qualifying each year are female. This compares with about 20 per cent some thirty years ago.

Many vets in general practice now study for extra qualifications in subjects that are of particular interest to them. This may be in surgery, medicine, dermatology (skin diseases), ophthalmology (eye diseases), imaging (X-rays, ultrasound scanning and their interpretation), cardiology (heart and circulation), and animal behaviour, to name but a few. Most of these

The author outside his veterinary hospital.

postgraduate qualifications are at certificate level, but an even higher qualification is a diploma. A very useful referral service for particular problem cases for the general practitioner is therefore, being created.

THE VETERINARY PRACTICE

A typical small animal veterinary practice will treat dogs, cats, rabbits, and indeed many smaller species still, such as rats, guinea pigs and so on. It will consist of veterinary surgeons, veterinary nurses and ancillary staff. Some practices, such as our own, will be fairly large (we have twelve veterinary surgeons, over twenty veterinary nurses, and eight receptionists in the practice), while others may consist of just one veterinary surgeon and one nurse. All veterinary practices are required to provide a 24hr emergency service every day of the year, or arrange for another veterinary practice to do this for them. For instance, our practice now takes on the out-of-hours work for another five practices in the area and employs dedicated night vets and nurses who don't do any day-time work. A large part of your vet's normal working day, however, will be spent dealing with your pet's more routine problems, or giving advice on preventative medicine, such as vaccination and worming. In the practice there will be one or more consulting rooms where the vet carries out routine examinations and treatments, an operating theatre, X-ray and possibly scanning facilities, and a dispensary where medicines are stored. In addition, there will almost certainly be a ward where patients may be hospitalized overnight, as well as during the day, and many practices will have an on-site laboratory to help with diagnosis, and residential facilities for vets or nurses who are on-call over night.

The RCVS, the veterinary profession's governing body, launched the Practice Standards Scheme on 1 January 2005. It is the only scheme representing the veterinary profession and was set up to:

- establish a quality assurance framework to promote and maintain the highest standard of veterinary care;

The author's veterinary hospital.

- to make more information available about veterinary practices, and so give clients greater choice.

Tier 1 is the basic level, which all veterinary practices should attain; Tier 2 is a higher standard, including the ability to train veterinary nurses; and Tier 3 is the highest standard reached by, for instance, veterinary hospitals. Every accredited practice has volunteered to undergo rigorous inspection by a qualified inspector every four years and must meet the criteria appropriate for its type.

A fairly recent phenomenon is the development of cat-only practices. If there is one in your area it may be that your cat would prefer to attend it as there will be no dogs in the waiting-room or wards. On the other hand, more practices now have specific cat waiting-rooms or areas in the waiting-room, and wards for cats. The Feline Advisory Bureau, a well-known and effective charity dedicated to promoting the health and welfare of cats through improved feline knowledge in the UK, have started to list so-called cat-friendly practices.

Before turning up with your cat for the first time, it is important to contact a practice by telephone, or even call in to get a feel of the surgery if you don't know the practice. Most practices have set surgery times, usually in the morning and evening, and some also have afternoon surgeries. More practices nowadays

Cat-carrier with top opening.

The best cat-carriers are sturdy but light plastic ones that open through the top, as no cat really likes being pulled out of the front of a box – much better to be gently lifted out.

It is a good idea to get your cat or kitten accustomed to the box at home. Line it with some bedding and encourage the cat to use it to rest in by leaving it open in a favourite place. Secure the box carefully for travel – cats do not appreciate being tossed about in a moving vehicle. When you arrive at the surgery, try to sit well away from dogs and consider covering the box with a towel. Your cat will also feel more relaxed if the box is above ground level on your lap or on a chair. If your cat is a nervous traveller, try using a pheromone spray in the carrier, spraying inside the box fifteen minutes before putting your cat inside.

On arrival at the practice, you should find neat and polite nursing staff, or a receptionist, who will most likely be wearing the practice uniform. Your pet's case history, either on the practice computer system or record card, should be readily to hand, so that the vet can refer back to previous illnesses, any allergies and treatments. If for any reason you have had to change from one practice to another, you should ask for your cat's records to be transferred before visiting the new practice.

The titles of veterinary practices may be confusing. Some are named after the veterinary

are offering an appointment system as an alternative to the 'sit and wait your turn' system. Some practices are open for consultations all day by appointment, and some have surgeries on Sundays.

Please always take your cat to the vet (and even the cattery) in an escape-proof cat-carrier. He will be safer and happier in this, both in the car and in the waiting-room. We hear of cats being carried to the vet in the owner's arms, suddenly realizing where they are, and making a leap for freedom and never being seen again.

A friendly, welcoming receptionist.

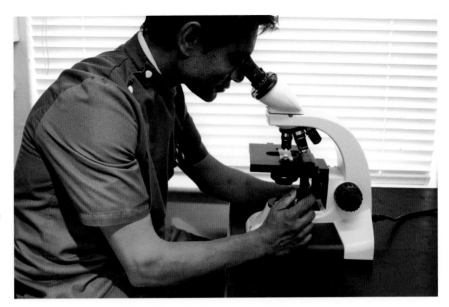

Microscope examination of samples of skin, blood, faeces, discharges and urine is important in establishing a diagnosis.

surgeons that own them, while others are called veterinary surgery, veterinary clinic, veterinary centre, or even pet health centre. These, in fact, are all the same type of general practice, although, of course, the services and facilities offered may vary. Look for the RCVS Practice Standards logo, which shows that they are accredited and inspected.

VETERINARY HOSPITALS

You may notice that some veterinary practices are called veterinary hospitals. These, as well as functioning just as all the other types of veterinary practices in the treatment of sick and injured animals, have a range of facilities, a standard of design and construction, and staffing of the suitable qualification and levels to be granted the title 'veterinary hospital' by the RCVS. These facilities include resident nurses or veterinary surgeons on the premises all the time, heated and air-conditioned dog and cat wards (suitable for long- or short-term patients, with adequate arrangements for their sanitary requirements), on-site X-ray facilities, laboratory facilities, properly equipped operating theatres and treatment rooms with suitable anaesthetic apparatus and resuscitation equipment, and many other facilities. In addition, the

construction, design, and wall and floor finishes have to be to a high standard to minimize spread of disease. Of course, adequate parking facilities have also to be available.

There are about 120 veterinary hospitals in Britain and Northern Ireland and about 4,000 other veterinary practices.

FEES AND SERVICES

The type of veterinary practice you choose will depend on your requirements. Service, personal attention and facilities vary and, of course, so do fees. There are no standard veterinary fees; these usually reflect the overheads and level of services being offered, although the geographical location of the practice can also affect them. For example, a practice in London is likely to charge more than a practice in rural Cornwall. Obviously, a practice that has purchased the latest available equipment, such as modern X-ray and ultrasound equipment, diathermy and cryosurgery, ultrasonic dental machines, and has hospitalization facilities with on-site staff 24hr a day, and an on-site laboratory for rapid diagnosis, will have higher fees than one offering just the basic services. Your veterinary surgeon has had to open or purchase and finance her own practice (there are no grants

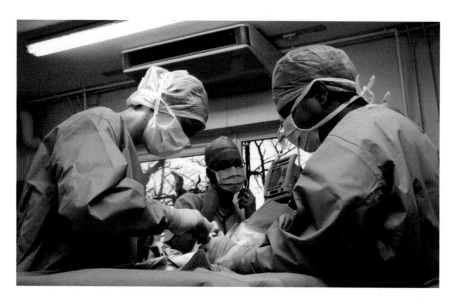

Sterility is important in the operating theatre.

available). Higher fees usually reflect a larger expenditure on equipment, facilities and staff to serve you and your pet. Veterinary hospitals tend to be the most expensive but, as already stated, they are guaranteed to provide a full and specified range of facilities.

A major part of any small-animal vet's day is spent in the operating theatre carrying out routine operations such as neuterings and dentistry, or complicated operations such as bone surgery, cancer removals or bowel surgery. Veterinary medicine and surgery has improved at roughly the same rate as human medicine, and our anaesthesia, for instance, is now usually identical to that used in human hospitals. Most surgical procedures are carried out with a veterinary nurse monitoring the anaesthetic while the surgeon operates, and pain relief is now so effective and safe that it is administered to most surgical cases routinely.

It may be that you prefer to attend a small practice where you know you will always see the same veterinary surgeon, who will get to know you and your pet very well. The slightly lower availability (no-one can be in two places at one time!) may be compensated for by the personal approach afforded by this type of practice. The veterinary surgeon will be equally qualified as those in the larger practices, and many small practices are well-equipped.

It is usual now for each visit to the surgery to be paid for at the time of attendance. This improves the cash flow of the practice, which helps to keep the fees down as less staff time is spent on accounts. Furthermore, this also allows for greater reinvestment in the practice to the benefit of patients and owners alike. And don't forget that your vet has to charge VAT on top of her fees, which she then must give back to the Chancellor!

When choosing a veterinary practice, it is important to first decide which type of practice you wish to register with, then ask around the local cat owners for their recommendations. When clients move away from Plymouth, we always suggest they choose their next vet by this method, unless we know a colleague to whom to refer them.

PET HEALTH INSURANCE

The fees charged may affect your choice of practice. However, in making that choice it is important to realize that veterinary medicine is improving all the time and paralleling human medicine. The extra benefits of modern treatment to your cat will cost more and more. There is, however, no need to worry about fees at all, as there are many reputable pet health insurance companies that will insure your cat against veterinary costs for a monthly premium roughly equivalent to a few pints of beer a week! Third-party insurance is also included in case your cat, for instance, damages other people or their property. Taking out pet health insurance is such an obvious thing to do that we cannot understand why at present only about 10 per cent of cats are insured. It means that, whatever diagnostic tests, treatments, medicines, operations or hospitalization are needed, your vet can carry on without the owner having to worry about where the fees are coming from. In other words, it means the patient has the maximum chance of survival, and diagnostics or treatments are not limited by cost.

Despite there being many pet insurance companies, there are only roughly three types of insurance available:

- Cover for life, whereby once insured, the company will pay for any illness or accident occurring during the pet's entire life.
- Annual insurance package, whereby the company will pay for any problem that year, but no longer for that condition if it continues or recurs in other years.
- Payment of vet fees up to a certain level (e.g. £3,000) over the pet's life, which means that if those fees have been paid out by the time the cat is, say, 5 years old, no insurance will be available for the rest of its life.

Your veterinary practice will be able to provide full information on the types of insurance available.

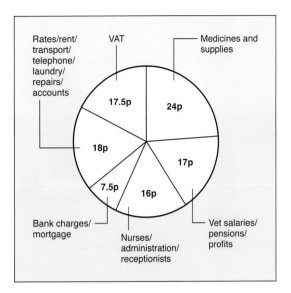

Fig 2 *Breakdown of veterinary costs. Average outgoings for every £1 of fees received.*

REGISTERING WITH A PRACTICE

When you have decided which practice to attend, you should telephone to enquire whether an appointment is necessary, or whether the system is one of open surgeries. You could also enquire whether the practice is willing to carry out house-calls, if necessary, and whether they provide or arrange an out-of-hours service. It is as well to register your pets with the practice before things go wrong, so that in an emergency, you are familiar with the system. A full case history will be kept and updated each time your cat attends. This is of great value in cases of drug allergies, or previous or current treatments, particularly if, for some reason, your usual vet is not available and one of her colleagues attends the case.

It is better for all concerned, if you are able see the same veterinary surgeon each time you attend the surgery. To this end, you should find out when he or she normally holds consultations, or enquire before you attend. Gradually, over the years, you develop a relationship (and often the pet does too!) and you should find it easy to communicate your worries and triumphs to your vet. For us, it is not just a job but a vocation, and we like to get to know

A new kitten's temporary pet insurance certificate.

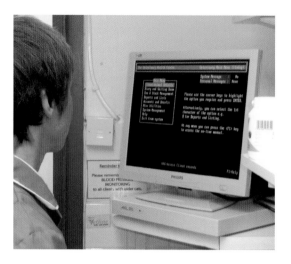

Your cat's medical history readily available on the computer twenty-four hours a day.

patients and owners, and follow cases through personally.

Your own vet will usually operate on your cat himself, should it be necessary, although as with the medical profession, complicated cases are often referred on to a vet with further qualifications or better facilities. However, we really do get highly involved with our cases, and one of the most rewarding aspects of our way of life is that, in most cases, we can diagnose the illness, administer the medical treatment, take the X-rays and operate, if necessary – all within our own surgeries without having to refer the case on to a consultant.

Loyalty of clients to the practice is very important to vets – and equally important for the cat. The case history notes and medical records over the years can be extremely important and even lifesaving to the patient.

SECOND OPINIONS

There may be occasions when, for various reasons, a second opinion is necessary. Your vet can arrange this for you with a neighbouring practice or a university or other referral service. You may, on the other hand, just decide you are dissatisfied with the treatment or results. In such a case, you are completely at liberty to seek another vet's advice and opinion but, if the case is 'under treatment', the second vet is bound, by our profession's ethical code, to consult the first vet, prior to seeing the case. This is mainly to

A health examination.

safeguard the patient and to ensure that no treatment is given that will cause an allergic reaction, or an adverse reaction to the drugs already in use on the patient.

In practice, a second opinion can be of benefit in a difficult case. Both vets should then discuss the case and decide on further action. It is usual for you to be referred back to the original vet for the continuation of the case, unless you really do wish to change practices.

This is, of course, possible – whether through dissatisfaction or for geographical reasons. At your request, your cat's medical records should be transferred to the new practice. If your cat is actively under treatment, the routine as outlined for second opinions applies.

THE CLINICAL EXAMINATION

The clinical examination of your cat differs from that of a human in that the vet cannot ask the cat how it feels or where it hurts. This is often an advantage, as it means we are not given any false or imagined information! So, the first part of the examination consists of history taking where the vet asks the owner questions about symptoms and behaviour. It is a good idea to write out a list of the things that are worrying you about your cat and take it with you to the surgery. This ensures you will not forget anything when explaining your worries to the vet, and it is of great help to him. An examination of the cat then follows, usually on the consulting-room table. The owner may hold the cat gently for this or perhaps a veterinary nurse is called in to help. The exact nature, or extent, of the clinical examination will be determined by the symptoms described by the owner. For example, a cat presented with a vague history of listlessness and lack of appetite, will require a full examination including temperature, pulse, chest, examination of eyes, mouth and throat, and palpation of his abdomen. On the other hand, a cat that has suddenly started to scratch his ear may well require merely an examination of this organ to reveal the cause.

This consultation may take from five to twenty minutes, but usually, an average of ten minutes is needed in an uncomplicated case to

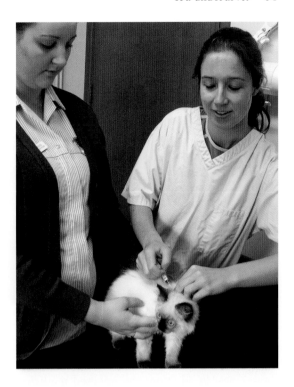

Vaccination time.

establish a tentative diagnosis, explain the situation and supply treatment. Sometimes, especially with behavioural problems such as destructive, spraying or aggressive cats, the consultation will take much longer and may even be held at the client's home. At the end of the consultation, the vet will either tell you what she thinks the problem is (the diagnosis) and what the likely outcome will be (this is called the prognosis) or, if in any doubt, may suggest further diagnostic tests. She may refer you, and your cat, back for a second examination either the next day (if she is particularly worried) or after a few days, or weeks, of treatment. If she does recommend that you bring the patient back to the surgery for her to re-examine after a course of treatment, you should ensure you attend. The vet is obviously the best person to judge whether the illness has cleared up, or further treatment is necessary.

At the end of an examination, many veterinary surgeons will start the treatment by giving an injection. This is for several good reasons. An ill cat will often not eat, or he may have sickness

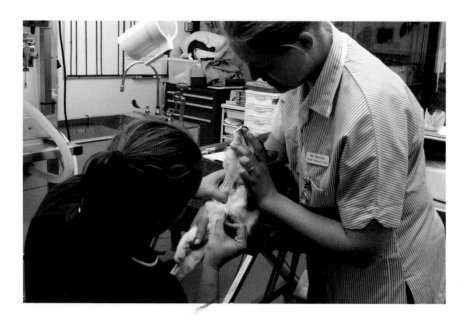

A blood sample being taken.

and diarrhoea, so medicines, which are often given hidden in food, would not be sensible in these cases. In addition, the injected medicine works more quickly as the drug is absorbed rapidly into the bloodstream. This will often mean that, when the second day's drugs are needed, they will be readily accepted in food or absorbed from the gut by then. It is fair to say that most cats are oblivious to the injection – they are not expecting it to hurt and, with the modern, disposable syringe and very sharp needle, it does not hurt. With cats it is often easier to give an injection than tablets.

With the help of the history and symptoms given by the owner and the findings at the examination of the patient, your vet will often be able to reach a diagnosis or suggest a line of treatment. If the cause of the problem is unclear, further tests may be necessary. Some conditions, such as diabetes or thyroid problems, can only be diagnosed after further tests.

DIAGNOSTIC TESTS

- Blood tests are useful in the diagnosis of certain conditions, e.g. liver or kidney disease, diabetes, thyroid problems, certain tumours, anaemias and leukaemia, and various virus or bacterial infections.

- Urine tests help in the diagnosis of bladder and kidney disease, diabetes and liver problems.
- Faeces samples can identify parasites, bowel disease, pancreatic disease, and so on.
- Sometimes small skin and hair samples or biopsies may be painlessly taken to aid investigation of skin and other disorders.
- Samples of pus taken on sterile swabs can be used to identify infections and the antibiotics needed to cure them.

All of these tests can be carried out by the surgery staff but some practices prefer to send samples to outside laboratories.

Your cat may need to stay in the surgery for a short while to have some of these tests performed, often under a mild tranquillizer. He will certainly have to stay for a while to have an X-ray or ultrasound scan taken, if this is deemed necessary for a diagnosis. Many X-rays now have to be taken under a general anaesthetic to comply with the 'exposure to radiation' regulations. Some patients have to be admitted into the veterinary hospital, or surgery, just for observation before a definitive diagnosis can be made. However, this is usually far more traumatic for the owner than for the cat! Surprisingly most cats settle down well when left at the surgery because they respond well to competent, careful handling.

WHEN HELP IS NEEDED

Your veterinary practice is not just a place to contact when you have problems. If you are unsure whether you need to attend, it would be worthwhile making a telephone call to the nurse or receptionist. The vet cannot spend her day answering routine enquiries or she would have no time to treat her patients. However, the veterinary team members are knowledgeable and trained to help with most enquiries. They will call their vet to the telephone if it is felt advisable, or if they are unsure.

Veterinary Nurses

Many practices now employ qualified veterinary nurses who have undergone training at approved training centres and have achieved the RCVS qualification of VN. These VNs are highly trained and skilled individuals, and their supportive role to their veterinary surgeons cannot be overstated. They capably monitor anaesthetics, perform most of the diagnostic tests, caringly nurse the patients and are there to also help the owners. Some practice also employ veterinary health advisors who are specifically trained veterinary nurses who will also deal with queries about your cat's diet, weight and general health questions. VNs will often run their own clinics with help and advice on diet and general health worries.

Veterinary Receptionists

Receptionists are in many ways the lifeblood of the practice. They are the first point of contact for a pet owner with the practice and are usually highly skilled, communicative and knowledgeable. They are there to help you, whether by offering advice on common queries, making you an appointment with the vet or nurse of your choice at a time to suit you, or ensuring a seriously ill pet is seen urgently.

Your local practice is there to help you – both with problems and with routine enquiries. Where better to telephone or attend for advice

A qualified veterinary nurse timing a heart rate.

on choice of breed of cat, whether pedigree or not, and where to get one from or what to look for in a new kitten? Advice is also frequently sought and given on boarding catteries, pet health insurance, feeding, micro-chipping, toilet training, behavioural problems, routine worming and flea control.

A day in the life of a small animal veterinary surgeon is full of interest. There will be many routine vaccinations against the killer diseases, but also treatment of cats that have these diseases, because they were not vaccinated. There will be routine claw clippings and operations on cats that have swallowed or inhaled a sharp blade of grass and other foreign bodies. There will be complicated road accident cases involving X-rays, transfusions and fracture repair, and there will be Caesarean births. All in all, nothing is too simple or complicated for your local veterinary surgeon to help with, so you should not hesitate to telephone or call if help is needed.

Chapter 4
The New Kitten

CHOOSING A SUITABLE KITTEN

Barring accidents or unforeseen problems, your new kitten should live for twelve to fifteen years or even longer, so it is necessary to ensure before taking on a kitten that you can, and will, care for this new member of the family for that length of time. You may be lucky and have your companion for longer – I have known a few cats live to be twenty years old or more.

Once you are convinced that you can, and wish, to look after a cat properly for that length of time, the next move is to choose the right breed or type of cat. There are many pure breeds of cat (pedigree) and each breed will have a standard appearance, a standard type of coat and,

A healthy litter of kittens with their breeder.

within reason, a standard type of behaviour pattern, but a 'Moggie' cat is just as likely to make a good pet. This is also a good time to decide how many cats you want. It is far, far better to take on litter mates at this stage if you feel you will want two or more cats, as they are much more likely to get on together than cats introduced at different times and ages (*see* Chapter 2).

Your local veterinary surgeon will be able to advise you on the correct choice of cat for your situation. Some cats can make very good urban pets in a flat or a small house with no garden, but if you are lucky enough to have a large garden in a quiet area, he will have more freedom. Interestingly, in America, many cats are house cats, never going out, but in the UK we prefer to give them more freedom. House cats need company and a varied environment containing interesting things to climb, play with and investigate, and should not be left on their own for long, if possible. If you keep a house cat with no access to outdoors, then you need to pay much more attention to providing a stimulating environment.

It is necessary to consider the amount of time you have available for grooming. A short-haired cat will merely need a quick brush most days, whereas a long-haired cat, such as a Persian cat, will need considerably more time spent on grooming. Probably half an hour a day is a reasonable estimate to avoid the coat becoming matted. Many cats of this breed end up at the vets to be de-matted under a sedative or general anaesthetic when owners fail to provide adequate grooming care.

The most important ingredient for success is time. You must have time available to spend with your cat and, initially, when he is a kitten, he will take up more of your time. Unless you will be

Two beautiful Silver Tabby kittens from the same litter.

with him frequently, or give him the company of another kitten or cat, there is no point starting a relationship at all.

SOURCES OF PEDIGREE AND DOMESTIC CATS

Breeding Catteries

These catteries usually specialize in one or two breeds, and a recommendation from your local vet or other satisfied customers is essential.

Individual Owner–Breeder

One or two cats are owned and bred as a hobby by an individual owner–breeder. This is a good source, particularly if the kitten is used to family life and a domestic environment when you buy him. However, a recommendation from someone you trust is advisable.

Stray-Cat Homes

These homes will supply not only kittens, but also adult cats, which, for one reason or another, had a previous unsatisfactory home. These cats need good homes and usually have been cared for well while on the premises. Disease, or predetermined behaviour patterns, may be a potential problem but the better stray homes will keep a record of the cat's behaviour and suitability for a variety of homes. This is usually the cheapest source of cats and some lovely cats are often available.

A rescue home is one source of cats.

Basic Rules to follow to maximize your chances of purchasing the ideal cat for you:

- Never be in a hurry or impatient to make the purchase. Do your homework first.
- Ensure that the kitten is from a reliable source, is fit and well, and will suit you. It is far better to wait for the right cat than to rush in and buy the first one of your chosen breed that becomes available.
- Ensure that any other cats on the premises are healthy; you do not want to start with a kitten with infectious disease problems.
- If possible, purchase a kitten from the premises where he was born. There are several advantages in doing this. You will at least be able to examine and assess the temperament of the queen. The kitten will not have been subjected to the stress of a journey from his original home and he will not have had his behaviour modified by anyone prior to you. You should, therefore, be able to gain an impression from the breeder and his premises as to the quality of the kitten.

AGE OF PURCHASE

The ideal age to take on a new kitten is from nine to twelve weeks. There is evidence to show that this is the best age for kittens to adapt to their new life-style and owners, having been taught to use the litter tray by their mother!

Over 80 per cent of kittens purchased in the UK are crossbreds (often called Moggies) but if your choice is to be a pedigree kitten, check with your veterinary surgeon if there are any breeders she could recommend in the area, and whether there are any inherited disease problems that you should avoid with that breed. This is much less of a problem than is the case with dogs but, in general, the short-haired cats have fewer problems than the long-haired cats, which need a lot more grooming or their coats become matted; eye discharge is more common in the flat-faced Persian-type cats. Tail kinks occur occasionally in Siamese, Burmese, Tonkinese, Foreign shorthairs and Turkish Angora cats, and less commonly in other types, but tail kinks have no health significance at all.

Kitten learning to use a litter tray.

There are both advantages and disadvantages in purchasing an adult cat from one of the many stray homes and rescue centres that offer cats for re-homing. On the positive side, you will know the coat type and, to some degree, the temperament and behaviour of the cat. The staff at the home should be able to tell you whether the cat will fit in with your way of life – they are caring people who wish the cat well in the future. One thing is certain – the cat is in great need of a caring home. Kittens from farms are fine, provided they have been raised in the farmhouse with the family and handled by people. Kittens raised in barns without contact with people may remain fearful of contact all their lives.

In general, you should never purchase a cat on impulse and, wherever possible, seek a recommendation from others.

WHAT TO LOOK FOR IN THE NEW KITTEN

Once you have decided on the breed or type of cat you require, and the source, you are now ready to choose your own kitten. What do you look for? Look at the queen first. She will give you an indication, but not a guarantee, of how your kitten will be when adult – both in looks, hair length and temperament.

Choose a kitten that is interested in you and certainly not the one that cowers in the corner. Never choose one that you feel sorry for. Life with your cat will be miserable if the kitten grows into a cat that refuses to sit on your lap or is frightened when you or visitors come into the room.

Check that he is in good bodily condition. Make sure he is bright and alert, not too thin, and that his eyes or nose aren't discharging. Some cats have a hereditary deafness, so make sure he is responsive to sounds. The coat should be glossy, and there should be no sores, bald patches or scabs on his skin. Make sure there is no obvious lameness, and check all his legs are sound and straight. Look around the pen to ensure there are no signs of diarrhoea or vomit, and that none of the kittens look unwell or are showing obvious signs of illness, such as sneezing. A pot-bellied appearance can be an indication of disease or severe worm infestation.

Vaccinations

Check with the breeder whether the kitten has received any vaccinations and, if so, against what and when. If he has, the breeder should provide you with a vaccination certificate and advise you when the next injection is due. The vaccination course must be completed for him to be protected against infectious diseases. Also enquire whether the queen, his mother, is up to date with her vaccinations, as this will have an important bearing on his level of immunity.

Worming

Ask the breeder if the kitten has been wormed and with what and when, as your vet is certain to ask you this. Worming should be carried out at the age of six weeks and then at such intervals and with a wormer suggested by your vet (*see* Chapter 6).

Pedigree Certificate

If you have purchased a pedigree kitten, you should be supplied with his certificate when you collect him. This shows his ancestry.

Pet Health Insurance

Ask if the breeder has taken out a temporary health insurance policy to cover any unexpected problems in the first six weeks. The better breeders do this for you and I advise you to continue this insurance. If the kitten is not insured, ask your vet for details at the first health examination and vaccination.

PARENTS	GRAND-PARENTS	G. GRAND-PARENTS	G. G. GRAND-PARENTS
		Gr Ch Miletree Owain Glyndwr Breed No 17 Reg No CS 228524	Tinkerbelle Top Hat Breed No 16
	Positively Wedgewood Breed No 16 Colour Blue Reg No CS 572952		Wellmar Miss Judy Breed No 28
		Witchwoods Silvestra Breed No 16 Reg No CS 491876	Kalpador Silvester Breed No 16
Petticote Goes West			Ch Miletree Mormghan Breed No 16
		Gr Ch Miletree Owain Glyndwr Breed No 17 Reg No CS 228524	Tinkerbelle Top Hat Breed No 16
	Positively Betsan Breed No 28 Colour Blue Cream Reg No CS 508366		Wellmar Miss Judy Breed No 28
Breed No 17 Colour Cream Reg No CS 602360		Catteractive Nimne Breed No 16 Reg No CS 263476	Gr Ch Positively Mab Glyndwr Breed No 16
			Adinnish Hollow Mallow Breed No 16 R
		Gr Ch Cloudmaker Lordharlequin Breed No 16 Reg No CS 548584	Gr Ch Adquash Cloudmaker Kyffin Breed No 14a CS 334745
	Ch Cloudmaker Freixenet Breed No 17 Colour Cream Reg No CS 604569		Ch Cloudmaker Harlequin Lady Breed No 22a CS 474417
		Cloudmaker Babycham Breed No 17 Reg No CS 484041	Ch Clovercat Champagne Charley Breed No 17 CS408513
Mardenka Miss Daisy			Gr Ch Icemoor White Diamond Breed No 14a CS396872
		Ch Wyrewood E Male Breed No 16 Reg No CS 442309	Ch Aspritous Wizardof Oz Breed No 17 CS 403665
	Mardenka Mustbemagic Breed No 31a Colour Blue & White Reg No CS 463886		Wyrewood Blue Cotton Breed No 16 CS 396844
Breed No 22a Colour Blue Tortie & White Reg No CS 637252		Mardenka Millymollymandy Breed No 22a Reg No CS 463602	Ch Scipus Blue Spangler Breed No 16 CS 273481
			Gr Ch & Gr Pr Loraston Lillie Langtry Breed No 31f CSSR 314374

I certify this pedigree to be correct to the best of my knowledge .... *Joan. Simmons.* Date ..29...6 - 05

A pedigree certificate.

A healthy new kitten.

MANAGEMENT AND CARE OF THE NEW ARRIVAL

Bedding

Before the kitten is brought into his new home, there are some purchases and arrangements that have to be made. A bed should be waiting for him; there is a lot of choice these days, e.g. soft cat beds, plastic ones in which you add a blanket, but I would avoid wicker beds, as they cannot be cleaned or disinfected easily. Choose one that can be washed in the washing machine or wiped down. Also, synthetic absorbent bedding materials that can be washed and dried are available. Most cats have their own bed in a warm, dry, draught-free area of the house, but some are allowed to sleep on the bed. This can be quite a comfort for some owners and, provided the cat is healthy, has no skin parasites and is not actually in the bed, there can be no serious objection to this.

Feeding

A food and water bowl should be waiting for your new kitten. Check with the breeder or rescue home which type of food the kitten is used to and make sure you have some ready for his arrival at his new home. You should be given a diet sheet, so make certain you ask for one. His water bowl should always be full of clean water. Feeding is discussed later in this chapter. There are very few diseases shared by humans and animals; these are called zoonoses. However, for basic hygiene reasons, cats should not use the same plates and dishes as humans, nor should they sleep in the bed with them.

Toileting

Until he is allowed outdoors, he should be provided with an indoor litter tray, so buy one and check with the breeder or rescue home which

A comfy bed for these four kittens, although wicker is not ideal.

Identification by microchip is a good idea.

type of litter he is used to and use that. It is most important not to change the litter type at this stage. Also, position the litter tray in a quiet place away from his food and water bowls and bed. If you have more than one cat, make sure they have at least one tray each; in fact, it is generally better to have one more tray than the number of cats.

Collar and Lead?

Should a cat have a collar or not? Certainly he should always have some sort of identification and the choices are really only a microchip injected under the skin of his neck (the best idea), or a collar with either his name and address on it or on a disc attached to it. Cat collars are generally safe and should have a break point in them so that if he gets a leg stuck in it, or gets the collar caught on a branch for instance, he can free himself. The microchip can be inserted at the time of his second vaccination as a kitten, or preferably while he is under the anaesthetic for the neutering operation at about five months of age. Or you could buy his identity disc from your vet at the first visit for his health examination and vaccinations, or at a pet shop or a key-cutting kiosk. Discs are much better than screw top name con-

tainers, which often unscrew and fall off. A lead is useful for the first few weeks when he goes into the garden or yard with you, until he is familiar with the surroundings, but it is best if this is attached to a soft body harness rather than a collar. Ensure the kitten gets used to the harness before you attach a lead to it, and let him move freely with you following!

Toys and Play Area

Cats are inquisitive, playful creatures that need plenty to do, especially when young. Obviously a lot of his fun will be playing with you but it's a good idea to supply him with some toys and a play area. Simple toys from a toy shop, e.g. catnip mice, balls, teasing toys on string from a stick and so on, are fine but he also needs to be able to amuse himself. So, to start with, cardboard boxes with holes in are fun, a climbing frame will be well used and enjoyed, and will give him the chance to escape attention when he wants to be alone. It's essential to allow your cats to have access to height, and a climbing frame is excellent for this. Most are carpet-lined. He also needs a scratching post to keep his claws in good condition so that your furniture and carpets will be less liable to damage.

A small play area.

The Homecoming

For the journey back home with your new kitten, remember to take a blanket to keep him warm, a kitchen roll in case he is travel sick and, if you are travelling alone to fetch him, transport him in an escape-proof basket. It is preferable for someone to accompany you, so that one of you is free to comfort and cuddle him in the car on this new adventure.

Remember that the first night with you will be his first ever night alone. It is, therefore, a good idea to collect him in the morning, if you can, so he has a longer time to adapt to his new surroundings and to get to know you before it is bedtime.

THE FIRST FEW DAYS

A new kitten will instantly alter your life! There will be upsets and delights as he messes and climbs, learns a new trick or enjoys playing with you. It is important to realize that his life has been totally altered too – from one of complete security with his mother, litter mates and familiar humans, to a life where he is, suddenly, on his own with a strange family in unfamiliar surroundings. This can be very stressful and, initially, he may not settle easily at night. Usually, however, this is transient and ceases once the kitten realizes he is, in fact, secure and his new friends are always there when he wakes up. It may be necessary to bring his bed or cat basket into your bedroom for a few nights, but it is better to try leaving a dim light on in his room overnight. Do make sure he is warm at night and has access to food, water and his litter tray.

The stress of change of ownership, environment and food can cause a few problems in the first few days. In my experience, kittens may have some diarrhoea during this period, which usually clears up if food is withheld for twelve hours and then a light diet of a chicken and rice-based food is fed until the problem is resolved. This possibility can be minimized by feeding the kitten the same diet that the breeder was using. If the problem persists, or the kitten seems unwell, you should contact your veterinary surgeon for advice.

It is much more likely that your new kitten will be healthy, with bouts of ceaseless energy interspersed with sudden periods of deep sleep. This is completely normal, but may take you by surprise. It is equally likely that he will get the timing wrong. He may collapse in a deep sleep just as you want to play with him, and then be at his most active at 11pm when you are ready to go to bed. Patience is essential – his biological clock will correct itself in time!

FEEDING YOUR NEW KITTEN

It is necessary to feed a balanced diet during your kitten's growing period and also during his adult life. This means he will be fed on the correct amount of protein, carbohydrate, fat, minerals and vitamins. All these will be provided in the normal course of events if a mixture of nutrients is given. Cats are obligate carnivores, which means they must have animal protein or they will not thrive and will suffer from a number of nutritional diseases. Do not try to convert your cat to a vegetarian! However, meat alone only provides some of the daily requirements; it is low in carbohydrate but, most important of all, it is very low in minerals and vitamins.

Life-Stage Diets

Feeding cats is very simple and effective these days due to the development by pet food firms of life-stage diets. These are formulated and developed to contain the correct amount of all the necessary ingredients in the correct proportions for your cat at the stage he is at. Importantly, because these foods would not sell

The more things to play in and with, the better.

if cats would not eat them, they are usually very palatable and tasty. I would suggest that you start your kitten on one of these but ask your vet's opinion as to which are the more nutritious and tasty ones; and remember, it's often best to use the same food as he was used to with the breeder for the first week or so and then *gradually* change. Most of these diets are extruded (or crunchy) diets and also have the beneficial effect, we believe, of helping to keep the teeth clean. It is a good idea, and a common practice, to feed a balanced wet and dry diet by offering tinned or sachets of kitten food and cooked chicken or fish at other times of the day; but check you are not overfeeding.

With a dry food, you can leave the bowl down all day, and most kittens will help themselves every few hours without overdoing it. Remember to leave a bowl of drinking water down all the time. Milk is not essential, as all the necessary nutrients are in the food and cow's milk should not be offered, as many cats are lactulose-intolerant. However, it is often a nice treat to give the kitten a small bowl of specific cat milk from the pet shop. Tinned or sachet food alone will not help in keeping teeth clean.

Normally, kitten food is fed for the first nine months and then changed to an adult variety, but it may be necessary to start him on adult food even earlier if he is gaining weight too fast.

THE FIRST VETERINARY HEALTH EXAMINATION

This will normally be carried out at the time of the first vaccination of the kitten at nine to twelve weeks of age. If your new kitten is lively and playful in between naps, eats well and has no obvious signs of illness, it may not be necessary to have a veterinary inspection before the first vaccination is due. If, however, there is anything that causes you concern, it would be advisable to take him to your local vet, or at least telephone for advice. It is wise to sort out any problems that may have been present at the time of purchase, as soon as possible.

Before vaccinating the kitten, your vet will ensure that he is fit and healthy and able to respond to the vaccination. To assess his overall condition she will carry out a full health examination, usually including his face, eyes, mouth,

Two kittens awaiting their first veterinary inspection.

ears, chest, pulse, abdomen, legs, coat and she may check his temperature. She will, of course, ask you questions about his health and behaviour, and she will check the kitten for any obvious faults or defects.

Unless you have noticed anything unusual, it is highly likely that your kitten will be completely fit and well. However, there are a few problems that may be identified at the first inspection.

Examination of the head will reveal whether the kitten has a congenital or hereditary problem in this area, but in cats it is only very rarely that any defects are seen:

- Hare lip and cleft palate are extremely rare problems caused by the centre of the upper roof of the mouth failing to join completely during development in the uterus.
- The upper and lower jaw should be the same length; any deviation from this is abnormal. If the lower jaw is longer than the upper jaw, it protrudes and the lower incisor teeth jut out in front of the upper teeth. This jaw is said to be undershot. Where the upper jaw is longer than the lower jaw, this is referred to as overshot. Kittens that are affected may well live a normal life, but they will not win any major cat shows. An exception to this rule occurs in Persian-type cats, which often have undershot jaws.
- More commonly, your vet will find minor problems, such as mild ear or eye infections, that you may not have noticed. These are usually fairly easy to cure.

A kitten has his chest examined with a stethoscope.

An examination of the chest by stethoscope may occasionally reveal a heart defect such as valvular disease, or congenital oddities like a hole in the heart. Fortunately, problems like this are extremely uncommon.

Palpation of the abdomen may reveal abnormalities or indicate an infestation of parasitic roundworms. Certainly, any unusual bowel obstructions will be noticed at this stage, as will hernias. In male kittens, the presence of both testicles can only rarely be confirmed at a young age.

The kitten's temperature is only likely to be taken if a problem is suspected, in order not to risk frightening him on this first visit. If so, a well-lubricated thermometer is inserted gently into the anus. If the temperature is raised, this may be an indication to the vet that the kitten has an infection. A thorough clinical examination should reveal the exact nature of the problem.

In addition to the detailed examination of various areas described, the vet will assess generally the appearance and condition of the kitten. She will note any abnormality of the coat due to deficiencies or parasites, or any abnormalities of the feet, legs and tail. If all is well, she will then progress to the vaccination of the kitten.

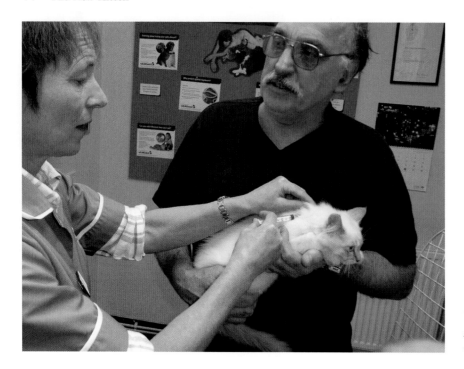

Twelve-week-old kitten having his second vaccination.

VACCINATION OF THE NEW KITTEN

Vaccination is the administration of a modified live or killed form of a virus, which does not cause illness in the kitten. Instead, it stimulates the formation of antibodies against the disease itself. This immunity against a disease is called 'active immunity'. The only other way a kitten can obtain active immunity is by surviving a bout of a disease, but as he cannot be guaranteed survival, vaccination is preferable. This active immunity takes over from the passive immunity due to antibodies given to him by his dam in her colostrum or first milk (called 'passive immunity'), which usually disappear by twelve weeks of age.

There are three major killer diseases against which all kittens should be vaccinated in Britain. These are:

• feline influenza (commonly known as cat flu);
• feline panleucopaenia (or feline enteritis); and
• feline leukaemia virus (FeLV).

There are some other diseases where vaccination is recommended in special circumstances and all these diseases are described in detail in Chapter 5.

The vaccination course varies according to the age of the kitten and the prevalence of disease in the area in which the kitten lives, and whether the kitten will be exclusively an indoor cat or will have access to the outside world.

Vaccination against feline influenza and feline panleucopaenia is invariably given as a combined dose, whereas that against feline leukaemia virus can be given combined with the first two or as a separate dose.

• Indoor cats require vaccination against cat flu and enteritis. This is because the flu virus is airborne and the panleucopaenia virus can live for a long time outside the body (up to a year). Thus both can enter the house: flu in the air or panleucopaenia carried in by people on clothing or shoes without any infected cat having been around. The vaccine containing both of these is given in two doses, three to four weeks apart, starting usually at nine weeks of age, but can be given at any age after that if you take on an older kitten or cat. An annual booster vaccination is recommended to maintain immunity.

- Cats that will be allowed to go out should also be vaccinated against feline leukaemia virus, as this is only spread by direct contact with other infected cats in their blood or saliva. This vaccine containing all three constituents is given in two doses, three to four weeks apart, starting usually at nine weeks of age, but can be given at any age after that if you take on an older kitten or cat. An annual booster vaccination is recommended to maintain immunity. However, if for any reason you decide not to vaccinate your kitten against all three diseases at once, the feline leukaemia virus vaccine can be given at any age later on in the usual two doses.
- Whichever course is decided upon, an annual booster is necessary to maintain protection.

Once vaccinated, your new kitten will also be able to stay in a boarding cattery, should this be necessary for your holidays and so on, although it's not a good idea to board a kitten at a very young age, and certainly not until his vaccines have had time to take effect. However, if it is likely that he will need to board during his life, it is a good idea to board him for, say, a weekend, to see how he takes to it; if so, be sure to choose a clean, well-run cattery. Your vet may be able to suggest some good local catteries, or a charity,

A clean, attractive cattery – FAB-approved.

such as the Feline Advisory Bureau (FAB), who keep a list of inspected and approved catteries, may be able to suggest one local to you.

Cat shows can be fun and rewarding if you take on a pedigree cat and if it appeals to you – and to your cat, of course. Some cats are very happy to be shown, others find it stressful and, if this is the case, it's kinder not to take him again to a show. If you do take your cat to a cattery, or to a cat show, ensure you carry him in a safe cat-carrier, and take his vaccination certificate with you.

Showing your cat can be both rewarding and good fun.

Chapter 5
Common Infectious Diseases

FELINE INFLUENZA

Feline influenza or cat flu, as it is commonly called, is a highly infectious virus disease, which often, but not always, affects cats under one year of age. This disease is still frequently seen, although widespread vaccination of cats by responsible breeders, rescue homes and owners has reduced the incidence considerably. It is a complex disease and is caused by either feline calicivirus (FCV) or feline herpesvirus (FHV), which is also known as feline viral rhinotracheitis (FVR). Occasionally it can be caused by a combination of both. The most serious cases are caused by FHV. These viruses are pres-

ent in tears, nasal discharges and saliva, and can last for one to seven days outside the body. FHV is the more fragile and lasts only up to 18hr in a damp environment, less in dry conditions. This means that cats can infect each other by direct contact with the various discharges, or by sneezing or coughing over a distance of up to two metres.

Once inhaled, the viruses divide rapidly in the tonsils or nearby lymph nodes, and after a day or two appear in the bloodstream, causing a temperature rise. The cat becomes dull, is usually off his food, and begins to sneeze and often cough. One of the first signs may be red discharging eyes and a runny nose.

Clinical Symptoms

Respiratory Signs. Cat flu can vary from a very mild infection to a severe fatal one. Initially, the symptoms are those of a respiratory infection as the virus attacks the lining of the nose, eyes, throat and lungs. Affected cats sneeze and often, just before the sneezing begins, the cat's temperature will rise to as high as 40°C (104°F) or more. The cat feels ill and is unable to smell his food because of his blocked nose, so often he will not eat. He begins to show a mild discharge from the eyes and nose, which, if untreated, often progresses to a thick purulent discharge. The eyes become very inflamed, appear reddened and adhesions may form between the third eyelid and the surface of the eye. This is serious, as the tear duct, which drains the tears from the eye through the nose, can be blocked leading to a permanent overflow of tears down the face. The discharge from the nose dries in the nostrils, making it difficult for the cat to breathe. Due to the effect of the virus on the

Cat with severe feline influenza. Note the nasal discharge and protruding third eyelids.

lining of the bronchi in the lungs and the trachea (windpipe), the cat will frequently wheeze or even cough as he tries to clear his windpipe and lungs of discharge. Painful ulcers often develop in the mouth on the lips, gums or tongue, and affected cats will often drool excessive amounts of saliva from their mouths. Especially in kittens or aged cats, pneumonia can follow due to a secondary infection with bacteria, and the cat may die.

Diagnosis. In a classic case, there is little that cat flu can be confused with, but another disease called chlamydia may appear similar, as it causes chronically discharging eyes, but this is usually a disease of multi-cat households. If necessary, diagnosis can be confirmed by your veterinary surgeon sending a throat swab to a veterinary laboratory where the virus can be identified as either FCV or FHV.

Treatment and Prevention

Like all virus infections, there is no specific cure for feline influenza, but your vet will aim to control any secondary bacterial infection with the use of antibiotics while the cat has to fight the infection by producing antibodies. As the disease can last for several weeks, careful nursing, food and drink are essential. In my experience, attention to making the patient comfortable and giving him a will to live is essential. His eyes should be bathed frequently with cotton wool soaked in warm, sterile water or saline, as often as is necessary to prevent the lids caking together with the discharge. They should be gently dried with a tissue immediately afterwards. The nose should be cleaned with Vaseline (not water, which will make it sore) and wiped away gently with tissues or a cotton bud. If the patient can smell his food, he is more likely to eat it, so attention to the nose is important — as is the use of strong-smelling, interesting foods, preferably warmed up to body temperature. Some cats just seem to give up — years ago, one of my own Siamese cats was so badly affected that he had to be given intravenous fluids to survive.

Your vet may inject antibiotics in the early stages of the disease, or supply palatable tablets or syrup, and, in addition, ointments or drops for the eyes. These are usually used until the discharges from the eyes and nose have ceased, and the sneezing has subsided. Your veterinary surgeon will decide. As it is so infectious, you must isolate the patient from other cats in the same house; this may be difficult but confining him to one room is better than nothing. Leave a coat in the room and wear it when attending to him to attempt to minimize spread. Surviving affected kittens can be left with life-long chronic sinusitis.

Vaccination

It is far more sensible to prevent cat flu, than to risk him getting the disease and then try and cure it. If the queen (mother) of the kittens is immune to cat flu, she will give them immunity in the form of antibodies in her colostrum. This is only temporary and fades by nine to twelve weeks of age, which is, therefore, the best age for vaccination against cat flu. However, if there is reason to suspect that the kitten was not given any immunity by the queen, or if the kitten is thought to be in a high-risk situation, then an additional vaccination can be given earlier — but the twelve-week dose is still necessary. The kitten will not have developed sufficient immunity to protect him from cat flu until about ten days after his second vaccination, so it is important to isolate him from other cats for this period.

A vaccination booster each year against cat flu is usually recommended throughout the cat's life.

FELINE CHLAMYDOPHILA

Feline chlamydophila (formerly known as chlamydia) mainly causes conjunctivitis in the cat, so can resemble cat flu in the early stages. Conjunctivitis is the inflammation of the conjunctival membranes that cover the inner surface of the eyelids and the white sclera. It is relatively common in cats, causing perhaps a third of all cases of chronic conjunctivitis. Cats of all ages can be infected, but it is most commonly seen in young kittens that have persistent or recurrent eye discharges. The disease is caused by a bacterium that is not able to survive well outside the body, so infection is usually transmitted by direct contact between cats. The disease is, therefore, more common in multi-cat households, breeding catteries and rescue homes.

Clinical Signs. These begin a few days after infection, as a watery discharge from one or both eyes, which may be partially closed. Shortly, severe swelling and reddening of the conjunctiva may be seen and the discharge becomes thicker and coloured. Affected cats may sneeze, have a nasal discharge and be dull. If the disease is untreated at this stage, the symptoms can persist for two months or longer, and the affected cat may shed the bacteria for many months.

Treatment. Antibiotic treatment is usually successful, especially if treatment starts early in the disease. Eye drops or ointment are used, usually combined with antibiotic tablets or syrup, and this treatment is continued for a period of four weeks. All cats in the household should be treated, even if they are not obviously affected.

Vaccination. Vaccines are available, which, although not always preventing infection, are helpful in preventing severe clinical disease. Some vets recommend vaccination only in high-risk situations, while others use it as part of a standard vaccination regime.

Note: Humans can be infected with chlamydia but the particular one that infects cats does not usually affect us and the risk appears to be extremely low. However, routine hand-washing after handling affected cats is recommended.

FELINE PANLEUCOPAENIA (FELINE ENTERITIS)

This disease is caused by the panleucopaenia virus, which is a very hardy virus, being able to survive in the environment for up to two years. It causes a disease that is frequently fatal and is very difficult to treat. The main sign is a rapidly ill kitten or cat, which will often vomit froth, and the virus is passed on in this way. However, as the virus can survive for long periods in the environment, infection is possible in two other important ways:

Inflamed eyes with conjunctivitis.

- By the cat sniffing or investigating an area where infected faeces were passed months previously.
- By the virus being brought into a safe area (e.g. house or garden) on shoes or clothing.

These two factors are extremely important when attempting the elimination of disease from your house, or boarding and breeding catteries.

This disease, however, is now uncommon in most areas of the UK, due to vaccination, but does still occur in young kittens and unvaccinated cats

Clinical Symptoms. Despite the alternative name, the main symptom is vomiting not diarrhoea, and the cat rapidly becomes very ill, dehydrated and very dull with a high temperature, usually over 40°C (104°F). In severe cases, the first sign may be a cat that is completely off his food, very dull and depressed, and may be completely collapsed. Cats suffering from this severe form of the disease are unlikely to recover. Sudden death may also be the first sign in acute cases. The incubation period of the disease is usually about two weeks.

If a pregnant queen is infected with FPV, her unborn kittens may be affected. Their brain becomes damaged, and when they start walking at about two weeks of age, they appear to have a wobbly gait.

Diagnosis. Usually your vet will diagnose this disease based on the clinical examination and signs that the cat is showing, but it can be diagnosed from blood or faeces samples, which your vet would send to a veterinary laboratory where they will be tested for antibodies or virus.

Treatment. There is no specific treatment of this disease, so good nursing is essential. Any treatment given is aimed at correcting the signs of illness shown, so it is very helpful to give intravenous transfusions of glucose saline to help counteract the dehydration, and to give drugs to stop vomiting and diarrhoea. Antibiotics are helpful but only to prevent or eliminate the secondary bacterial infection, which usually occurs.

Infected Premises. It is very difficult to eradicate the disease from infected premises, such as breeding or boarding catteries, where many cats are present. Vaccination of kittens may fail because of the high level of maternal antibodies, which may then wane before the next vaccine is given, leading to disease. A plan of action must be undertaken:

- Vaccination of kittens from six weeks of age and then every two weeks.
- Thorough mechanical cleaning of the premises using pressure hosing, if possible.
- Disinfection of the cleaned premises. Panleucopaenia virus is very resistant to disinfection and is only killed by potent substances, such as hypochlorite (bleach) or formalin. Products are available commercially.
- Compartmentalization of the cattery, so that kittens can be reared in isolated batches.
- Personal hygiene and attention to detail by the staff, e.g. boots disinfected after each isolation cat pen, thorough washing of hands and separate overalls for each cat pen.

Prevention. Vaccination of young, susceptible kittens and repeat vaccinations every two to three years, as recommended by your vet, prevents development of the disease.

FELINE LEUKAEMIA VIRUS (FELV)

Feline leukaemia virus (FeLV) is similar to the human immuno-deficiency virus (HIV) only in that its main effects are those of causing a deficiency of the immune system of the cat, leading to multiple infections, tumours or anaemia. Luckily a vaccine is available, which if administered before the cat has met the virus, and preferably as a kitten, protects the cat from this disease. The virus is present in an affected cat's saliva and there has to be direct or almost direct contact for the infection to spread. Being bitten or licked by an infected cat, or sharing a drinking or food bowl, can cause the infection but the virus is rapidly destroyed within hours outside the body. FeLV can also cross the placenta, and usually all kittens born to an FeLV-infected queen will develop the disease.

Clinical Signs

These will depend on the effect the virus has on the cat. The incubation period (the time from when the cat meets the virus until the first symptoms are seen) is very long and can be months or even years. However, by far the majority of FeLV-infected cats die within three to four years of becoming infected.

Immunosuppression. If the immune system is suppressed, a cat will keep getting various infections, so if this appears to be happening, FeLV is suspected. A blood test will rapidly find out whether this is the cause. This immunosuppressive effect causes most deaths from FeLV.

Anaemia. As the virus suppresses the bone marrow where red blood cells are manufactured, anaemia can result. Your vet would normally check to see if your cat has FeLV, if she suspects anaemia.

Tumours. Various types of a tumour called lymphosarcoma can be caused by FeLV. Younger cats often develop this tumour in an organ called the thymus in the chest, where the signs are often of breathing difficulties. In middle-aged cats, it usually causes cancer in many of the lymph nodes, which can be felt as hard little lumps. In the older cat, the tumours are usually found in the intestine in the abdomen. However, it must be stressed that by no means all of the intestinal tumours are caused by FeLV. Other organs, such as kidney, liver and especially the eye, can develop these cancers. FeLV also causes abortion, still birth and infertility.

Diagnosis. Most veterinary practices can now carry out a rapid test on a sample of blood in the surgery, which detects a bit of the virus. But because false-positives are possible, all positive in-practice FeLV test results are usually confirmed by virus isolation at one of the UK University Veterinary Schools. The blood sample will also confirm the presence of large numbers of abnormal white blood cells, and usually fewer red blood cells, i.e. a concurrent anaemia.

Treatment

This will depend on the signs shown by the affected cat. If the problem is multiple, repeated infections, antibiotics will be needed, possibly almost continually. If the cat has the lymphosarcoma cancer, chemotherapy may be tried, which can prolong life if the tumour regresses but the cat rarely survives more than a few months.

Prevention

If you have a FeLV-positive cat, you should not introduce another new cat into the house, and ideally keep your cat in to prevent it affecting other cats. If you have several cats, some of which are FeLV-positive and others are negative, it is better not to allow them to mix, even if the negative cats are FeLV vaccinated.

Vaccination

Several makes of FeLV vaccine are available and your vet will recommend the one which she feels is most suitable for your cat. However, it should be realized that vaccination is not always 100 per cent effective; but, apart from keeping your cat in permanently, it is the only protection you can offer. Because the virus cannot survive outside the body, house cats that never go out do not need FeLV vaccination but of course should always have their cat flu and feline enteritis vaccinations. Some vaccine manufacturers, and some vets, recommend that the cat is tested for FeLV before vaccination, because if the kitten is already positive for the virus, the vaccine will have no effect – but it will not harm the kitten either. However, this has to be weighed up against the desirability of the extra procedure in the young kitten.

The FeLV vaccine is usually given in two doses, three to four weeks apart, starting at nine weeks old at the earliest. It is recommended that this vaccine is given combined with the other vaccines the kitten needs, so that he does actually only have the two injections initially. There are normally no side-effects to vaccination; occasionally the cat may be quiet for a day or two, and occasionally a small lump may form at the injection site, which usually disappears after a week or two. An injection-site tumour seen in the USA, which may be linked, does not seem to occur to any great extent in the UK – certainly the benefits of prevention far outweigh this very rare occurrence.

An annual vaccination booster is usually recommended, again combined with the other vaccinations the cat needs.

Boarding Catteries and Rescue Homes

Because cats can only become infected by direct or almost direct contact, provided cats are kept apart and have their own or thoroughly disinfected bowls, there is no reason for an FeLV-positive cat to be excluded from a cattery. In a rescue home, it is probably kinder to euthanase any FeLV-positive cat, rather than risk other cats becoming affected or that cat slowly dying in a new home. Any well but FeLV-positive pregnant queen, should be spayed rather than give birth to a litter of FeLV-affected kittens.

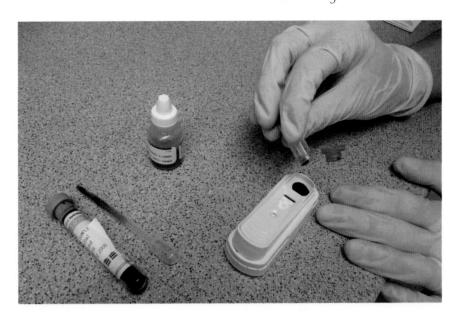

FeLV-FIV blood test in progress.

FELINE IMMUNODEFICIENCY VIRUS (FIV)

FIV is another cat virus that attacks the cat's immune system. It is very similar to the human HIV and can lead to the cat's own acquired immune deficiency syndrome, or FAIDS. FIV can also cause the cancer known as lymphosarcoma, although this tumour is more commonly associated with FeLV. As distinct from FeLV though, many FIV-infected cats seem able to lead completely normal lives. FIV is not transferable to humans, nor is HIV transferable to cats.

FIV is also shed in the saliva and is mainly transmitted by fighting, as in the case of FeLV. But this virus also is unable to survive outside the body, so the same comments apply as in FeLV cases – it is safe to board them, and you cannot transmit the disease to any other cats on your clothes or hands. Unfortunately there is no vaccine available yet to prevent this disease. It is worth remembering that as tom cats bite the neck of queens when they are mating, FIV could be passed this way to the queen, and possibly even from the queen to the tom. It is recommended that cat breeders test their cats annually for FIV and require that any visiting studs or queens are also regularly tested. FIV is not thought to cross the placenta to the unborn kittens.

Clinical Signs. After infection with FIV, a cat may show surprisingly few signs. He may initially be a bit unwell for a few weeks and your vet may be able to detect that his lymph nodes are a bit enlarged, but most appear completely normal. This may last for years until in old age he begins to show signs of immune deficiency, becoming prone to repeat infections, weight loss, dullness and possibly tumours. However, surveys have shown that FIV-positive cats do not necessarily have a shorter life-expectancy than non-infected cats!

Diagnosis. As with FeLV, your vet can perform a rapid in-house blood test for this disease, and in fact the test is usually a combined FeLV/FIV test. If there is any doubt, a sample can also be sent to a veterinary laboratory.

Treatment. Because there are few signs, especially in the early stages, even if your cat is proved positive on a blood test, treatment is not necessary unless he is ill.

Prevention. There is no vaccine available as yet in the UK but there is in the USA. Several laboratories are working on this worldwide. Female neutered cats tend to have a small territory of usually the yard or garden, so are not really a risk to other people's cats. Entire tom cats, however, roam much further and fight, so castrating them usually helps by reducing fighting and their urge to roam in search of mates. Where there are very few cats, such as in the countryside, there is no reason to keep them in.

FELINE INFECTIOUS PERITONITIS (FIP)

Feline infectious peritonitis (FIP) is a disease caused by a coronavirus infection, which invades and grows in certain white blood cells. These infected cells carry the virus throughout the cat's body causing an intense inflammatory reaction. This reaction between the body's own immune system and the virus is responsible for the disease.

Most cats become infected by inhaling or ingesting the virus, which is shed by infected cats in their saliva and faeces. The virus can survive for a number of weeks in the environment, so cats become infected either by direct contact or by contact with virus-contaminated surfaces like clothing, bedding, feeding bowls or toys. The virus is, however, rapidly inactivated by most household detergents and disinfectants. An inexpensive and effective disinfectant is household bleach using 25ml of bleach per 1ltr of water.

Clinical Signs. There are often no signs at all that the cat has been infected with the coronavirus, although a mild respiratory illness may occur – sneezing, runny eyes and so on, and sometimes diarrhoea. Most cats recover completely from these early signs, some remain as carriers and only a small proportion develop the lethal form of the disease some long time afterwards – weeks, months or perhaps years later.

When the lethal form of the disease occurs, it may be very sudden particularly in kittens. In other cases, the signs come on gradually but are very vague – perhaps off food, weight loss, poor coat and depression. Gradually the disease progresses to the lethal form, which can be of two types: the so-called wet FIP or the dry FIP, both of which can revert to the other type.

- Wet FIP. In this form there is an accumulation of fluid in the abdomen and chest, which causes enlargement of the abdomen and pressure on the lungs so the cat has difficulty in breathing.
- Dry FIP. This usually develops more slowly and the signs are vaguer. There is usually weight loss, depression, anaemia and the temperature rises. Increased thirst and frequency of urination often occur as the kidneys fail; the liver and pancreas can fail, so jaundice, vomiting, diarrhoea or diabetes can occur. Other organs are often affected, such as the nervous system causing loss of balance, behavioural changes, fits or eye disease leading to blindness may be seen. Any or all of these signs can be seen in various combinations, and because of this, FIP can mimic other diseases and can be very difficult for your vet to diagnose. Luckily it is a relatively uncommon disease in the general cat population, but in multiple-cat households, rescue homes and catteries the disease rate can be much higher.

Diagnosis. There are blood tests that detect the presence of coronavirus antibodies in a cat, but not necessarily one that causes FIP. If the test is negative, it means the cat has not been exposed to a coronavirus and thus has not got FIP. Recently, however, new tests have been developed that can detect parts of the virus itself, but for confirmation, a biopsy of affected tissue is necessary.

Treatment. Unfortunately there is no treatment that will cure this disease, but some treatments may lead to short-term remissions in some patients. A combination of corticosteroids and antibiotics, while maintaining food and fluid intake, may be helpful in some cases. Immunotherapy with a drug called interferon, is also an option. A vaccine exists in the USA but because of doubts as to its effectiveness, it has not been approved or licensed in the UK.

FELINE INFECTIOUS ANAEMIA (FIA)

This is a disease of the blood stream caused by a bacterial parasite called *Mycoplasma haemofelis*. This attaches to the surface of the red blood cells which it destroys, leading to a type of anaemia called haemolytic anaemia. It is still not fully known how the disease is spread between cats, but as very young kittens can be infected, it is thought that it could be spread from the mother. However, non-infected and infected cats are known to have been housed together for long periods with no transmission between cats, so saliva and urine are not thought to spread infection. Although FIA is not a common disease, it seems that older male, non-pedigree cats are the most likely to be infected, which suggests that fights and fleas may be involved in transmission of infection between cats. It is known though that infection can be spread by an injection of infected blood, as in a blood transfusion from an infected donor, and during cat bites where a healthy cat bites an infected one.

Symptoms. Clinical signs of anaemia include tiredness, depression, a reduced appetite and pale gums. There may be a raised temperature in the early stages, respiratory signs and weight loss can occur.

Diagnosis. This is not always easy and usually relies upon the microscopic examination of blood smears to identify the bacterium on the surface of red blood cells. However, because the parasite is not present on the red cells all the time, but appears in cycles, this method is not always reliable. A new technique called a polymerase chain reaction (PCR) assay is more reliable, and only requires a small blood sample.

Treatment. Very specific antibiotics are used to treat FIA, sometimes with the addition of corticosteroids to suppress the immune-mediated destruction of red blood cells. The PCR assay can be used to monitor how treatment is progressing. In severe cases, blood transfusions may be required, along with supportive care such as encouraging the cat to eat, and when the cat is dehydrated, rehydration therapy is helpful. While the antibiotic treatment can often be successful in treating the anaemia, cats may remain symptomless carriers of the disease for life. In times of stress, however, they may have relapses.

Prevention. There is no vaccine available but as fleas and fights are thought to be involved, it is another reason to use regular flea prevention on your cat, and try to avoid aggression with other cats.

BORDETELLA BRONCHISEPTICA

Bordetella bronchiseptica is a bacterium that the veterinary profession has known for some long time as the major cause of kennel cough in dogs but only fairly recently has it been discovered that it could also cause respiratory disease in cats. It has been found in cats with respiratory disease in breeding colonies and it is now thought that it may play a significant role in some cases of feline respiratory tract disease. It has been shown that *B. bronchiseptica* is fairly widespread in the cat population but that disease itself often only occurs when the cats are stressed. Examples of this would be in breeding and boarding catteries, and during pregnancy and giving birth.

Clinical Signs. Affected cats may cough, have a runny nose, runny eyes, sneeze and occasionally be dull with a high temperature; very similar to those of cat flu. They become infected by inhaling the bacteria into their noses. In young kittens, the disease can progress rapidly to bronchopneumonia and death.

Diagnosis. The disease can be diagnosed by your vet taking a swab from the cat's throat or from the nasal discharge of affected cats.

Treatment. Antibiotic treatment in either tablet or palatable syrup form is usually successful if the disease is caught early.

Prevention. A vaccine to prevent disease caused by *B. bronchiseptica* is available, which can also reduce the severity of disease in infected cats. It is in droplet form into the nose but is not usually used unless the cat is to enter a high-risk area such as a cattery or where contact with the disease is suspected or likely. Your own vet is the best person to advise on this.

GIARDIA

Clinical Signs. This disease is caused by a protozoan parasite, *Giardia lamblia*, which can cause gastrointestinal tract disease. Diarrhoea is the commonest sign of infection, and the parasite is passed on in the faeces to other cats that become infected by exposure to an infected cat (e.g. through grooming, through contaminated litter boxes or by drinking contaminated water) or by eating infected prey species. As with several cat diseases, giardiasis seems to be more of a problem in multi-cat households.

Diagnosis. Examination of a sample of faeces under the microscope by your vet may reveal the parasite but it's usual to examine three different samples, as the parasite is not shed every day.

Treatment. No medicines are licensed specifically to treat *Giardia* but some of the treatments for worm parasites in cats are used effectively, especially fenbendazole.

Giardia vaccination is not available in the UK, although a vaccine that has some effect is used in the USA.

TOXOPLASMA

Toxoplasmosis is a disease of cats and other mammals that, like *Giardia*, is caused by a parasitic protozoan. These are single-celled organisms and are among the simplest creatures around. Although infection with *Toxoplasma* is fairly common, actual disease caused by the parasite is relatively rare.

Toxoplasma has a complicated life-cycle involving more than one animal, but cats are the definitive host of the parasite and are the main reservoir of infection to other animals. They are important in transmission of *Toxoplasma* to other animals, including human beings, which become involved only as intermediate hosts of the parasite. Eating raw meat is also an important method of transmission. Cats become infected by eating any of the stages of the parasite, usually by eating an infected mouse or other prey species. The *Toxoplasma* then multiplies rapidly in the cat's intestine and the cat passes these out in its faeces in large numbers. If this form of the parasite is eaten by another mammal, it becomes infected and the life-cycle continues. Sometimes the parasite penetrates the cat's intestinal wall and finds its way to other organs, where it forms cysts and remains dormant for up to long periods of time.

Clinical Signs. Most infected cats show no clinical signs of infection with *Toxoplasma* but occasionally, usually in kittens and young adults, disease does occur. If so, lethargy, depression, loss of appetite and a raised temperature occur. Respiratory signs and pneumonia can be a main sign in many cats, but other organs can be affected. Hepatitis can occur causing diarrhoea, vomiting, weakness and jaundice. Toxoplasmosis can affect the eyes and also the central nervous system causing odd behaviour, circling, fits and loss of control over urination and defecation.

Diagnosis. If toxoplasmosis is strongly suspected from the signs of illness, a blood test may show an increase in antibodies to *Toxoplasma*. To make a definite diagnosis, a microscopic examination by your vet of tissue samples for characteristic pathological changes and the presence of parasites, is necessary. However, if high antibody levels are present in a healthy cat, this suggests that the cat has been previously infected and now is most likely immune and not excreting the parasites.

Treatment. This must be started as soon as possible after diagnosis and continued for several days after signs have disappeared. An antibiotic is fairly effective in treating this disease, but there is no vaccine as yet available to prevent toxoplasmosis in cats, humans or other species.

Human Infection

Toxoplasma is a zoonosis, which is the name given to any disease that can affect both man and animals and can be passed between them, either directly or through a so-called intermediate host. *Toxoplasma* can infect people with weakened immune systems, and women who become infected during pregnancy, can produce children with severe illnesses. People usually become infected by eating undercooked or raw meat, or from contaminated soil on unwashed or undercooked vegetables. However, people are highly unlikely to become infected from direct contact with their cats, but from parasites surviving from a previous infection.

RABIES

Rabies is a virus disease that affects the central nervous system. Many species are affected throughout the world. The main hosts are the dog, cat, fox, vampire bat, skunk, mongoose and, of course, humans – as rabies is another zoonosis.

Rabies is present in the continents of Europe, America, India and Asia, but not Australasia. However, within these continents certain countries are free of rabies – notably Britain and Ireland, Portugal, some Scandinavian countries and Japan. France has historically had many cases each year, especially in the fox population, but due to widespread vaccination of foxes in bait, this is now reducing.

Spread of the Disease

The virus is spread by a susceptible cat being bitten by an infected animal. The virus itself cannot penetrate intact skin but can gain entry through a pre-existing cut. The virus enters a nerve ending in the skin and travels from here up the nerve to the spinal cord; from here it travels slowly up to the brain. So far the animal is symptomless and the original wound will have healed. Once in the brain, the virus spreads down the nerves to the salivary glands and into the saliva in the mouth. It then spreads to another animal when this saliva is introduced through a bite.

Signs

The virus travels along the nerves and in cats usually takes two to six weeks to reach the brain, when for about two days the cat shows odd, variable, erratic behaviour patterns. From this initial phase, rabies usually develops into one of two types:

- Furious rabies. The cat becomes more excitable, restless and develops an odd behaviour pattern. He may roam, so the potential for spread from bites is tremendous, and he becomes aggressive and hypersensitive to sights and sounds. An affected cat will then become weaker as paralysis sets in, will have difficulty swallowing and become progressively more comatose until death occurs.
- Dumb rabies. In cats this is the less common form and is more difficult to diagnose. The cat just becomes duller as paralysis sets in, and coma and death follow.

In both forms, death usually occurs within five days of the start of the classic symptoms. Affected cats should not be handled or euthanased, but should be confined in a cage or cat-carrier and the case reported to DEFRA. Any in-contact cats or cats should also be isolated until a diagnosis has been established.

Diagnosis

There have been no cases of rabies in the UK outside quarantine for just on a century. Quarantine for six months still exists in Britain for animals that have come from a country outside the EU and where rabies still occurs, but was abolished in favour of vaccination several years ago for animals coming in from the EU and various other rabies-free countries. However, the above signs in a cat in quarantine would be sufficient to isolate the cat. Food and water are pushed through the bars but no-one contacts the cat. If death ensues, post-mortem examination of the brain will establish a diagnosis. There is no treatment possible for rabies and, even if there was, people are not allowed to come in contact with rabid dogs or cats, once suspected.

Prevention

Quarantine

As rabies is always fatal, once a human, cat or any other animal becomes infected, any cat entering from a rabies-infected country abroad is vaccinated and placed in quarantine for six months. This isolation has proved totally successful at keeping rabies out, and Great Britain has been free of rabies since 1908.

Vaccination and the PETS (PEts Travel Scheme)

Vaccination against rabies in cats (and dogs) is now widely available and very successful, so this PETS travel scheme has been adopted in the UK to facilitate travel between the UK, European and some other countries. For the UK there are several requirements:

- the cat must first be micro-chipped to specifically identify it;
- the cat must be vaccinated against rabies;
- the cat must then have a blood test (usually two to four weeks later) to show the vaccine has taken;
- if so, a PETS passport is issued;
- rabies vaccination must be boosted every two to three years (this timing is subject to change so ask your vet);
- your cat can travel to any of these countries immediately after vaccination but cannot return until six months after passing the blood test, to ensure it is not incubating the disease; this is a one-off delay only.

A very useful leaflet is published by the British Veterinary Association's Animal Welfare Foundation called 'Taking your pets abroad'. This explains all the regulations, and outlines some of the exotic diseases your pet may be exposed to in some European countries.

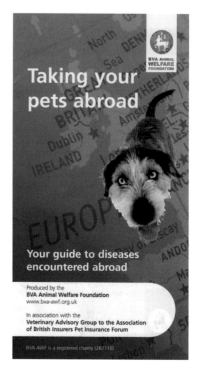

The BVA-AWF leaflet about taking your pet abroad.

Rabies in Humans

Safe vaccines are now available and people in high-risk situations can be protected. This applies both to people bitten abroad or people working in Great Britain in situations where they may be exposed to rabies, e.g. in quarantine kennels or vets working in any situation where rabies may occur.

Chapter 6
Parasites of the Cat

A parasite is an organism that benefits from a prolonged and close association with another (host) animal, which is harmed to a greater or lesser degree. In general, parasites are much smaller than their hosts, show a high degree of specialization for their mode of life and reproduce more. Parasites reduce host fitness in many ways and increase their own fitness by exploiting hosts for food, habitat and dispersal. Parasites can be outside the animal (external parasites) or inside the animal (internal parasites).

EXTERNAL PARASITES

Fleas

Fleas are extremely common and are the single most common cause of skin disease in cats. They are small, reddish-black, sideways-flattened insects that can move rapidly between the cat's hairs because of this shape. Adult fleas can live for several weeks and spend all this time on the cat. They mate and the females lay about 500 tiny white eggs during their life on the cat but these are very smooth and rapidly fall off wherever the cat is at the time. In many cases this is in the house, so there are numerous eggs around in any house where the cat has fleas. These eggs hatch out into minute, whitish, maggot-like larvae. In the winter, if the temperature is low, this can take months, but in the warmer environment of summer or in a warm, centrally heated house, this can be as short as a few days. High humidity also speeds the hatching up. These larvae feed on debris in the carpets or cat's bedding, grow and then form a pupa or chrysalis before emerging as an adult flea. The pupa can remain in this inactive state of development for up to a year, or can emerge as an adult flea much quicker. This whole life-cycle in ideal and warm conditions can be as short as three weeks.

Hatching of the pupa into a flea is dependent on temperature and movement in the house. In warm conditions, it happens more rapidly. If the house is empty for a period, hatching seems to be postponed until movement of animals or people in the house stimulate the fleas to hatch out. This explains why people often get bitten by fleas if they return home after a holiday during which the cat has been in a cattery – it is not fleas from the cattery but pupae stimulated to hatch by the movement of returning inhabitants!

During a feed, a flea bites the skin of a cat and injects saliva into the skin to stop the blood from clotting. It then sucks up some blood, digests it and passes it out later on as small, shiny, black droppings.

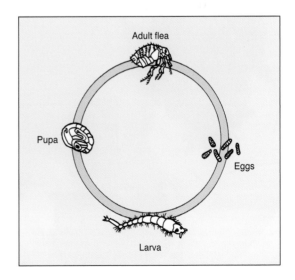

Fig 3 *Life-cycle of the flea.*

Prevention of Fleas

Cats are sociable creatures and if allowed an outdoor life, will mix with, or pass through, areas where other cats (and dogs, and hedgehogs) have been, and if these have fleas, your cat stands a good chance of picking a few up. So it is safer to assume that your cat will be exposed to, and pick up, fleas, especially in the warmer months and especially towards the south of the UK. This, therefore, means that the most effective treatment is to prevent a flea infestation by the regular use of a product that will achieve this. There are two general methods of achieving this, and either, or possibly both, could be the correct method for your cat.

Fleas in the hair (greatly enlarged).

- An adulticide. Use an effective veterinary spot-on application on your cat regularly throughout the year. In the past, fleas used to rapidly develop a resistance to insecticides, but much less so to the modern veterinary treatments, so ask your vet which one she recommends for your cat. These are usually applied to the skin on the back of the neck every four to eight weeks and are extremely safe for the cat. It is applied as a very small volume from a tiny ampoule and is much more tolerated than a spray. However, if a spray is preferred, these are available too, as are insecticide collars but these are usually much less effective and I have seen skin problems around the neck from these. However, as cats groom themselves so thoroughly, it is vitally important to use the correct safe treatment on your cat and under no circumstances use treatments aimed at dogs, as these may well be toxic to cats.

Applying a spot-on flea treatment.

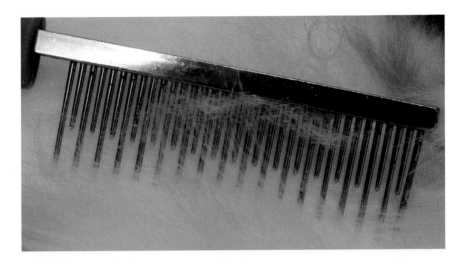

Dark flea droppings and loose hair on a flea comb.

- Insect growth regulators. These are flea contraceptives but are administered to the cat! Take your cat to the vet once every six months for an injection of a medication called lufenuron. This lasts in the cat for six months and prevents any flea that bites the cat from breeding. It does not kill fleas but, if the odd one gets on to the cat, it dies off naturally without leaving any offspring behind in the house. Usually, this twice-yearly injection alone will solve any flea problems, and because one dose can be given at the cat's annual vaccination and health examination appointment, it only means one extra visit to the vet a year. This medication is also available in liquid form given monthly by mouth.

Most vets agree that the most effective way to prevent or eliminate fleas is to use adulticides in combination with insect growth regulators, which is known as integrated flea control.

Note: Some treatments are available that will prevent or treat combinations of fleas, ticks and mites, so it may be worth discussing with your vet which product is best for your cat.

Fleas can affect cats in two ways:

- Flea infestation. The cat becomes infested with fleas from another cat or his environment and becomes irritated by the mere presence of large numbers of fleas, which are biting him. He will generally be itchy, especially in the summer months, and spend a lot of time licking himself, often on his back near the base of the tail or between his back legs. Flea dirt will be seen or even fleas moving rapidly over the skin between the hairs, or if they cannot be located immediately, a fine toothcomb (flea comb from your vet or pet shop) will soon reveal them.
- Flea allergic dermatitis (FAD). A much more serious problem occurs if a cat becomes hypersensitive to, or allergic to, the flea saliva due to repeated exposure to flea bites. In this case, merely one bite every few days will render the cat permanently itchy and ensure that he scratches sufficiently to inflame the skin and lose hair over widespread areas, again especially over his back and towards the base of his tail. In this case it may be difficult or impossible to find a flea, as there may only be the odd one or none at all present at the time.

Flea Infestation
Diagnosis. This is often straightforward. The cat will be very itchy, restless and constantly licking and biting himself. Fleas will usually easily be seen by parting the hair or combing the cat, or flea droppings seen which appear as small black particles in the coat. If the black particles are thought to be flea dirt, a useful test is to place some on a damp white tissue when flea dirt will soften and turn red within a short period as it is mostly dried blood. The diagnosis

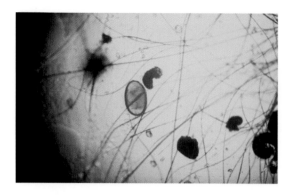

Microscope view of hair, a flea egg and numerous dark flea droppings.

is also based on the absence of effective flea prevention – there are now several very effective ways of preventing flea infestations, but there are also many products available to which fleas have become resistant, so do ask your vet to supply or recommend the best way of preventing or treating fleas in your cats.

Treatment. To remove the adult fleas that are on your cat, use a flea comb initially, and if flea droppings are present in profusion, it is wise to wash, rinse and dry the cat, if possible, as these droppings can be irritant also. If it is a very severe flea infestation, there is also a tablet available from your vet containing nitenpyram, which will kill all the fleas on your cat within minutes but has no lasting effect. So, as with prevention, preferably use an effective veterinary spot-on application on your cat regularly throughout the year after this.

Because the fleas on your cat will have been breeding and producing numerous eggs, larvae and pupa in your house, it is necessary to use a spray that will kill off eggs and larvae, or prevent them from maturing on all the flooring, carpets or furniture where your cat has been. This smells a bit but does not stain; however, it is dangerous for fish, so remove fish tanks from the room on the day you spray, and don't use the room yourself that day.

It is worth mentioning here that the cat flea (and louse) acts as an intermediate host to the *Dipylidium* tapeworm of cats and dogs. The flea larvae will eat tapeworm eggs that are deposited

in the environment when the mature tapeworm segment dries and ruptures, scattering them around. The egg develops into a cyst inside the flea and remains dormant until the adult flea irritates a cat, which licks and swallows the flea. The cyst is then released and develops into an adult tapeworm in the cat. Thus, routine tapeworm treatment should be considered in any cat that is shown to have a flea infestation.

Cat fleas will bite humans and may cause intense irritation. As stated earlier, this is especially so on return from holiday to an empty house, where the developing fleas have had no chance to feed for a few weeks as the cat has been to a boarding kennels. Numerous flea bites may appear around the ankles and the fleas may themselves be seen.

Flea Allergic Dermatitis (FAD)

Diagnosis. In this condition, the cat will be as itchy, if not more itchy, than a cat with a flea infestation but it may be difficult to find a flea. Because of the allergic reaction, there are often sores along the back, or under the abdomen, and these can become so irritating that the cat turns these into ulcers due to excessive licking with his very rough tongue. The presence of one positive dropping on a cat that shows the characteristic lesions along the back, is enough to make a tentative diagnosis of flea allergic dermatitis, despite the frequently encountered retort 'my cat has never had a flea!'. Cat fleas do not indicate a dirty house – rather a pleasant, warm environment with deep-pile carpet, which is very attractive to fleas.

There are also various tests available to the vet for FAD but usually the signs in a cat that is not receiving an effective flea prevention programme are so obvious, that the cause is strongly suspected.

Treatment. The fleas themselves are treated as for a flea infestation but, in addition, it is necessary to reverse the allergic reaction. This is usually achieved by the vet administering an anti-inflammatory medication, either in long-acting injectable or tablet form. Once diagnosed, an effective flea-prevention programme must be established using both an adulticide and an insect growth regulator.

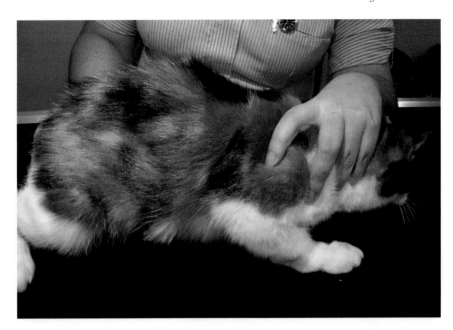

Baldness due to flea allergic dermatitis.

Lice

A louse is a wingless insect that lives on your cat's skin and feeds on its skin debris. Lice can be seen with the naked eye as small, white or pale-orange dots crawling very slowly between and up the hairs. They are not seen as commonly on cats as fleas and are much easier to treat because they spend their whole life on the cat laying eggs, which they attach to the hairs and, therefore, do not affect the environment at all. The white, single egg attached to the hair is known as a nit. Lice do not cause a serious skin problem but, if present in sufficient numbers, they can produce small, itchy scabby areas of eczema.

Cats and dogs have their own species of lice, neither of which infect humans. Kittens or debilitated cats are more likely to be affected.

Diagnosis. The presence of the lice or their eggs is considered diagnostic in an itchy cat. A hand lens may be useful to see them.

Treatment. Modern parasiticidal preparations used for the treatment of fleas will also kill and prevent lice effectively. Usually one treatment alone, of an effective spot-on treatment, as for fleas, will kill the lice and also last in the coat long enough for the eggs to hatch out and be killed. A good thorough combing a week later should remove the dead lice. It may be wise to repeat the spot-on one month later, however, to be certain. As the parasite completes its life-cycle entirely on the cat, the environment does not have to be treated. Again it is worth mentioning that the cat louse can act as an intermediate host to the *Dipylidium* tapeworm of cats.

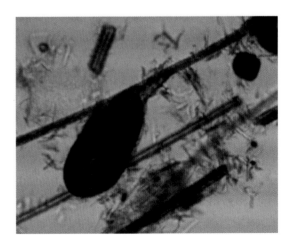

Microscope view of cat louse egg on hair.

Ticks

The ticks that are found on cats, especially in the summer months, are usually parasites of sheep, cattle and hedgehogs. They are not insects but parasitic members of the spider family, and the small adult tick is brushed on to the cat from the grass then crawls over the body, finds a suitable place to stay and bites on to the skin. It now remains in this one spot for up to a week, sucking blood and swelling until, in some species of tick, it becomes the size of a pea. It is usually beige or reddish in colour, and will now drop off the cat and, if female, lays eggs in the environment. These hatch into larvae, which repeat the above process, and become attached to any passing host, which may be a sheep, cow, cat, dog, rodent, hedgehog or human. After a feed, this larva drops off, undergoes change and finds another host. After two to three larval stages, depending on the species of tick, the adult form of the tick is reached and the cycle recommences. This is the method by which ticks from the countryside are brought into the parks and gardens of towns and cities.

Diagnosis. Surprisingly the presence of a tick does not usually make the cat itchy, although in the case of hedgehog ticks, they can be present in such large numbers that they are very irritant. I have seen literally scores of small hedgehog ticks on cats' faces, around the eyes and ears. Ticks are usually found by the owner during grooming.

A sheep tick feeding on cat blood.

Treatment. There are several ways by which the tick can be removed, but the easiest, quickest and least painful way is to use a 'tick remover', which can be obtained from any vet or pet shop. This is like a plastic miniature claw hammer about two inches long. It is gently slid along between the tick and the skin and then slowly rotated, not pulled. After about the third rotation, the tick magically become detached and is left in the tick remover to be destroyed. A tick can also be pulled off with fine forceps, which grasp the tick where it is attached to the skin, or it can be killed with cotton wool soaked in spirit or a parasiticide and then removed, as above. It must not be removed by burning, as is sometimes mentioned by clients! This is very painful for the cat. By any other method than the specific tick remover, the tick's mouthparts can be left in the skin and cause a foreign body reaction or abscess, so I would only recommend this method.

Occasionally, the bite wound will become infected and need treatment. In some countries, ticks are the carriers of disease. Currently the only one of concern in the UK is Lyme disease, caused by a bacterium called *Borrelia*. This can also affect humans, so it is wise to remove a tick as soon as it is seen, and even more sensible to use a parasiticide, which will kill ticks during the warmer months. Abroad, other diseases, such as tick borne fever and heartworm, are carried by ticks and the potential arrival of such diseases is a worry for the UK with global warming.

Mites

There are several species of mite that affect cats.

Feline Scabies

This is an uncommon disease of cats and is caused by tiny mites called *Sarcoptes* (and even more uncommonly in Europe, *Notoedres*), which affect cats very much like they affect dogs. Mites are tiny members of the spider family and spend their entire life on the cat. The female mite burrows into the skin laying eggs and in three to eight days, the eggs hatch into larvae reaching adulthood within two to three weeks.

Symptoms. The disease usually start with hair loss and itching on the ears and then spreads to

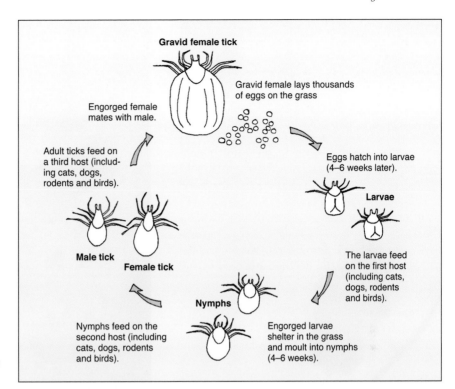

Gravid female tick

Gravid female lays thousands of eggs on the grass

Engorged female mates with male.

Adult ticks feed on a third host (including cats, dogs, rodents and birds).

Eggs hatch into larvae (4–6 weeks later).

Larvae

Male tick

Female tick

The larvae feed on the first host (including cats, dogs, rodents and birds).

Nymphs

Nymphs feed on the second host (including cats, dogs, rodents and birds).

Engorged larvae shelter in the grass and moult into nymphs (4–6 weeks).

Fig 4 Life-cycle of the sheep tick.

the face, eyelids, neck and elsewhere. The skin becomes thickened, wrinkled and covered with crusts.

Diagnosis is usually based on the symptoms and microscopic examination of skin scrapings taken by your vet.

Treatment is by the use of insecticides, but remember that most insecticides that will kill the mites will *not* be safe to use in a cat, as they are much more sensitive to some of the insecticides that are used on dogs. You must be guided by your vet on this.

Demodex

This microscopic, cigar-shaped mite only rarely affects cats, where it causes a non-itchy patchy hair loss.

Diagnosis is by eliminating other causes and by identifying the mites with a microscope examination of skin samples.

Treatment. The cat has to be dipped in a solution of a parasiticide called amitraz weekly for two to three weeks and must wear an Elizabethan collar to ensure it cannot take the solution in by grooming.

Cheyletiella

This white mite lives on the skin and is just about large enough to be seen with the naked eye. It can be present in such numbers as to resemble dandruff. Because they move, it is often referred to as 'walking dandruff'! Cats have their own *Cheyletiella* mite but can also be infected by the rabbit version called the rabbit fur mite. It lives on the surface of the skin especially along the back, and causes intense irritation leading to the excessive dandruff seen. This irritation and dandruff are the main signs of the problem.

Diagnosis. The mite is similar in size and appearance to a grain of salt and can be seen moving under a microscope or magnifying glass. If it is suspected, the mites can easily be found by pressing a short length of Sellotape on to the suspected area and examining it under a microscope.

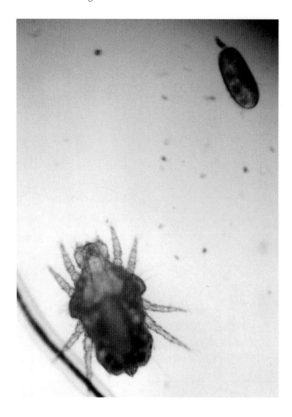

A Cheyletiella mite and its egg under the microscope.

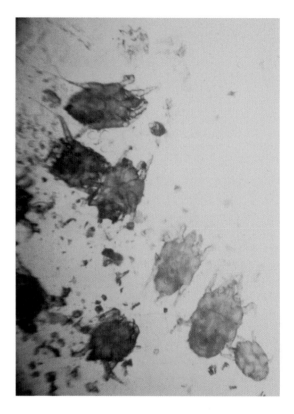

A large group of ear mites (Otodectes) under the microscope.

Treatment. As with Feline scabies, most insecticides that will kill the mites will also not be safe to use in a cat, as they are much more sensitive to some of the insecticides that are safe to use in the dog. You must be guided by your vet on this.

Harvest Mites (Trombiculids)

Harvest mite infestation occurs in the late summer, starting about the middle to late July. The little, orange harvest mite larvae infect the ear flaps, feet, legs and skin of the belly, where they cause intense irritation.

Diagnosis. The orange mites can just be seen with the naked eye or a hand lens, often on the legs especially, but a skin irritation that regularly develops in the late summer or early autumn on a cat is likely to be caused by these mites.

Treatment. Most insecticides that will kill the mites will also not be safe to use in a cat, as they are much more sensitive to some of the insecticides that are safe to use in the dog. You must be guided by your vet on this.

Ear Mites

These tiny, parasitic members of the spider family are called *Otodectes*. They live and breed in the ear canals of cats and dogs. They graze on the lining of the ear canal and cause intense irritation. The ear produces a lot of wax in response, which can block the canal leading to infection by bacteria and yeasts called *otitis externa* (*see* Chapter 11).

It is a common problem, especially in kittens, usually in both ears, and in the early stages there may be little to see apart from an increase in wax. As the disease progresses, the ear begins to smell, the discharge increases and the cat shakes his head, scratches his ear or rubs it along the ground. The ear may become very painful and the cat resents examination. If only one ear is affected, the cat may hold his head towards that side. It is very contagious between cats and to dogs (but not to humans), and the kittens have invariably caught it from their mother or other cats in their immediate community. It is much more common in farm or feral cats, or other situations where a number of cats live together and are not closely examined or contacted frequently.

Diagnosis. Your vet will firstly examine the ears with the naked eye and then with an auriscope (an instrument for looking in ears). She will usually be able to see the tiny white mites moving about in the canal but, if a lot of wax is present, she may gently remove this with a cotton bud and examine it for mites under a microscope.

Treatment. If caught in the early stages this condition responds very well to treatment. First, a thorough cleaning of the canal with a wax solvent may be needed. Then it is necessary to instil drops into the ears, which will kill the mites and remove the waxy debris. So you will be supplied with drops and advised to apply these into the ears on a daily or twice-daily basis until the problem is cleared. Because the mites breed in the ears and lay eggs that are resistant to the drops, it's wise to continue treatment on

an occasional basis for up to six weeks, in some cases, to ensure there is no recurrence.

If the condition has been unnoticed, untreated and allowed to progress, it may be necessary for your vet to clean the ears out removing all the accumulated debris and wax under an anaesthetic before providing treatment. In very severe cases, surgery is needed to open up the ear canal.

INTERNAL PARASITES

There are two groups of parasitic worms that commonly infect the intestines of cats – roundworms and tapeworms – and these include two species of roundworm and two species of tapeworm. The adults of all four types live and feed in the intestines of the cat. There is also a roundworm that affects the lungs of cats, but this is relatively uncommon.

Tapeworms

Both tapeworms require an intermediate host to complete their life-cycle, so there is no direct transmission of these from cat to cat.

Dipylidium caninum
This tapeworm is commonly found in the cat. A single *Dipylidium* can grow up to 30cm (11.8in)

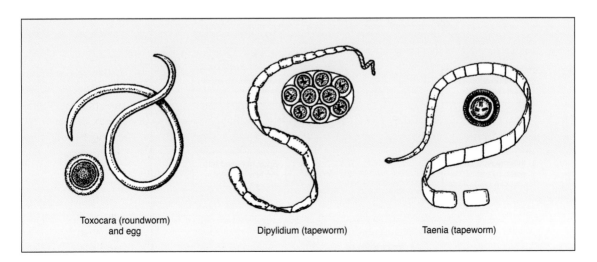

Toxocara (roundworm) and egg   Dipylidium (tapeworm)   Taenia (tapeworm)

Fig 5 Intestinal worms of cat.

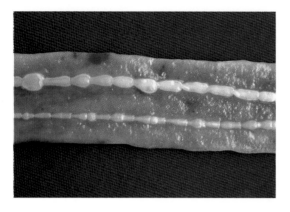

A Dipylidium tapeworm at post mortem.

A dried Dipylidium segment on fur of a cat.

long and consists of a small, pointed head and a long, flattened, segmented body.

Life-cycle. The head of the tapeworm is embedded in the intestinal wall and the rest of the tapeworm consists of gradually maturing segments containing eggs. Mature segments break off from the rear of the tapeworm in the cat's large intestine and are passed out by the cat in its faeces or even alone. Fresh segments are mobile and can be seen moving in a caterpillar fashion on the faeces or even crawling across

the cat's fur in this area. Once exposed to the air, the segments dry and closely resemble grains of rice. Once dry, each segment ruptures and releases the eggs it contains into the environment.

To complete the life-cycle of *Dipylidium*, an intermediate host is required and, in the case of the cat, it is the flea or louse. The tapeworm eggs in the environment are eaten by the flea larvae, which are also in the environment in the carpets and so on, then hatch and burrow through the flea's intestines into its body where they develop

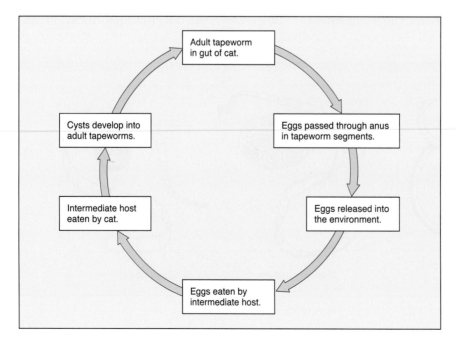

Fig 6 Life-cycle of tapeworms.

into cysts. These cysts do not develop further until the cat, irritated by the presence of the flea on its skin, licks and swallows it. The flea is digested, releasing the tapeworm cyst, which develops into a mature tapeworm in the cat's intestine, completing the life-cycle.

Note: Humans can also very occasionally become infected with *Dipylidium* in the same way as cats, if they happen to swallow an infected flea.

Taenia taeniaeformis

Taenia is a much longer tapeworm than *Dipylidium* and can grow up a metre or longer.

Life-cycle. This is similar to *Dipylidium* but the intermediate host is usually a rabbit, mouse or other small rodent, which the cat must eat raw to become infected. In this case, the mature segments containing the tapeworm eggs are again shed at the cat's anus, are mobile and can be seen crawling around this area when fresh. They dry, rupture and release the eggs into the environment. These eggs are eaten by the intermediate host and form cysts in its liver, where they remain dormant until the cat eats the rodent. The digestion of the rodent by the cat releases the tapeworm cyst, which latches on to the bowel lining, matures and completes the life-cycle. This tapeworm cannot affect young kittens until they are old enough to catch and eat prey.

Signs of Infection by either Tapeworm

The presence of tapeworms in small numbers does not normally cause any clinical signs in the animal, but a heavy infection with many tapeworms present may cause diarrhoea. In addition, the segments moving on the coat around the anus may cause irritation and so the cat may be seen licking its anal area excessively.

Treatment. The first priority when segments are noticed is to give the cat treatment for tapeworm. This can be administered in any one of three ways:

- By mouth in the form of a single tablet containing praziquantel obtainable from your vet or chemist.

- Where it is difficult to give a cat a tablet, an injection of the same medication can be given by the vet.
- By using a 'spot-on' treatment specially formulated for cats, which is applied to the skin at the scruff of the neck

Only one treatment is needed to kill any tapeworms present in the cat at the time but some vets recommend a second treatment in three weeks, because the owner will need to control the fleas to control tapeworms. This could take at least a month or so during which time the cat could become re-infected with *Dipylidium*.

Roundworms

Intestinal Roundworms

There are two species of roundworm that commonly parasitize cat's intestines: *Toxocara cati*, which is the more important, and *Toxascaris leonine*, which rarely causes any ill effects. To understand the signs and implications of infection, it is necessary to understand their life-cycles.

Life-Cycles

Toxocara cati. The male and female adult worms live in the intestine of the cat and the females produce eggs. These thick-shelled but microscopic eggs are passed in the faeces into the environment. Within these eggs, larvae develop and after about three weeks (and only after this time – fresh eggs are not infective)

Cat roundworms found at post mortem.

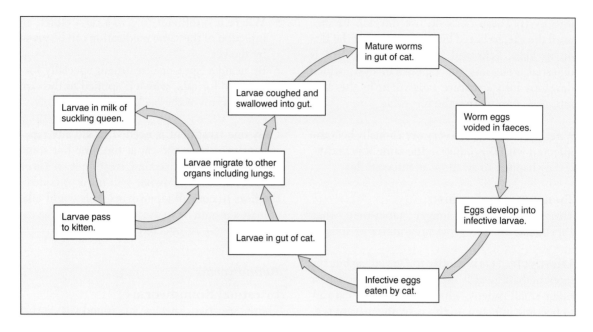

Fig 7 *Life-cycle of Toxascaris roundworms.*

they are at the infective stage to cats and other animals. When these are inadvertently eaten by a cat as it licks and investigates the environment, the larvae are released from the eggs into the cat's intestine, where they travel via the liver and lungs to be coughed up and swallowed to mature in the cat's intestine and complete the life-cycle.

In older cats, the larvae may not complete this cycle and end up dormant in other tissues, where they cause little harm. In nursing queens, however, the larvae can migrate to the mammary glands and pass to the kittens as they suckle.

A third possibility occurs if prey species such as rodents or birds eat the infective eggs. The life-cycle is completed when the cat becomes infected through eating the prey.

Again, humans can become infected through accidentally eating the infective eggs in the environment – biting soiled fingernails and so on.

Toxascaris leonine. The life-cycle is similar to, but much more straightforward than, that of *T. cati*, in that infection occurs in cats by eating infective eggs in the environment or prey species, which have eaten these eggs and become infected. In cats, the larvae do not migrate through other parts of the body but pass straight to the intestines to complete the life-cycle. In the prey species, however, the larvae do migrate to other tissues and remain dormant until the prey is eaten by the cat.

Signs of Infection

In heavy infestations, both species may be seen in the vomit or faeces of cats, and are relatively large. The worms resemble white or pale pink earthworms and are 10cm (4in) or more in length. They can occur in large numbers, especially in kittens, as these have little resistance to them, and are seen in bundles when vomited, rather like spaghetti. A kitten with a large infestation, apart from vomiting and possibly having diarrhoea too, will look unthrifty, have a ravenous appetite but not gain weight, and will have a pot-bellied appearance. In adults, the worms rarely occur in large numbers and cause few if any signs of disease, as a balance seems to set up whereby neither the host cat nor parasite are harmed. However, these adult female worms are passing out large numbers of eggs in the faeces into the environment where the cat lives and will cause re-infection and, of course, infect other cats.

Prevention and Treatment

Due to the cat's hunting and roaming life-style, the recommendations of the British Small Animal Veterinary Association (BSAVA), with which I totally agree, are to worm your adult cat with an effective wormer every three months. If either of the two species of roundworm is diagnosed or suspected, it is sensible to worm the cat again. As kittens can be infected through the milk, it is recommended that they are wormed starting at six weeks of age and repeated according to the manufacturers' recommendations until they are twelve to fourteen weeks of age – consult your vet, as several products are available but it is important to use a safe one at the correct dose. Thereafter, worming should be carried out at six months of age and then two to four times a year for the rest of their lives. House cats, which spend all their life indoors, probably need to be wormed less often but as the worm eggs are sticky, they can be brought into the house on shoes.

It is important to use a modern veterinary wormer, such as those containing either fenbendazole, pyrantel embonate or milbemycin oxime. All of these products will treat either species of roundworm and are available from several manufacturers, while the latter two are available combined with praziquantel, which will kill off any tapeworms present at the same time. Your vet will be able to supply or prescribe them.

Lungworms

One species of roundworm, *Aelurostrongylus abstrusus*, parasitises the lungs of cats, the adult worms living and feeding in the cat's lungs, and requires an intermediate host, a snail or slug, to complete the life-cycle.

Life-Cycle. The adult female worms lay eggs in the lungs, which develop into larvae and are coughed up, swallowed and passed out of the cat

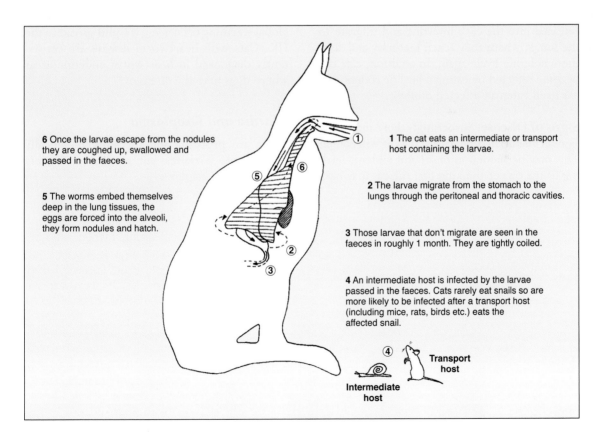

Fig 8 Life-cycle of the cat lungworm.

The snail is an intermediate host for the cat lungworm.

in the faeces. These develop to an infective stage and are eaten by molluscs, such as slugs and snails, where they remain until eaten by a cat or transport host. If this happens, the larvae are released into the cat's intestine and migrate to the lungs, where they reach maturity and start the whole life-cycle again. In addition, cats can become infected by eating a bird or rodent that has itself eaten an infected mollusc.

Signs of Disease. Surprisingly there may be no signs at all but, in other cases, the cat will cough. This may be sudden in onset and violent, leading to the owner thinking that the cat may have a fish bone stuck in its throat. In severe infections the cat may have difficulty breathing.

Diagnosis. This condition is suspected if the coughing does not clear up with treatment for the usual cause of coughs in cats. An X-ray may show odd patterns in the lungs but an examination of fresh faeces under a microscope is the most reliable method of diagnosis, when the larvae can be seen.

Treatment. A wormer called fenbendazole is licensed for treatment in cats and is available from your vet or elsewhere in granule or liquid form. Treatment will need to be repeated.

Heartworm

This infection in cats, by a worm called *Dirofilaria immitis*, is a problem with an increasing incidence and awareness worldwide, but as yet it is absent or very rare in the UK. It does occur in Europe, and the worry is that, with global warming occurring, it could spread to the UK. Cats with heartworm disease are consistently diagnosed in heartworm endemic areas where dogs have the disease.

Giardia and Toxoplasma

These are protozoa and therefore technically microscopic parasites but are more sensibly dealt with in Chapter 5.

Chapter 7
The Digestive System

NORMAL STRUCTURE AND FUNCTION

The digestive system consists essentially of the mouth, throat or pharynx, oesophagus, stomach, intestines, liver and pancreas. The function of the digestive system is to convert food that the cat needs for energy, growth, and maintenance of body tissues into a form that the body can use. Food is taken in through the mouth; chewed, where it mixes with saliva, which starts the digestive process; swallowed; and then broken down in the stomach and intestines by enzymes. These are substances that are

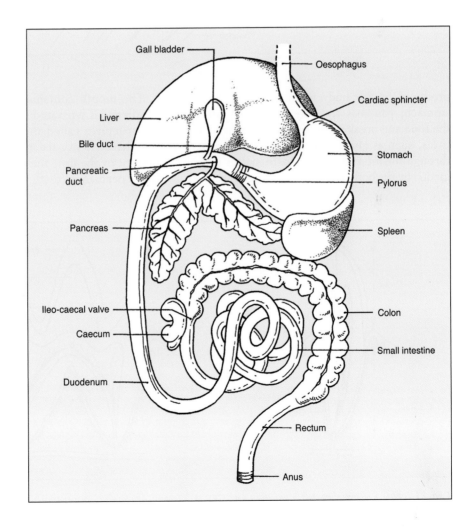

Fig 9 The digestive system.

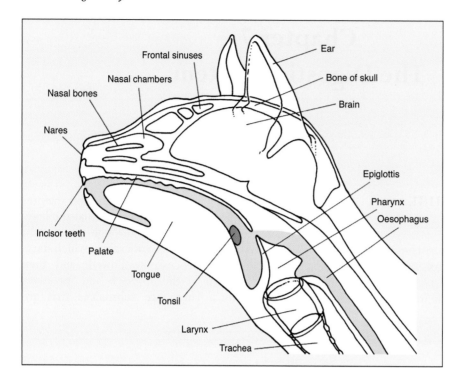

Fig 10 Section through head showing mouth and pharynx.

produced by the body in the salivary glands, stomach, pancreas and intestines; they attack the food and break it down into very small particles, such as glucose, which can be absorbed through the intestinal wall. Waste matter is discarded by the body via the rectum then the anus.

The mouth contains the teeth, tongue and tonsils and is separated from the nasal chambers by structures called the hard and soft palates. Cats have twenty-six milk teeth, which are all present by the time the cat is six weeks old, and thirty permanent teeth, which have replaced the

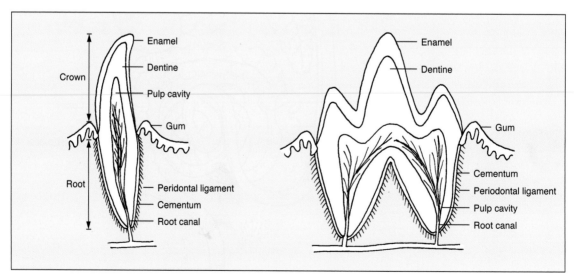

Fig 11 (LEFT) Section through a canine tooth; (RIGHT) section through a molar tooth.

milk teeth by six to eight months of age. There are three salivary glands on each side: the parotid gland, the sublingual, and the submandibular, which discharge saliva into the mouth. This lubricates the food and starts the process of digestion. Although mouth breathing is not normal, the mouth is also used for breathing when the cat is at full exercise, stressed, short of oxygen or is involved in heat loss through panting.

The air passages from the nose join the mouth at the pharynx, which is the area at the back of the throat at the entrances to the oesophagus and larynx. The pharynx leads air from the nose to the larynx but also starts the process of swallowing food into the oesophagus, which is a straight muscular tube passing from the pharynx through the chest to the stomach. The oesophagus has only one function and that is to convey food to the stomach.

The stomach is a muscular sac that receives, stores and mixes the food. It produces an acid secretion and enzymes, which continue the process of digestion. This partly digested food passes from the stomach through the muscular pyloric sphincter into the small intestine, which is a long tube in which the food is finally broken down into its components, which are then absorbed through the intestinal wall. The liver produces bile salts and the pancreas produces enzymes, both of which are secreted into the small intestine just below the pylorus.

The caecum, which is the equivalent organ to the appendix in humans, is situated at the junction of the small and large intestines. In the cat it is a small sac-like structure, and inflammation of the caecum (appendicitis) is extremely rare in this species. The first part of the large intestine is called the colon, and here some food absorption takes place but, more importantly, water is removed to both conserve it and to produce dry faeces, or stools. The faeces, which consist of undigested food, roughage and gut bacteria, are stored in the last part of the large intestine, the rectum. The large intestine also produces mucus, which lubricates the faeces and aids in their evacuation. The exit from the rectum is controlled by a strong muscular ring: the anus.

The part of the body that contains the stomach, intestines, liver and pancreas, along with the spleen, kidneys, adrenal glands, bladder, uterus and other organs, is known as the abdomen. The walls of the abdomen and abdominal organs are covered by a shiny tissue called the peritoneum, which allows free movement of the organs within the abdomen.

DISEASES OF THE MOUTH AND PHARYNX

Inflammation of the Mouth

This can be caused by infection, injuries, licking or swallowing toxic substances, such as acids, or food that is too hot, or can result from a generalized disease, such as cat flu or even kidney failure. The lining of the mouth becomes inflamed and, in severe cases, there will be blisters or ulceration of the gums, tongue or palate, causing excess salivation and a reluctance to eat or drink.

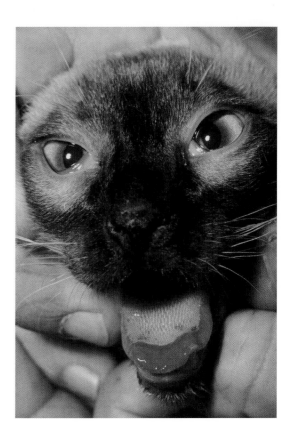

Severe tongue ulceration – glossitis.

Treatment is with antibiotics, usually either by injection, if the mouth is very painful, or by palatable antibiotic syrup, and the cat should be offered soft food at body temperature. Concurrent diseases, such as kidney failure must also be treated.

When the gums are inflamed, this is called gingivitis, and a more serious version of this, when the mucous membranes of the mouth become chronically inflamed is called chronic stomatitis.

Chronic Stomatitis

This is often a very painful condition and, when the angle of the mouth at the throat is affected, the cat will often cry out when opening his mouth. It is a difficult condition to manage and antibiotics have either little or no long-term effect. Some cases are thought to be due to a fault in the cat's immune system but others are because the cat is a carrier of one of the feline influenza viruses.

Treatment. Scaling and polishing the teeth will often help, but in some cases, the only way to heal the gums and remove the pain is to extract all the upper and lower teeth behind the canines. This sounds drastic but the cat is then out of pain, much happier and can eat very well with his now healthy, healed gums.

Pharyngitis (sore throat)

This is fairly common and because the pharynx is inflamed and may be ulcerated, it causes the cat to 'gulp' or retch, so that the owner will often suspect that this is an obstruction of the throat. The cat may be depressed, have a raised temperature and be off his food, but this condition usually responds quickly to treatment with antibiotics.

Tonsillitis

This can occur in young cats and produces symptoms similar to pharyngitis, but there may also be a soft cough. It readily responds to antibiotic therapy but may be a recurring problem. If so, or if the tonsils enlarge and cause airway obstruction, surgical removal (tonsillectomy) is the treatment of choice. However, as the tonsils are responsible for 'mopping' up infection from the pharynx and preventing it from spreading further, they are very useful and are not removed unless absolutely necessary.

Foreign Bodies

The mouth is often injured by foreign objects because the cat uses his mouth for investigating and swallowing objects, and also for chewing bones, if he is given any or finds them. Fish bones, other small pieces of bone and fish hooks are the commonest offenders. The symptoms caused and action to be taken are dealt with in Chapter 20 under first-aid, accidents and emergencies.

Dental Problems

Dental Caries (Tooth Decay)

This is far less of a problem in cats than in dogs or people, but occasionally occurs in the flat molar teeth at the back of the jaw. By the time the cat shows signs of this and the vet finds the caried tooth, the cavity is usually quite large and the tooth has to be extracted. Small cavities however can be drilled out and filled.

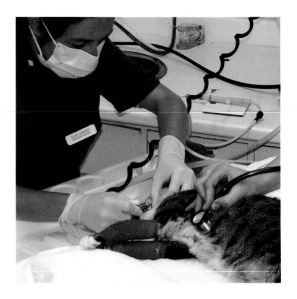

Dentistry is a common veterinary procedure.

Severe calculus formation and some periodontal disease of the gums.

The same cat after the teeth have been scaled and polished.

Periodontal Disease

This, however, is very common in the cat. The periodontal tissues are those around the tooth and consist of the gingiva (gums), ligaments, cement and supporting bone, all of which hold the tooth in place. When things go wrong in this area, the gum inflames, becomes painful and recedes, and the tooth can loosen. Surveys show that more than 85 per cent of cats older than four years have periodontal disease to some extent. The process starts where plaque forms on the teeth. This is a hard deposit composed of minerals and dead bacteria, which slowly accumulates on the teeth, starting at the gum margin. Plaque starts forming very quickly, e.g. within eight hours after a thorough dental cleaning. When plaque is not removed, mineral salts in the saliva precipitate, forming hard calculus. This irritates the gums causing inflammation known as gingivitis, and the gum recedes exposing the root. Infection can then enter the tooth socket causing further inflammation, loosening and eventual loss of the tooth. Cats with advanced gingivitis have an appalling mouth odour. Even with the most advanced dental disease, most cats will continue to eat but must be in considerable discomfort.

Prevention. Only prevention of plaque formation will prevent the above sequence of events, and the best way to do this is to train the cat as a kitten to have his teeth brushed. Using tasty, special cat toothpaste on your finger to start with, gently stroke the outside of his teeth and he should rapidly begin to accept and even like this. Progress through a finger brush slowly to a small soft toothbrush and most kittens will accept this. If you are able to, or take the time to brush his teeth, say, even just three times a week, this will delay any dental problems or possibly even prevent them. Occasionally, a cat can be persuaded to chew raw bones, or dental chews or toys, which also help a lot. There are now specific foods developed that your vet can supply or advise, which help to prevent plaque and calculus from developing.

Treatment. Once dental calculus has formed on the teeth, periodontal disease will follow unless this calculus is removed by a dental scaler. Regular removal of dental plaque under general anaesthetic is routinely carried out by vets and the proportion of dental cases in a normal day's work is quite high. Ultrasonic scalers are now commonplace in veterinary surgeries. The regular gentle scaling and polishing of cats' teeth results in a higher proportion of patients retaining their teeth into old age. Some cats may never need to have their teeth scaled, while others may require scaling as often as every six months. If periodontal disease is advanced and loose teeth are present, these must be extracted and the remaining teeth scaled and polished. Many cats lose their teeth unnecessarily, as their owners have been unaware of the need for regular dental care.

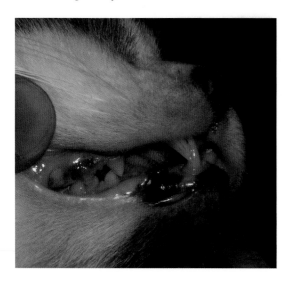

The red areas are resorptive lesions on the molar teeth.

Resorptive Lesions of Teeth

Feline tooth resorption seems to be peculiar to domestic cats, where it is a common and painful condition. The lesions were originally called feline 'neck lesions' because the area of the tooth affected was usually in the 'neck' region of the tooth near the gum. The full correct name is feline odontoclastic resorptive lesion (or FORL). Studies have shown that well over 50 per cent of adult cats develop this at some stage of their life.

In the early stages, the appearance is of a reddened area looking as though the gum tissue is growing into the tooth or covering the base of the tooth, but it is the enamel that has been lost exposing the dentine. It has been removed by the cat's own immune system for reasons that are not known, and the underlying exposed dentine is very painful to the touch. Once it begins, the area enlarges until the whole tooth is 'dissolved'. Cats are very careful not to show pain and must keep eating, so a regular examination of your cat's mouth is essential. Vets often spot this at the cat's annual health examination and vaccination consultation.

Treatment. As the affected area always continues to enlarge, the only treatment is to remove the tooth under a general anaesthetic.

Broken Teeth

Teeth may become broken through accidents or fights, and the teeth mostly affected are the canines. How these fractures are dealt with depends on their severity and position. Some small fractures can be ignored, provided the pulp cavity has not been exposed. Where the fracture is severe and irreparable, it may be better to remove the affected tooth. Because cats' teeth are relatively small, it is unusual but still possible for your vet to carry out root treatment and repair some defects, or refer you to a dental veterinary surgeon. Undetected fractures can result in the formation of a root abscess, which is usually first noticed when the cat refuses food and has a painful swelling below the eye. If left untreated this abscess may rupture and discharge down the cheek. The damaged tooth must then be removed under anaesthetic, the abscess drained and antibiotic treatment instigated.

Tumours

In the cat, the mouth is a common site for the development of tumours. Many are malignant and grow quickly; some readily spread to other organs. The most common site of tumour growth in the mouth is the gum; it can be mistaken for dental disease in the early stages. The first sign the owner may see is excess salivation or drooling, which is often blood-tinged. The cat will resist having his mouth opened and may find it difficult to eat or swallow, and, especially in the later stages, there is an unpleasant smell on the breath. If the mouth can be gently opened, a lump along the line of the upper or lower jaw may be seen. As some tumours develop further back in the mouth or in the throat, it may be necessary for your vet to examine the patient under an anaesthetic.

Treatment is difficult because the tumour will usually have already invaded the hard tissues of the mouth, such as the jaw bone or hard palate. If the tumour is detected early, cryosurgery (the killing of tissue by freezing) is often successful. Far more radical surgery, such as the removal of a portion of the jaw bone, is possible so long as there is no evidence of tumour spread to other organs; but cryosurgery is a gentler technique.

PROBLEMS OF THE OESOPHAGUS

Blockage of the oesophagus can be caused by small bones, such as chop bones, which can be chewed and swallowed but are too large or too sharp to pass down into the stomach. The cat will appear very uncomfortable, off his food and will usually regurgitate any food immediately. The obstruction can usually be detected on an X-ray or by looking down the oesophagus with an endoscope, and should be removed as soon as possible before serious damage is done to the oesophageal wall. Sometimes the object can be removed with long forceps through the mouth or gently pushed into the stomach, but any that are firmly embedded must be removed surgically by open chest surgery.

PROBLEMS OF THE STOMACH AND INTESTINE

Vomiting

Gastritis

Inflammation of the stomach lining can be caused by an infection, or by eating unsuitable food. The cat becomes depressed, usually off his food and repeatedly vomits either food or stomach fluid, which can be blood-stained. In mild cases, treatment consists of withholding food for twenty-four hours to allow the stomach to recover, and then feeding a light diet, such as boiled white fish, chicken, scrambled eggs or a proprietary food for this purpose that your vet can supply. In severe cases, antibiotics and gastric sedatives may be necessary.

Hair Balls

Because cats spend so much time grooming themselves, they will always swallow quantities of hair. Normally these pass through the digestive system with no problem, but if large quantities are swallowed, they will form into a ball in the stomach as it churns and cause vomiting. Very often the hairball will be vomited up, or passed through and out at the anus, but if the cat persists in vomiting, a hair ball must be suspected.

Prevention. A malt-flavoured lubricating laxative product in a tube should be used as a preventative measure in any cat that suffers from hair balls. Most varieties are pleasantly flavoured and readily available from your vet or a pet shop. If given by mouth regularly, especially to long-haired or moulting cats, this laxative will usually prevent the hair from balling in the stomach and will lubricate its passage through the bowels.

Treatment. If the hair ball is causing an obstruction, often diagnosed by palpation or X-ray, your vet may need to operate to remove it, although a dose of the lubricating laxative used for prevention may sometimes allow it to be passed out.

Other Foreign Bodies

Other foreign bodies, such as stones or small bones, can completely block the pylorus or intestine. This is very serious and will produce a very sick cat that will repeatedly vomit. This vomit at first is yellow or white but gradually it will become brown and foul-smelling. The cat will often not eat, drink or defecate, and will be depressed. If the vet is unable to feel the object, an X-ray of the abdomen may be required to confirm its presence. Once diagnosed the obstruction must be removed surgically, as soon as possible.

Sometimes a foreign body, such as a small plastic bag, will be eaten if it smells or tastes of food, and produce a partial obstruction. The symptoms will be similar to above but not always as severe, and the cat may pass some faeces. This type of foreign body can pass through the intestine, possibly taking several days to do so, but if it stops moving, surgery will be required. Diagnosis of this is more difficult as it may not show up on X-ray. In this case, a contrast medium such as barium must be fed to the cat prior to the X-ray to show up the foreign body.

Intussusception

This condition is encountered mainly in kittens, especially during, or following, a bout of diarrhoea. Excess bowel contractions in diarrhoea lead to a length of intestine telescoping into the following section, causing a blockage. The kitten will start to vomit, often regurgitating blood and will become depressed and refuse food. The vet can often diagnose an intussusception by palpation through the body wall, when a very characteristic painful sausage-shaped swelling will be felt.

Treatment. An emergency operation is invariably required to reduce this intussusception. If the disease has been diagnosed early, the telescoped portion can be gently manipulated out of the normal intestine with no further surgery necessary. However, if the intussusception has been there for a few days, the two portions of intestine will often have adhered to each other and it will be necessary to remove surgically the damaged section by an operation called an enterectomy.

Tumours

Tumours of the stomach occur very rarely in the cat but can cause vomiting. They are not always easy to diagnose; some may be visible on X-ray but others can only be diagnosed by an exploratory operation to examine the stomach. Unfortunately, stomach tumours are usually malignant and, once diagnosed, euthanasia is often the treatment of choice.

Localized tumours of the intestine are also fairly uncommon. When they occur, these tumours cause no symptoms in the early stages and it is only when they are large enough to obstruct the bowel that symptoms of intestinal obstruction begin. Persistent vomiting occurs and the cat will usually pass a reduced amount of faeces. These tumours can often be diagnosed by palpation of the abdomen by your vet or they can be seen on an X-ray, sometimes with a barium swallow. Small bowel tumours can be removed surgically, provided there is no evidence of spread to other organs.

Malignant lymphosarcoma tumours are, however, more common in domestic cats and often infiltrate the digestive tract and other organs (e.g. lymph nodes, liver, kidneys and spleen). Common signs include inappetance, weight loss, vomiting, diarrhoea, bloody stools and jaundice. They are usually inoperable and euthanasia is the kindest option.

Note: Vomiting may also be due to other causes such as a metabolic or endocrine disease, rather than intestinal disease; these are mentioned elsewhere in the book.

Diarrhoea

Enteritis

Enteritis is the name given to inflammation of the small intestine and can be caused by specific infections, such as the virus of feline enteritis/ panleucopaenia, various bacteria including *Campylobacter* and *Salmonella*, both of which are zoonoses, a heavy worm burden, or unsuitable or unaccustomed food. Vaccination against panleucopaenia is essential to avoid this serious disease.

Signs. These can vary enormously. In mild cases, the cat is perfectly normal except for softish faeces. At the other extreme, the cat will be depressed and off his food, and have frequent, watery, blood-tinged diarrhoea. A cat that will not drink and has severe diarrhoea can become dehydrated very quickly.

Diagnosis. It may be that the history given to the vet and the clinical examination will reveal the cause, but if not, samples of the cat's faeces will be needed to examine for bacteria or parasites, and in some cases blood samples may be needed.

Treatment. In mild cases, simply withholding solid food for twenty-four hours, while ensuring an adequate intake of water, may be the only treatment necessary. In more severe cases, depending on the cause, besides withholding food, antibiotics or intestinal sedatives and fluid therapy by mouth may be required. In the severely dehydrated patient, fluid replacement by intravenous therapy will be instigated as soon as possible by your vet, and antibiotics may also be required. Once the diarrhoea is under control, a light diet of boiled white meat or fish, or a prescription diet from your vet should be fed for several days.

Colitis

This is the inflammation of the large bowel, and usually produces less severe diarrhoea than enteritis. The faeces tend to be soft rather than watery, and often contain spots of blood and increased amounts of mucus. The cat appears to be healthy in all other respects. Mild colitis may respond to dietary management alone, along similar lines to treatment of enteritis, but more severe cases may require antibiotics and/or anti-inflammatory medications.

Stress Diarrhoea

Any cat changing from one home to another, or from one type of food to another suddenly, especially new kittens, may develop a mild diarrhoea. These cases respond to dietary treatment, by withholding food for twenty-four hours, followed by a low-fibre diet and a gradual introduction of the new diet over a few days.

Inflammatory Bowel Disease (IBD)

IBD is a common cause of gastrointestinal problems in the cat. Although cats of any age can be affected, middle-aged or older cats are more susceptible to IBD. The cause of IBD is unknown, but because of characteristic microscopic changes in the bowel, it is thought that the disease is a problem of the immune system. To diagnose the problem, your vet may need to rule out other causes of gastrointestinal disease by performing various diagnostic tests, but the most definitive test is the microscopic examination of small samples of the intestinal lining.

Treatment. Dietary management and medical treatment with corticosteroids will usually both be needed, and this should successfully manage, but not cure, IBD in most cats. Because there is no single best treatment, your vet may need to try several different combinations in order to obtain the best results for your cat.

Tumours

Intestinal tumours, other than lymphosarcoma, tend to produce vomiting rather than diarrhoea. Lymphosarcoma produces a diffuse thickening and destruction of the intestine by the deposition of white blood cells in the wall and is diagnosed by biopsy. Chemotherapy may provide relief, but not a cure; again, euthanasia may be the kindest option.

Parasitic Worms

A heavy roundworm burden, or the presence of tapeworms, can produce diarrhoea, particularly in kittens.

Straining

This can be caused by irritation of, or blockage of, the rectum. When the lining of the rectum is inflamed, the cat will usually strain to pass faeces, even though there is hardly anything in the rectum, and this leads to a persistent watery diarrhoea.

The presence of foreign bodies in the rectum will cause straining in an attempt to remove them. Small bone fragments that have passed through the digestive system are the commonest cause of problems at this site. Surprisingly, sewing needles are sometimes found in the rectum, where, having successfully passed through the entire digestive system blunt end forwards, the increased movement in this area causes the needle to be lodge painfully just inside the rectum.

Cats have scent glands just inside the anus called anal sacs and these can cause straining and pain if they become impacted or infected. The cat would also be likely to spend more time licking his anal area. Your vet will empty the sacs and treat any infection that is present.

Constipation

When faeces accumulate in the rectum, the cat is said to be constipated. Straining occurs in an attempt to evacuate the rectum but the accumulation can be so great that the cat cannot pass the faeces.

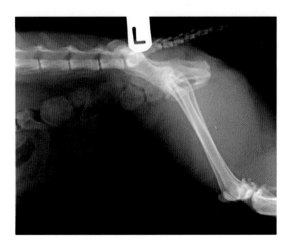

An X-ray of a constipated cat.

Diagnosis is possible by palpation of the abdomen, or by the vet gently feeling inside the rectum with a well-lubricated, gloved finger. If there is any doubt over the diagnosis, an X-ray will help.

Treatment. Mild cases can be treated with a lubricating cat laxative, available in a tasty form in a tube. In more severe cases, your vet may have to use an enema, which she will gently insert into your cat's anus. This lubricates and stimulates the rectum. Occasionally, however, it may be necessary to manipulate the faeces out under a general anaesthetic.

PERITONITIS

The specific disease of feline infectious peritonitis has been dealt with elsewhere in this book but there are other types of peritonitis, where bacteria are involved. Peritonitis is an inflammation of the lining membrane of the abdomen and is an uncommon but serious disease. It is characterized by a depressed cat, off his food, with vomiting and diarrhoea, a raised temperature and severe abdominal pain. The infection gains entry to the abdomen through a ruptured intestine, by a foreign body penetrating the intestinal wall, from leakage of pus from an infected uterus, missile injuries, bite wounds or, occasionally, following abdominal surgery.

Diagnosis. Peritonitis is not always easy to diagnose. The symptoms may be sufficient for a diagnosis, but sometimes it is necessary for the vet to perform an exploratory abdominal operation for a detailed examination.

Treatment. Antibiotics are always required in the treatment of peritonitis but surgery may be required to repair any damage to the intestine, or to remove the cause. If the abdomen contains pus, this can be flushed out with sterile saline. Severe peritonitis may leave the cat with adhesions between the various organs in the abdomen.

DISEASES OF THE PANCREAS

The pancreas is a very important organ in the body and has two different functions:

- It is an 'exocrine' organ and produces enzymes that are needed for digesting proteins, carbohydrates and especially fats. Pancreatic fluid is released into the intestinal tract in response to eating food.

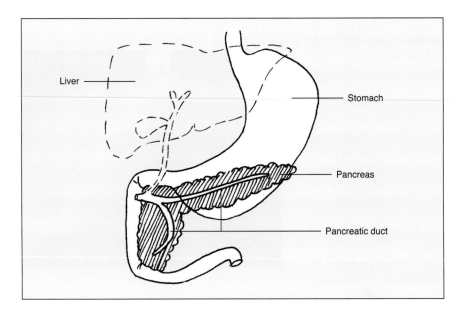

Fig 12 The pancreas and duct.

- The pancreas is also an 'endocrine' organ and produces hormones that regulate body functions, especially the regulation of blood sugar. When certain cells of the pancreas detect an increase in the blood sugar concentration, insulin is released directly into the blood, where it acts to carry glucose into the body's cells. The higher the blood sugar, the more insulin is secreted. Thus, insulin lowers the blood glucose concentration. This Endocrine function is dealt with in Chapter 16.

The signs of pancreatic disease depend on which function of the organ is malfunctioning.

The Exocrine Function

Pancreatitis or inflammation of the pancreas can be caused by trauma, infection, parasites and even odd reactions to certain drugs, but most cannot be linked to any one specific cause. Siamese cats seem to be at greater risk than other cats, which suggests it may be, at least partially, hereditary.

Signs. Cats affected by the acute form of pancreatitis will usually have a poor appetite, are lethargic and suffer weight loss, dehydration and diarrhoea. Vomiting and abdominal pain are not common signs. In cats, pancreatitis tends to be a chronic, intermittent problem, where the symptoms either persist for longer or recur from time to time.

Diagnosis. Pancreatitis can be suspected by the symptoms the cat is showing but tests for pancreatitis have not always been reliable. However, currently a blood test to detect feline pancreatitis is being evaluated and preliminary studies look promising. At this time, however, there is no single diagnostic test, other than a biopsy, that is completely reliable in diagnosing feline pancreatitis.

Treatment. Supportive care, such as intravenous fluid therapy, is the mainstay of therapy, and efforts will be made to try to identify and treat the cause, if known. As the pancreas aids in digestion, resting it by withholding food for a few days may help. Treatment to control pain and vomiting may be indicated, and antibiotics may be needed if an infectious cause is suspected.

Pancreatic Insufficiency

Pancreatic insufficiency or loss of pancreatic function can arise if the cat is born with a defective pancreas, or follow repeated bouts of acute pancreatitis, or through a slow degeneration of the pancreas of unknown cause. This type of pancreas problem is rare in the cat, but when it occurs, a cat is unable to properly digest his food. This results in persistent diarrhoea, weight loss and a ravenous appetite.

Diagnosis. Pancreatic insufficiency is diagnosed by laboratory testing of blood and faeces.

Treatment. Cure is not possible, but to control the disease, replacement enzymes are mixed in the food and the cat is fed an easily digestible diet.

DISEASES OF THE LIVER

The liver's main function is to produce bile to aid in the digestion of food, but it has several other important functions also. These include regulating the storage and use of carbohydrate and fat, and the removal of toxic substances from the body. The liver is a large organ and has an enormous reserve capacity, so that by the time the cat starts showing signs of liver failure, a large part of it is usually affected. However, it also has the capacity to repair itself well, which means that cats can often recover from even severe liver disease.

Signs of Liver Disease. These are usually very vague. The cat may be off his food, drink more, vomit, be lethargic, lose weight and sometimes have a raised temperature. In the advanced stages, jaundice may occur colouring the gums and skin yellow. Because of the disturbance in fluid circulation, excess fluid may build up within the abdomen. This is called ascites and gives the cat a very pot-bellied appearance.

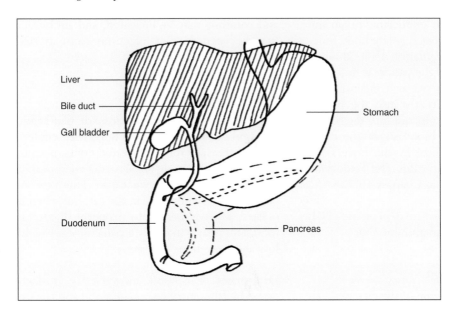

Fig 13 The liver and the bile duct route.

General Diagnosis. If liver disease is suspected, your vet will usually confirm it by a blood test. This could reveal the cause, or it may be necessary to investigate further using X-rays, ultrasound scans or even a biopsy.

Hepatic Lipidosis

This is probably the commonest form of liver disease in cats, particularly of overweight cats, and is a condition where fats infiltrate the liver, causing widespread damage. It seems to occur when, for some reason, a cat stops eating and results in the release of fats from stored fat deposits into the bloodstream. It is a severe disease and unless treated promptly, many cats will die.

Diagnosis. It will be necessary for your vet to take a biopsy to diagnose this but this may be simply by using a fine needle inserted through the skin while the cat is conscious or perhaps sedated. This is a procedure called a fine-needle aspirate, and microscopic examination will reveal the fat cells in the liver.

Treatment. The most important treatment for this disease is to start the patient on a high-carbohydrate diet and in most cases, because the cat is off his food, this needs to be given through a pharyngostomy tube or even a gastrotomy

tube inserted through the body wall directly into the stomach. As this latter may be left in for a long period of time, once in place, an owner can use this at home where the cat is happier. Recovery can take some time, sometimes months, during which time your vet will supply or recommend a special diet and often other nutritional supplements.

Cholangiohepatitis

This is one of the commoner causes of jaundice in cats and is a bacterial infection of the liver causing inflammation. Because of the easy access to the liver and pancreas through their ducts into the small intestine, it often occurs in conjunction with disease of the small intestine and/or the pancreas.

Signs. Typical signs of this and other liver disease, such as inappetance, increased thirst, vomiting, lethargy, weight loss, sometimes a raised temperature and jaundice.

Diagnosis. A biopsy may need to be taken for evidence of liver inflammation and the presence of bacteria.

Treatment. Antibiotics are required. If the appropriate antibiotic is ascertained by testing a culture from the biopsy, and started promptly, the prognosis is often good, although relapses can occur.

Lymphocytic Cholangitis

This condition occurs when there is inflammation around the bile ducts within the liver. The cause of this is not known but due to the large presence of particular cells called lymphocytes, it is thought that it may be due to an abnormality of the cat's immune system.

Diagnosis. A biopsy of the liver is the only way to confirm this, and to exclude bacterial infection.

Treatment. A course of anti-inflammatory corticosteroids is the only treatment, but the prognosis varies depending on the severity. However the disease is controlled rather than cured, and relapses can occur so permanent treatment may be required.

Feline Infectious Peritonitis (FIP)

FIP can be highly involved in the cause of liver disease (*see* Chapter 5).

Damage by Drugs or Toxins

Although toxic hepatitis is not often seen in cats, it is worth remembering that they are very susceptible to liver damage caused by a wide range of substances. These will include insecticides formulated for other species that are licked off during grooming, or common drugs that may be quite safe in humans and other species. It is, therefore, essential that you should never give your cat, or use on your cat, any treatment of which you are unsure, without consulting your vet. If your cat does become ill, you must be able to inform your vet of any drugs or toxins you may have given your cat or with which he may have been in contact.

Tumours

Liver tumours may occur either as primary tumours or because malignant tumours in other parts of the body readily spread to the liver. The symptoms are those of chronic liver failure, whatever the cause.

Diagnosis. This usually requires an X-ray or scan, and often direct inspection of the liver by the vet through an operation and a biopsy. Only very rarely is the tumour confined to one part of the liver and able to be surgically removed. In the vast majority of cases the tumour is spread throughout the liver and the kindest action is to put the cat to sleep.

Chapter 8
The Respiratory System

NORMAL STRUCTURE AND FUNCTION

The respiratory system consists of the nose, pharynx, larynx, trachea, bronchi and lungs. It has two main functions: gaseous exchange to provide the body with fresh oxygen and at the same time to remove carbon dioxide; and, secondly, temperature regulation by panting, as the cat is unable to lose heat by sweating except through the paws.

The nose of the cat is a short bony box containing a myriad of fine bones called the turbinate bones, which are covered with a blood-rich membrane. Cats breathe normally through the nose and air is drawn in through the nostrils, where it is warmed and filtered of dust or other foreign particles. This warmed, clean air then passes across the pharynx at the back of the throat into the larynx. During swallowing the entrance to the larynx is closed by a flap of cartilage, the epiglottis, which prevents food particles from being inhaled. On each side of the larynx are the vocal cords, which are used both to produce sound and to narrow the diameter of the larynx, and to help prevent dust and food from entering the lungs. The larynx leads down into the trachea, which is simply a non-collapsible tube consisting of rings of cartilage and which runs the length of the neck and into the

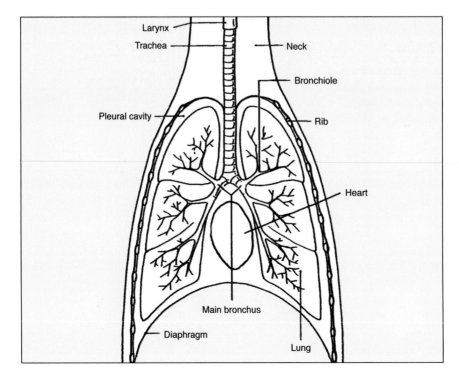

Fig 14 The respiratory system.

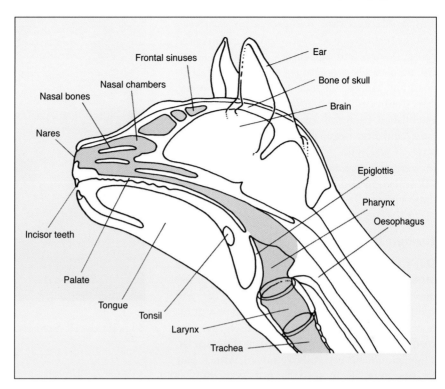

Fig 15 *Section of head showing nasal passages.*

chest. It divides into two bronchi at the level of the heart, one of which enters each lung. These bronchi then subdivide into smaller tubes, bronchioles, which terminate in the air sacs or alveoli. The walls of the alveoli are richly supplied with blood vessels and it is here that the exchange of oxygen and carbon dioxide takes place.

The lower section of the trachea, the bronchi and lungs, are contained in the chest, which is bounded by the rib cage and the diaphragm – a thin sheet of muscle between the chest and abdomen. During inspiration, the chest expands as the ribs move outwards and the diaphragm moves downward; whereas during expiration, the chest contracts as the chest wall relaxes to its resting position.

A cat's resting respiratory rate varies from sixteen to forty breaths per minute, and in the normal resting cat, breathing will be shallow and regular, and the tongue and gums will be pink. A cat with severe oxygen shortage will have laboured, rapid breathing even at rest, and the tongue and gums will be a blue colour. Such a cat is said to be cyanotic.

DISEASES OF THE NOSE

Infection (Rhinitis)

Nasal infections are fairly common in the cat, usually following or during one of the respiratory virus infections. They can also be caused by bacteria and fungi, usually as a secondary infection that invades the lining of the nose, which is already damaged by a virus.

Signs. Sneezing is often the first sign shown by a cat with an infected nose, accompanied by a clear watery discharge. After a day or two, as the disease progresses, the sneezing becomes more frequent and the discharge may become purulent or blood-stained. This may form crusts around the nostril, causing a nasal obstruction, and often the cat will have to breathe through his mouth.

Treatment. The signs of a nasal infection are usually obvious, although unless it is part of a general respiratory virus infection like cat flu, the cause may be difficult to pinpoint. Consequently the cat will usually be treated with antibiotics, but if there is no response, further testing may be necessary to identify the cause. X-rays and laboratory testing of blood and nasal discharge samples may lead to a diagnosis and the appropriate treatment. However, infections caused by fungi or yeasts and by well-established bacterial infections are difficult to treat, and may require surgical drainage of the nose. Cats with chronic rhinitis are often immuno-suppressed by concurrent FeLV and FIV infection and would normally be tested for these viruses.

Foreign Bodies

Due to the cat's habitual sniffing, grass seeds (or other foreign objects such as blades of grass) may be inhaled into the nostrils. The cat will suddenly start to sneeze violently and paw at his nose, often after being outside in the grass, and seeds may be seen protruding from the nostrils. They should be carefully removed with a pair of tweezers. If a seed is not removed, it will progress up the nose and a blood-stained purulent discharge will appear at the affected nostril within a day or so. It is essential that a vet examines the cat, as the foreign body must be removed as soon as possible.

Sometimes a blade of grass, which has been taken into the mouth of the cat, will become lodged in the pharynx and find its way back into the nasal passage, where it enters the pharynx. The signs of this will be urging, sneezing or gagging.

Treatment. The grass blade is usually visible or detected under an anaesthetic and removed.

Tumours

Tumours can occur both on and in the nose. The squamous cell carcinoma, due to ultraviolet sun rays in white cats, occurs on the end of the nose as well as on the ear tips (*see* Chapter 11). They are slowly invasive and in this position are much more difficult to remove than on the ears, but cryosurgery (freezing) can be helpful.

Tumours can also occur within the nose where they replace the delicate turbinate bone tissue. The first sign is usually an intermittent

A squamous cell carcinoma on the nose.

haemorrhage from one nostril; an X-ray will reveal a mass in one or both nasal chambers. Most tumours are highly malignant and surgery is of little help. Radiotherapy can sometimes reduce them in size.

Polyps

These are benign tumours but when they occur in the nasal passages where they enter the pharynx, they produce noisy breathing and gagging.

Diagnosis. Usually by X-ray and examination under an anaesthetic.

Treatment. Surgical removal, again under an anaesthetic.

Nasal and Face Shortening

This is a feature of the flat-faced breeds, such as the Persian cat, where it can cause noisy breathing for one of two reasons. Firstly, the nasal passages themselves are shortened and tortuous but also the soft palate is sited slightly backwards nearer the larynx, which it partially obstructs.

Severe right-sided nasal discharge due to a tumour inside the nose.

However, it rarely causes this breed type any real problems. The cat makes an intermittent snorting or snoring noise but surgery is only rarely required to shorten the soft palate in cats.

DISEASES PRODUCING A COUGH – THE LARYNX, TRACHEA, BRONCHI AND LUNGS

The cough is a reflex, which, by forcing air out of the chest, clears irritating foreign matter from the bronchi, trachea and larynx. Severe inflammation of these structures will also stimulate the cough reflex.

Laryngitis, Tracheitis and Bronchitis

Inflammation of these structures can be caused by an infection, especially with *Bordetella* bacteria (*see* Chapter 5).

Signs. Usually all the airway is affected at the same time, and the cat will cough and may also have some difficulty in breathing. In most cases, the patient is relatively well in the early stages and will continue to eat, but if the larynx is affected the cat may lose his meow for a while.

Treatment. These infections usually respond readily to antibiotics. During treatment, the cat should be kept in until he has recovered. These respiratory conditions are usually extremely infectious, and affected cats should be isolated.

Asthma

This an allergic respiratory disease in cats, most commonly affecting young to middle-aged cats and a small percentage of older cats. An allergic reaction causes spasms in the bronchi, leading to inflammation and swelling of the lining of the airway.

Signs. This inflammation and swelling restricts the airflow, causing respiratory distress, wheezing, coughing and laboured breathing, and can become life-threatening in a matter of minutes. There is also a chronic progressive form of the disease that can also be potentially life-threatening, causing constriction and obstruction of the airway.

Treatment. Asthma is incurable but can usually be controlled by bronchodilators and anti-inflammatory medications, enabling the affected cat to lead a normal life.

Chronic Bronchitis

This is a major problem in the older cat and can follow on from asthma. It is caused by persistent or repeated low-grade infections or irritations, which produce irreversible changes in the bronchi.

Signs. The cough develops slowly, being only produced on exertion, and in the majority of cases the cat is otherwise normal. Many cases will not develop further but some progress until the cat seems to cough almost constantly.

Treatment. As with asthma, there is no cure, but a combination of antibiotics, steroids, bronchodilators and medicines to break up the mucus can greatly reduce the amount of coughing and improve the quality of life.

Lungworms

These form small nodules in the trachea, usually where it divides into two bronchi, and they cause an intermittent cough (*see* Chapter 6).

Foreign Bodies

These are uncommon but blades of grass and fish bones seem to be the commonest offenders in cats. Both tend to have a sudden onset causing gagging, coughing and often the cat will paw at his mouth. Some of these foreign bodies can be difficult to locate, and a thorough examination of the throat and larynx, using an endoscope under general anaesthesia, is invariably needed. The foreign body must be removed with forceps and, surprisingly, in cats, a grass blade will often be found in the throat passing back into the nasal passage (*see* page 86).

DISEASES PRODUCING LABOURED BREATHING

Conditions that cause the cat to have difficulty in breathing are normally those that occupy space within the lungs or chest, thus reducing the volume of lung tissue available for gas exchange.

Pneumonia

This is an infection of the lung tissue, which produces an inflammatory reaction in the air sacs. Pneumonia is uncommon in the cat but can follow, or be caused by, viruses, bacteria, fungi or foreign material. It is seen more commonly as part of a generalized disease, especially feline influenza. A cat with pneumonia will be very dull and off his food, and will have difficulty breathing. If the inflammation also affects the bronchi, there will also be a cough.

Diagnosis is usually made on the clinical signs and an X-ray of the chest, when the lung changes will be seen.

Treatment consists of high doses of antibiotics, complete rest or confinement, and in severe cases, oxygen therapy may be needed.

Pleural Effusion

The pleura is the membrane lining the inside of the chest and if it becomes inflamed or irritated, it produces fluid that fills the free space between the lungs and the chest wall, thus putting pressure on the lungs and causing laboured breathing. One of the commonest causes is a bite from another cat, whose long canine tooth penetrates the chest wall between two ribs and introduces infection into the chest. This rapidly produces pus in the chest and is a very serious condition requiring immediate treatment. Another cause is chylothorax, where the body fluid, called chyle, is present due to damage to the lymphatic system (*see* page 89).

Signs. The cat becomes very dull, has a high temperature and difficulty in breathing. A penetrating wound may or may not be obvious in the chest wall, and it may be known that the cat has recently been involved in a fight.

Diagnosis. Any bite wound would be suspicious but diagnosis is confirmed by either, or both, an X-ray and a chest drain to ascertain if pus is present in the chest.

Treatment. The pus is drained using a drain inserted into the chest, and a soluble antibiotic often then introduced into the chest using the same drain. Antibiotics are also invariably needed either by injection or by mouth, and in most cases the cat recovers well if the condition is caught early enough. If the problem is due to chylothorax, drainage will help but, unless the original problem can be detected, the condition will recur.

Accidents

Cats do seem to have more than their fair share of road traffic accidents (RTAs) and dog fights, and respiratory failure is a common sequel to trauma from this sort of occurrence. There are several injuries that may be encountered, all

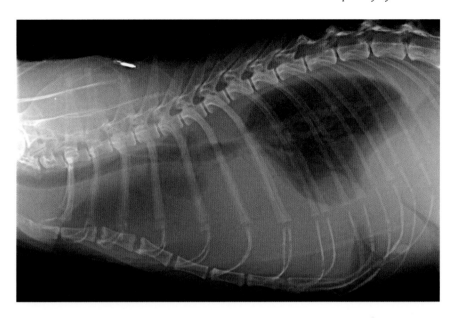

X-ray of chest. The white area below the dark lung is pleural fluid. Also note microchip in neck.

resulting in a cat that is quiet and has difficulty breathing. These various injuries are diagnosed by your vet on clinical signs and X-ray examination. After a severe accident, the vet's main priority is to correct any chest injuries and ensure the cat can breathe to maintain life, before any other injuries, such as fractured legs, are dealt with. The signs the cat shows in the four following conditions are all very similar but may be complicated by other injuries.

Haemothorax

This occurs when there is haemorrhage into the chest. The usual cause is a rupture of blood vessels in the lung releasing blood, which fills the air sacs; so the cat will have laboured breathing, may cough up blood and will have pale mucous membranes. As the lungs can rapidly fill with blood, a severe haemorrhage may result in death.

Diagnosis is based on the history of an accident, the breathing difficulty the cat is showing, the presence of blood in the chest, using a fine needle inserted into the chest or X-ray examination.

Treatment is difficult as this free blood cannot always be removed. Your vet may attempt to drain some using a chest drain, but in all cases, the cat must be kept quiet, often in an oxygen tent in the vet's surgery, until his own body reab-

sorbs and removes the blood clot. Surviving cats will often show a marked improvement after about five days rest.

Pneumothorax

This occurs when a lung has been ruptured. If an accident has broken one or more ribs, a lung may be penetrated or ruptured by the impact, which allows air to leak into the chest cavity. This will compress the lungs because it occupies space that should be occupied by the lungs, and the cat will have great difficulty in breathing.

Diagnosis is based on the history of an accident, the breathing difficulty the cat is showing and by X-ray examination when the air will be seen around the lungs and, if present, a broken rib will be seen.

Treatment. Your vet will usually drain the free air from the chest cavity by the insertion of a drainage tube. In most cases, the tear in the lung will heal without surgery unless a fractured rib is depressed inwards and aggravates the condition.

Chylothorax

Chyle is a milky fluid containing lymph and triglycerides, which arises from the intestines and is carried by the veins into the lymphatic

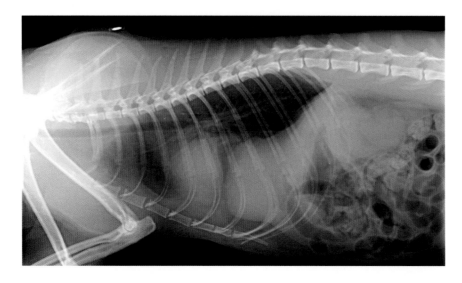

X-ray of diaphragmatic hernia. Note how the liver and some intestines have moved into the chest.

system. Part of this system is a duct in the chest called the thoracic duct, and when chyle leaks out from here, it drains into the chest cavity causing pressure on the lungs and causes difficulty in breathing. A rupture of the duct during a road traffic accident can also cause this and, in these cases, the chyle is often tinged with blood.

However, an RTA is not the only cause of chylothorax, as any condition that increases the pressure in veins can cause chyle to leak from the thoracic duct. These would include heart problems, tumours and thrombosis, so these causes should also be investigated, if an RTA has not taken place.

Diagnosis. An X-ray will show free fluid in the chest and a chest drain inserted by the vet will reveal the milky chyle fluid. Chest examination by stethoscope and X-ray, and blood tests may reveal other causes.

Treatment. If caused by an RTA, draining the chyle may be all that is needed. If other causes are present, the underlying problem, such as heart disease, should be treated. In my experience, however, chylothorax of unknown origin is very difficult to treat and the outlook is very poor.

Ruptured Diaphragm

The impact in a road traffic accident involving a cat, often causes the diaphragm to rupture, and this breaks down the barrier between the chest and the abdomen. The consequence of this is that abdominal organs, such as the liver, spleen, stomach or intestine, can and do move forward into the chest cavity.

Diagnosis. This condition will be suspected in any cat having difficulty breathing after an accident, and X-rays will confirm it.

Treatment. Surgery is required both to replace these organs into their normal position, and to repair the tear in the diaphragm. Closed-circuit anaesthesia with positive pressure is essential as, due to the rupture of the diaphragm, once the abdominal incision is made, the chest cavity is connected to the outside air and the cat, therefore, is unable to breathe for himself.

Chest Tumours

These do occur in cats and cause respiratory difficulties in two ways – by occupying lung space instead of air, and also by causing obstruction to the flow of fluid, such as chyle, which then leads to the accumulation of fluid in the chest. Primary tumours arising from the lung tissue are uncommon, but the lungs are a common site for tumour spread from other parts of the body. They are almost always inoperable.

Chapter 9
The Circulatory System

The circulatory system consists of the heart, arteries, veins, capillaries and the blood they contain, as it flows around the body. The design is that of a continuous tube running in a figure-of-eight with the heart at the crossover point. One loop of this supplies the lungs, while the other supplies all the other tissues of the body. The circulating blood provides the body's transportation system. A second circulating system, the lymphatic system, is responsible for combating infection and also for returning fluid to the heart that has leaked from the blood vessels.

NORMAL STRUCTURE AND FUNCTION

The heart is a very active, four-chambered muscle, which has the sole function of pumping blood around the body. Two chambers are the larger ventricles, right and left, which pump blood out – the left ventricle to the main artery, the aorta, and the right ventricle to the lungs. The other two chambers are the smaller atria, which receive blood from the body tissues and from the lungs. The arteries are thick-walled,

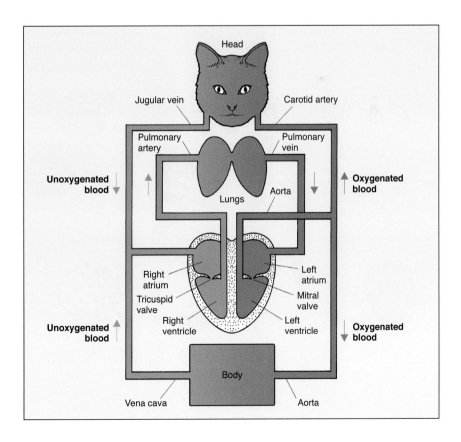

Fig 16 Schematic diagram of heart and circulation.

elastic blood vessels, which carry oxygenated blood away from the heart to all the parts of the body, and the much thinner walled veins return blood from these tissues to the heart. This returning blood is then pumped to the lungs to be re-oxygenated, then back to the heart to start the cycle again. This circulation is extremely rapid. The cat's blood pressure is much higher in the arteries than in the veins, hence the thicker, elastic walls.

The sino-atrial node, an area in the wall of the right atrium, controls the strength and rate of the heart beat. It releases electrical impulses that spread through the heart, causing the heart to contract in such a way that blood is forced out through the arteries; this can be measured and recorded using an electrocardiogram (ECG). The sino-atrial node receives nerve messages from the brain through the autonomic nervous system, which change the rate and strength of the heart beat to supply the different volumes of blood required by, say, a cat that is resting or one that is hunting.

Blood full of oxygen in the left ventricle of the heart is pumped out via the main artery, the aorta, and from here to all the other organs of the body, such as the brain, muscles and liver. In these organs, oxygen and nutrients are extracted from the blood and new nutrients enter the bloodstream from the breakdown of food in the intestine. This unoxygenated blood (blood low in oxygen) returns to the right atrium of the heart via a large vein, the vena cava, then via the right ventricle of the heart through the pulmonary artery to the lungs. Here the blood exchanges its carbon dioxide for oxygen and returns to the left atrium of the heart through the pulmonary vein, then into the powerful left ventricle to begin the cycle again. The carotid artery, one of the first branches of the aorta, is the main arterial supply to the brain and the jugular vein returns the blood to the heart after it has circulated through the brain.

The fluid part of blood is the plasma, and this carries the blood cells suspended in it. Red blood cells contain haemoglobin, which transports oxygen to all the tissues and organs of the body. White blood cells attack and rid the body of infections and other foreign material. Platelets and other clotting substances in the blood are required for the control of haemorrhage. Food and hormones are carried in the plasma. Red blood cells, most white blood cells and platelets are produced in the bone marrow,

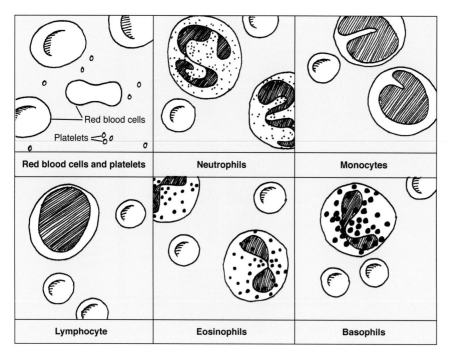

Fig 17 Typical blood cells.

which is the soft fatty tissue inside bone cavities. Some white blood cells, lymphocytes, are also produced in the lymph nodes, spleen and thymus gland. Serum is the fluid portion of blood remaining after blood has clotted.

The lymphatic system is responsible for combating infection and also for returning fluid to the heart that has leaked from the blood vessels. Lymph nodes link this system and are scattered throughout the body and are composed of white blood cells. The superficial lymph nodes, such as the ones under the throat, can be felt underneath the skin and your vet will often feel these nodes for evidence of enlargement, which may indicate disease. The cat's tonsils are similar in structure and function to the lymph nodes, and play an important part in preventing infection spreading further into the body. The spleen, a large organ situated alongside the stomach in the abdomen, is part of the lymphatic system and helps fight disease, as well as acting as a store for red blood cells. The thymus is an organ situated in the entrance to the chest and is composed of white blood cells. It is fairly large in the young cat and helps fight disease, but in the adult it almost disappears.

VETERINARY EXAMINATION OF THE CIRCULATORY SYSTEM

The examination of this complex system will depend on which part of it the vet suspects is not functioning well. There are various methods available to the vet to ascertain the function of this ultra-important organ, the heart, and the rest of the circulatory system:

- The stethoscope is is an acoustic device for listening to the internal sounds of an animal's body. It is mostly used to listen to heart sounds, but is also used to listen to lung sounds, blood flow in arteries and veins (for instance, when taking a cat's blood pressure), and occasionally to listen to sounds in the intestines. Listening through a stethoscope, a vet can count the number of heart beats per minute, can hear if the heart is making the normal 'lub dub' sound or has a 'murmur', and she can obtain some idea of the size of the heart.

- X-rays will reveal the size, shape and positioning of the heart. A diseased heart will often be larger than normal.
- An ECG (electrocardiography) examination can be very helpful in diagnosing cardiac problems. Small leads are clipped on to the cat's skin and the electrical output of the heart is measured, recorded and printed out. This is carried out in the conscious cat, as there is no discomfort.
- An ultrasound scan will also reveal the size and shape of the heart but will also reveal the function of the heart because moving pictures are obtained. It will reveal whether the valves in the heart are working well, and whether the heart is pumping correctly.
- The pulse of the cat, felt on the inside of the cat's thigh by your vet, will give some idea as to the efficiency of the heart by how strong a pulse is produced. It is also useful to correolate the number of heart beats felt via the pulse with what is heard through the stethoscope.
- Blood samples are taken to allow microscopic examination of the blood cells in the diagnosis of diseases such as leukaemia and anaemia.

HEART DISEASE

Diagnosis of Heart Disease. By listening to the heart through a stethoscope, the vet will be able to hear if the heart has any obvious defects, such as heart murmurs, heart enlargement and an irregular or fast heart beat. She will also feel for the pulse with finger pressure on the inside of a hind leg to see if this is weak – an indication of poor cardiac output. If a thrombosis in a leg artery is also present, the pain, paralysis and often absence of a pulse will be diagnostic. In many cases, the examination of the heart sounds, along with the other clinical signs, may be enough to make a diagnosis of heart failure. In more complicated cases it will be necessary for the vet to X-ray the cat's chest to detect any abnormality in the size or shape of the heart, or the presence of pulmonary oedema. An ECG machine is also a useful aid in the diagnosis of heart conditions.

Ultrasound scanning is now widely available

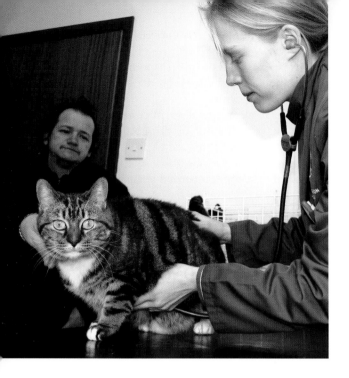

Heart examination with a stethoscope.

to the veterinary profession and is proving very useful in diagnosis of heart disorders, especially in Veterinary Hospitals and at specialist referral centres. The heart can be seen actually functioning on a video monitor and detail recorded of the valve function. This method of diagnosis is easily performed on a conscious cat and has no harmful effects on either the patient or operator.

Heart disease in cats can be congenital or acquired during life. When it occurs it is usually a problem of the heart muscle and is called a cardiomyopathy. Heart problems in cats can be very difficult to diagnose due to the cat's life style – even normal cats spend a lot of time resting and alone which makes the early symptoms difficult to identify.

Congenital Heart Disease

This is to be suspected when a kitten shows difficulty in breathing or can't exercise or play, and may collapse with blue mucous membranes. However, sometimes the signs do not occur until the kitten has matured, when the demands on the heart are greater. Congenital heart problems are very uncommon in the cat, perhaps one case in every 1,000 cats.

Septal Defects. These are the commonest congenital defects and they occur when the dividing walls in the chambers of the heart fail to fuse completely. A heart murmur may be heard using a stethoscope. The cat may or may not be affected by this, and surgical repair, even if possible in a referral centre, will be very risky and expensive. The common name for this is 'a hole in the heart'. Other less common congenital defects are:

- Aortic stenosis. An abnormal narrowing of the aortic valve. Untreatable.
- Endocardial fibroelastosis. This is a thickening of, and the replacement of, the heart muscle with fibrous tissue. It leads to heart failure and there is no cure. Mostly seen in Burmese and Siamese.
- Mitral valve dysplasia – abnormal mitral valves.
- Patent ductus arteriosus. An extra, small artery bypassing the normal circulation is very uncommon in cats but in some cases can be cured by surgery.

Acquired Heart Disease

Most cases of feline acquired heart disease (problems that they were not born with) are types of cardiomyopathy, which literally means 'disease of the heart muscle'. Cats can develop one of three main types:

- Dilated cardiomyopathy: where, because the heart muscle is weakened, it enlarges as it attempts to deliver the normal amount of blood around the body. One of the causes was a deficiency in the diet of an amino acid called taurine but that is now added to commercial cat foods and as a result this condition is now uncommon.
- Restrictive cardiomyopathy: which is seen in older cats due to scar formation in the heart muscle, which prevents the heart from beating normally.
- Hypertrophic cardiomyopathy: which is a thickening of the wall of the left ventricle of the heart and leads to a reduced capacity of the ventricle. This in turn causes blood to accumulate in the left atrium because it can't

get out, and the outcome is too little blood circulating round the body. This cycle of events progresses slowly but surely over time and may not be noticed in the early stages, but when crisis point is reached, the cat may appear to become very ill very quickly, or even die suddenly. Hypertrophic cardio-myopathy is the most common form of cardiomyopathy in the cat.

As well as being a primary disease, cardiac hypertrophy can be caused by one of the commonest hormonal problems of the older cat – feline hyperthyroidism. It leads to an increased blood pressure, which causes the heart to enlarge in response.

Symptoms. In practice, the commonest first sign of a cardiomyopathy is difficulty in breathing (dyspnoea) due to both poor heart function and also the accumulation of fluid that builds up in the lungs due to the poor circulation. This is called pulmonary oedema. The cat will usually be off his food, lethargic, may vomit and sometimes will faint. Coughing occurs only in a few cases.

Treatment of any type of cardiomyopathy is aimed at resting the patient, clearing the lungs

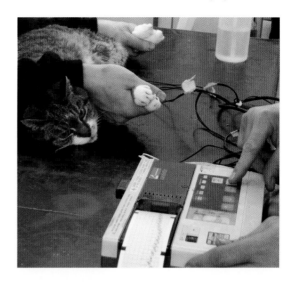

Heart examination using an ECG machine.

of fluid to make breathing easier and medications to improve the heart beat. Some cats will show a marked improvement after a few days rest. Oxygen treatment in an oxygen tent may be needed in severe cases in the initial stages. Your vet may be able to withdraw fluid from the chest using a catheter, and medication with a diuretic will help the body remove the fluid. To improve the efficiency of the heart, various

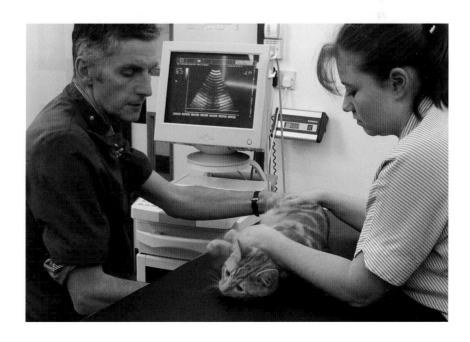

Heart examination using ultrasound.

cardiac drugs are available. It is, however, a serious complaint and the prognosis is usually poor, as by no means all cats are able to continue with a good quality of life. However, if the problem is related to hyperthyroidism, treatment of this condition will bring about an improvement in the heart complaint.

Thrombo-embolism. A common sequel to cardiomyopathy in cats, especially the hypertrophic type, is a condition called thrombo-embolism. This is the development of a sudden thrombus (a type of clot or obstruction) in the diseased left atrium, which passes out into the aorta and becomes lodged, where it divides into two arteries, the iliac arteries, each one of which supplies a hind leg. Here it blocks one or both of these arteries, causing the cat severe pain. A sudden onset of loud crying coupled with some paralysis of the hind legs are the usual signs; this is a very serious problem called iliac thrombosis. There is little that can be done to

help the cat once this has occurred, both because of the difficulties of surgery and the poor risk of anaesthesia due to the heart problems. Usually the pain and paralysis are such that the cat, in most cases, is gently put to sleep, although some do recover, partially or fully, if they can be nursed through the initial crisis, by forming some sort of accessory circulation to the limb.

Hypertension

Hypertension (high blood pressure) is common, particularly in older cats with chronic kidney failure. Blood pressure can now easily be measured in cats in the veterinary surgery, and is often carried out by a qualified veterinary nurse in the owner's presence. A raised blood pressure causes damage to blood vessels, and it seems that the blood vessels in the retina of the eye are particularly sensitive to this, resulting in retinal detachment. This is one of the commonest causes of sudden blindness in cats.

Symptoms. When this occurs, affected cats appear confused and disorientated, and walk into obstacles. On examination, their pupils are widely dilated and your vet will diagnose the problem using an ophthalmoscope, when the retina is seen billowing out into the body of the eye. This condition is an emergency, as blindness will become permanent unless the retina reattaches within a few days. Unfortunately, by the time most cats are brought to the vet, the blindness is permanent. If caught early and the cat is found to have hypertension, medicines that lower blood pressure (hypotensive agents) can help the retina to reattach, or at least prevent further detachment.

The cat's blood pressure is measured in a very similar fashion to the test in humans. A cuff is inflated round the cat's leg, usually while held gently by the owner, and the readings noted by the vet or nurse. It is not a difficult procedure for the cat, but may have to be carried out in a quiet room in which the cat has time to calm down.

Other diseases can also lead to hypertension, so your vet may have to undertake tests to find the cause. In cats there is almost always a separate cause, as primary hypertension, as in humans, rarely occurs.

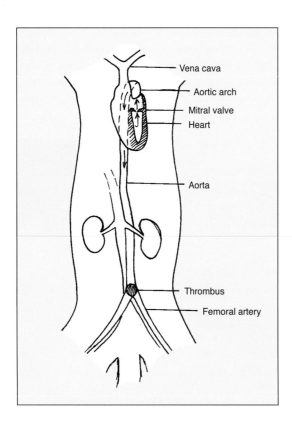

Vena cava
Aortic arch
Mitral valve
Heart
Aorta
Thrombus
Femoral artery

Fig 18 *Iliac thrombosis.*

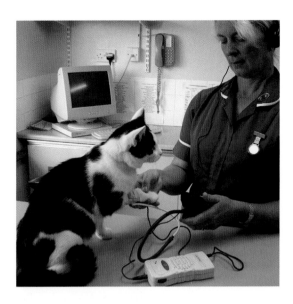

A veterinary nurse measuring a cat's blood pressure.

Heartworm

This infection in cats, by a worm called *Dirofilaria immitis*, is a problem with an increasing incidence and awareness worldwide, but as yet it is absent or very rare in the UK. It does occur in Europe and the worry is that with global warming, it could spread to the UK. Cats with heartworm disease are consistently diagnosed in heartworm endemic areas, where dogs have the disease (*see* Chapter 6).

DISEASES OF THE BLOOD AND LYMPH

Anaemia

Anaemia is caused by a reduction in the haemoglobin in the circulating blood, and can be due to a fall in the number of circulating red blood cells in the bloodstream or by their destruction in the blood. It is not a disease as such but a symptom of a disease that causes it.

Signs. These will be due to both the anaemia and the cause of the anaemia. Usually the cat will appear pale and, in extreme cases, the gums and tongue will be almost white. He will be weak, reluctant to exercise or play, have a poor appetite and a fast respiratory and heart rate. However, because cats are generally quiet, the early signs may not be noticed. In the case of a haemorrhagic cause, bleeding may be seen. Although the clinical signs provide evidence of severe anaemia, confirmation is provided in the laboratory by the examination of a blood smear. In this way, anaemia is not confused with leukaemia.

Causes. Anaemia is quite a common finding in the cat and has several causes:

- Haemolytic anaemia due to red blood cell destruction.
- Haemorrhagic anaemia caused by either small, repeated haemorrhages, such as in warfarin poisoning (rat poisoning), or a sudden, large haemorrhage from, for instance, a road traffic accident.
- Aplastic anaemia due to a reduced red blood cell production, for instance, in the bone marrow. Tumours of the bone marrow will prevent the formation of new red blood cells and lead to anaemia.

Treatment of Anaemias. Any cat suffering from severe anaemia will require a blood transfusion to replace the lost blood cells but then the underlying cause must be attended to. Vitamin K injections will be given for warfarin poisoning, haemorrhaging tumours may be surgically removed and infections treated with antibiotics.

Haemolytic Anaemia

- Feline infectious anaemia. This disease is caused by an infectious organism in the bloodstream called *Haemobartonella felis*, which destroys the red blood cells (*see* Chapter 5).
- Immune-mediated haemolytic anaemia. The cause of this type of anaemia is not fully understood but it is a problem with the cat's immune system. It is diagnosed on blood tests by eliminating other causes. Treatment with corticosteroids can help.
- Paracetamol poisoning. Anaemia is one of the signs of this distressing condition caused by well-intended but ill advised owners administering paracetamol to their cat. Treatment is often of no use.

Haemorrhagic Anaemia

This type of anaemia is commonly seen in veterinary practice, usually as a result of a road traffic accident or other trauma. Treatment is by blood, plasma or saline transfusions, depending on the severity, while other damage to the body is assessed. Other causes do occur, particularly poisoning with mouse or rat poison (warfarin). Here, as well as any treatment for the haemorrhage, an antidote, vitamin K, is available and given by injection by your vet.

Aplastic Anaemia

This is quite common in cats and is due to a reduction in the production of red blood cells in the cat. It can be caused by various conditions, including feline leukaemia virus, kidney failure, various toxins and any chronic inflammatory disease, such as feline infectious peritonitis, long-term abscesses, pyometra and various tumours. In this type of anaemia treatment of the disease causing it is most important.

Leucopoenia

Leucopoenia is the name of the condition when the animal has too few white blood cells. It is quite common in cats, often severe and potentially more serious than anaemia because, as well as being life-threatening itself, it is always caused by an underlying disease. One such disease is feline enteritis and the leucopoenia caused gives rise to its alternative name – panleucopoenia (*see* Chapter 5). [CROSS REF]

Signs. Both acute and, more commonly, chronic types of leucopoenia occur. In the acute form, the cat may have an acute haemorrhagic gastro-enteritis, the classic form of feline enteritis, or a severe generalized infection with the presence of pus. In the chronic form, the cat may just be depressed, off food and not thriving for weeks, or have repeated bouts of skin or other infections.

Diagnosis. A blood test will show whether the cat is leucopoenic, and whether it has feline leukaemia virus or feline enteritis.

Treatment. This is unlikely to be successful, but if the underlying cause is discovered, treatment of this may help.

Leukaemia

Leukaemia is an excess production of white blood cells and is the name for a number of cancers of the white blood cells, which are the cells that fight infection in the body. Blood cells are produced in the bone marrow, which is the spongy tissue that forms the centre of the bone. In leukaemia, white blood cells multiply in an uncontrolled and abnormal way, and gradually take the place of the other cells that normally make up the blood. There is then little room in the bone marrow for the other types of blood cells and for new blood cells to be produced; this can cause a shortage of red blood cells, which leads to anaemia and severe bleeding (because platelets, the cells helping normal blood clotting are absent), or serious infection as a result of a weakened immune system.

In cats there is a virus that causes leukaemia – the feline leukaemia virus, which is described in Chapter 5. However, not all cases of leukaemia are caused by this virus, and indeed the cause of many of these is not known.

Signs. Loss of condition, weakness, recurrent infections, enlargement of lymph nodes or spleen, or anaemia are all signs that alert the vet to consider leukaemia.

Diagnosis. A blood sample examined under a microscope should reveal the preponderance of abnormal white cells suggesting leukaemia, and a rapid in-house blood test at the surgery will reveal whether it is caused by the FeLV virus. Enlargements of the various lymph nodes, which your vet can feel, is also very suggestive of this problem, and a biopsy of a lymph node would also confirm the diagnosis.

Treatment. The long-term prognosis is not good, but if the cat suffers from recurrent infections, these can be treated with anti-biotics. General supportive treatment is helpful but there is no specific treatment currently available.

Prevention. The FeLV virus is only transmitted cat to cat by direct contact, such as bites and scratches, and sharing food and water bowls, so if your cat will spend time outdoors and meet other cats, it is essential to vaccinate him against the FeLV virus. Indoor cats with no chance of contact need only be vaccinated against feline influenza and feline enteritis (*see* Chapter 5).

Lymphosarcoma

This is a tumour of particular white cells of the blood called lymphocytes, and is, therefore, related to leukaemia. It is fairly common in the middle-aged and old cat; the affected white blood cells infiltrate various organs of the body to produce lymphosarcoma tumours. Sometimes there is an increase in the circulating white blood cells to produce leukaemia. The symptoms are governed by which organ is affected, but lymphosarcoma develops slowly. The first signs are lethargy, often a poor appetite and weight loss. If the nervous system is affected, the cat will become uncoordinated and weak. Infiltration of the lungs, liver or kidney will result in failure of these organs. Intestinal lymphosarcoma produces vomiting and diarrhoea. Often, lymphosarcoma will affect the lymph nodes around the body and produce large superficial lumps, especially under the throat.

Diagnosis. Lymphosarcoma is not easily diagnosed from an examination of the blood and will often require a biopsy of the affected organ.

Treatment. Lymphosarcoma can be treated with chemotherapy using anti-neoplastic drugs, which kill tumour cells, as in the treatment of leukaemia in humans. However, this treatment does not usually kill the tumour but it may slow the progress of the disease for several months. Remissions can and do occur.

BLOOD-CLOTTING DEFECTS

Failure of the blood-clotting mechanism is rare in the cat but occasionally occurs due to platelet abnormalities, haemophilia or poison-ings. Haemophilia has been seen in Devon Rex cats. It will result in severe haemorrhage, even from small wounds, and small spontaneous haemorrhages will occur in various parts of the body, especially in the joints and in the chest.

Blood-clotting disorders can only be diagnosed by laboratory testing of blood, although warfarin poisoning can be diagnosed on clinical signs, if rat poison has been used locally. The antidote is vitamin K. Low platelet counts can often be reversed by steroid therapy.

DISEASES OF THE SPLEEN

Splenic Tumours

The spleen is rarely affected by disease but it can be a site for tumour formation, usually in cats over eight years old. These splenic tumours in cats are usually, but not always, benign and this type does not spread elsewhere.

Signs. The cat becomes thin, except for an enlarged round abdomen; he will have a poor appetite and become lethargic. Splenic tumours can rupture easily and bleed into the abdomen, and if this occurs, the first sign is a collapsed cat. The abdomen can become much distended through the accumulation of free blood, and death can occur very rapidly.

Diagnosis. Splenic tumours can be diagnosed by the vet, when she palpates the abdomen, and confirmed by an X-ray.

Treatment. The entire spleen, along with the tumour, must be removed surgically by an operation called a splenectomy. This is a serious operation but, if successful, has no detrimental effect on the cat's health. A blood or plasma transfusion is normally necessary because, by removing the spleen, a storage organ for blood, this volume needs to be replaced.

Splenomegaly

Literally, enlargement of the spleen. This can occur as part of other diseases especially leukaemia.

Chapter 10
Skin and Associated Structures

The skin is the tough, outer, protective covering of the body and is the largest organ in the body. Its functions are to protect the rest of the tissues of the body from dangers, such as trauma and infection, and, together with the cat's fur, to maintain the internal temperature of the body by insulating it from excessive heat and cold. Also, importantly, via nerve endings, the skin relays messages about the environment to the brain and warns of painful stimuli, also via reflexes. It also provides a waterproof layer for the body and is important in water conservation.

NORMAL STRUCTURE AND FUNCTION

The skin consists of two layers: the outer tough epidermis and the underlying dermis from which the epidermis grows.

- The outer epidermis is composed of flat, dead cells which are being constantly produced from the deeper layer and continuously worn away from the surface. In certain areas, where there is excessive wear and tear, such as the pads, the epidermis has become much thicker.

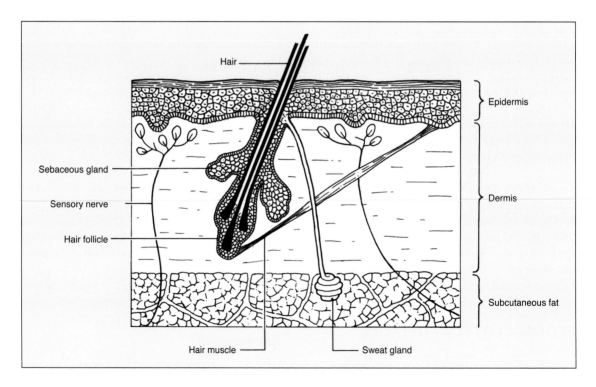

Fig 19 *Structure of the skin.*

- The dermis is a thicker layer and contains the blood vessels, nerve endings, sebaceous glands and hair follicles. Each hair follicle has an associated small muscle, which when it contracts, causes the hair to erect – vividly demonstrated by the tail of an angry or frightened cat.

A few areas of the skin and hair have become very specialized:

- The anal sacs are small scent glands, which lie on either side of and slightly below the anus. These sacs are normally emptied every time the cats defecates and this is one of the ways in which the cat is able to mark his territory.
- The claws are formed from a specialized part of the skin, the nail bed. The inner part of the claw, the quick, contains blood vessels and nerves, which is why it is essential to be careful not to cut the cat's claws too short when clipping them (*see* diagram later).
- The cat's whiskers are specialized hairs, which are mechanoreceptors and are extremely sensitive to touch.

The skin, because of its external position and protective role, is prone to disease, so the vet in

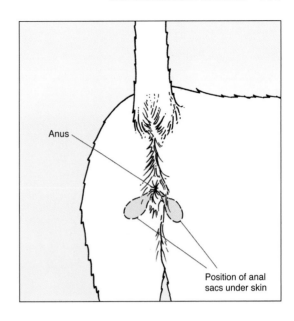

Fig 20 *Rear view of cat showing position of the anal sacs.*

general practice will be called on to treat many skin problems. In fact, about 30 per cent of our case-load in small-animal practice concerns skin cases. As many skin diseases are a reaction between the cat's skin and his environment, many of these diseases can become chronic, intermittent or seasonal, and as such require constant or intermittent treatment. Some of these diseases cannot be cured because of the impracticality in changing the cat's environment, but they can be controlled.

DISEASES OF THE SKIN

General

In cats, allergy accounts for a large proportion of skin diseases since, unlike in dogs, mange, hormonal skin disease and pyoderma (bacterial skin disease) are not common. Of the allergies, flea allergic dermatitis (FAD) is the most common (70 per cent) followed by atopic dermatitis (25–30 per cent) and food allergy (5–10 per cent). However, multiple allergies may occur, especially FAD and atopic dermatitis. Atopic dermatitis is an inhaled allergy (e.g. house dust mite and pollen allergy), which in

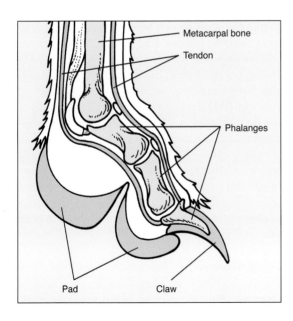

Fig 21 *Structure of the foot.*

Flea allergic dermatitis: note the sores on the skin.

humans causes eczema, asthma and hay fever. In cats, however, this and other allergies cause skin problems and itching, called pruritus. The problem in diagnosing allergy in cats is that they all show in these similar ways – generalized itch, alopecia (hair loss) and spots, sores or scabs. Interestingly, it appears that the incidence of atopic allergy is increasing in cats, as it is in humans, for reasons that scientists have not worked out, but genetic predisposition probably plays a large part.

Fleas, lice, ticks and mites can all cause itchy skin disease in cats (*see* Chapter 6). However, fleas deserve a special mention here because they are the commonest cause by far of itchy skin disease in cats for three main reasons:

- The flea is a very successful parasite, which breeds and lives well in warm, clean surroundings. Our centrally heated houses provide exactly this sort of environment for them, enabling them to breed all year round.

- Cats easily develop an allergy to the flea saliva, which means that even very infrequent flea bites can cause almost continual irritation.
- Many cat owners do not understand both of these facts and omit to permanently undertake an effective flea-prevention programme.

Flea Allergic Dermatitis (FAD)

Flea allergic dermatitis is without doubt the commonest cause of itchy skin problems in cats, and fleas, or an allergy to fleas, must be ruled out before any other condition is considered.

The usual sign of a flea allergy is an itchy cat with patchy hair loss and numerous small scabs over the entire body, especially the back and sides. This is often called miliary eczema. However, the face can be involved as the cat scratches and rubs it. A useful tip as to whether your cat has a flea or two is to brush or comb him with a fine tooth comb on to a light coloured surface and examine the debris that falls off. This is more effective after a flea spray or spot-on. Flea droppings may be seen as shiny comma-shaped black granules, which turn red on a damp surface as they contain the cat's blood. FAD usually, but not always, starts at about three to five years of age.

Atopic Dermatitis

While the signs shown by a cat that is allergic to something he inhales, like certain pollen grains, dander or house dust/mites, are similar to FAD above, i.e. itchy skin, hair loss and scabs, he may also have a runny nose. It is very important to rule out FAD first by a thorough examination of the fur and skin, a search for fleas or flea droppings and an assurance from the owner that they are using a flea-eradication programme. Initially atopy usually starts at about one to three years of age and produces a seasonal itchiness, though after several years, the duration of the itchy period extends. Finally, the cat is itchy nearly all year round.

Food Allergy

If a cat is allergic to something he eats, which, amongst other items, can be fish, milk or beef, in addition to the same skin signs, he may also vomit or have diarrhoea.

Diagnosis of Allergies. This is based on a thorough history from the owner, especially about flea prevention, a thorough examination of the cat by the vet, the age at which the problem started, the season of the year and various diagnostic tests that are available.

Treatment. Firstly a full flea-prevention routine must be set up as multiple allergies occur — a cat that is allergic to one allergen is likely to be allergic to others. In food allergies, the food to which the cat is allergic must never be fed. Atopic inhaled allergies are more difficult to control, so medication may be needed, usually with a cortisone-type medication.

Bacterial Infections

Apart from cellulitis and abscesses, mainly from cat fights, bacterial skin disease is rare in the cat.

Cellulitis

This is an inflammation of the skin and underlying tissues usually caused by a tooth or claw penetrating the skin during a fight. Cats carry the bacterium, *Pasteurella*, in their mouths and when this is taken through the skin of a cat, the bacteria multiply. Initially, the area becomes hot, swollen and painful, and if the affected area is a leg, the cat will limp. Other common sites for wounds like this are the head, face and tail.

Diagnosis and Treatment. In most cases careful examination of the affected area will reveal a small scab or puncture wound. It is strongly recommended that you immediately bathe the area in warm saline, and then contact your vet, as antibiotics will bring about a rapid healing to what would otherwise be likely to develop into a painful abscess.

Abscess

If the infection is not brought under control at the cellulitis stage, an abscess is likely to develop. This will appear as a discrete swelling at the site of the bite, as the area gradually fills with pus.

Treatment. At this stage, you should encourage the abscess to burst and release the pus by bathing in hot water or saline. It may be wiser to contact your vet, as she may be able to lance it and release the foul-smelling pus. This will shorten the time that your cat is in pain. Lancing is often straightforward, if the abscess is a discrete mature abscess, and can often be carried out by your vet in the consulting room using a new, disposable, very sharp scalpel blade that the cat will hardly feel. However, in multiple or long-standing abscesses, your vet may need to administer an anaesthetic to thoroughly irrigate and eliminate the abscess. Antibiotics are almost always used where a cat has treatment for an abscess.

If the wound or abscess fails to heal, your vet may suspect that some foreign material, such as hair, a claw, tooth or even air gun pellet, has entered the cat through the wound and further investigation will be necessary. Another reason for non-healing may be the presence of a disease such as feline leukaemia virus, or feline immuno-deficiency virus.

A cat bite abscess above the left eye.

Viral Infections

Feline Leukaemia Virus, FIV, and the Cat Flu Viruses

These diseases (covered in Chapter 5) suppress the immune system or the cat's resistance to infection, so can result in repeated abscesses or generalized skin disease, which can take many forms. Tumours can appear or a general seborrhoea, or ulcers.

Cowpox

This is particularly a disease of the hunting cat, as infection is usually spread by a rodent bite. Skin lesions caused by this virus are occasionally seen in cats, where they cause ulcers and nodules to appear and some hair loss. Affected cats may be itchy and may recover without treatment.

Fungal Disease

Ringworm

Ringworm is a common skin complaint of the cat and is not caused by a worm but a fungus or yeast. The disease develops when the hairs and

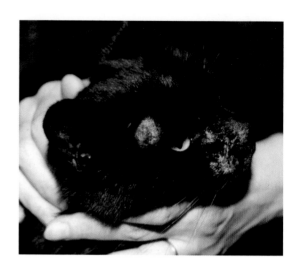

Ringworm affecting the nose and face.

skin become invaded by the ringworm fungi. The hairs become weak and break off at the level of the skin, leaving bald, scaly patches, sometimes resembling cigarette ash. Ringworm in cats is usually caused by a fungus called *Microsporum* but there is another species of ringworm called *Trichophyton*, which can also cause

(LEFT) Cowpox areas on the head; (RIGHT) cowpox areas on the foot.

(LEFT) A Wood's lamp can detect ringworm; (RIGHT) but only in a darkened room.

the disease. Various species of this fungus affect cattle, horses, hedgehogs and rodents, all of which can transmit the infection to inquisitive cats. Infected cats are often a source of this infection for the dog, and both species can also pass the infection on to humans, especially children.

Ringworm usually starts to develop on the face or forelegs as single or multiple areas of hair loss. As the disease progresses, these areas can become quite large and they can become infected, producing a purulent sore. Initially, the cat is not itchy.

Diagnosis. The majority of ringworm infections caused by *Microsporum* will fluoresce a lime green colour in the dark under an ultraviolet light called a 'Wood's lamp'; if this occurs, the test is usually diagnostic, but if the suspected lesion fails to fluoresce, or if confirmation is needed, hair samples can be examined and cultured in a laboratory, either by your vet in her surgery or sent to an outside lab. Examination of the hairs under a microscope may be immediately diagnostic but if not, growing the fungus is necessary, so the result may not be available for two weeks or so. As ringworm is a zoonosis, it is important to ascertain whether the disease the cat has is ringworm because of the risk of transfer to people.

Collecting hairs for testing is tricky, as you do not want to risk exposure of yourself to the fungus. Wearing thin, rubber gloves, stand your cat on a large sheet of newspaper and comb or brush the hairs out on to this. Then funnel the hairs and skin debris into a paper envelope, seal it and put your cat's and your name and address on this, then place it in a polythene bag and seal that before taking it to your vet.

Treatment. When handling cats with ringworm, the owners must be very careful and should wear rubber gloves. The area surrounding the lesion should be clipped to remove as much infected hair as possible, and the skin thoroughly cleaned with an antifungal wash; these clippings should be burnt. Sometimes vets find it necessary to shave the entire cat. In mild cases, antifungal ointment or lotion may eliminate the

A ringworm test. The left dish shows a positive result.

A squamous cell carcinoma on the nose.

lesions, but usually an antibiotic, called griseofulvin, which kills the fungus, is given in tablet form for between four and eight weeks. Further brushings of the coat may be examined at this stage to see if any fungus remains. An examination with the Wood's lamp every two weeks or so will provide an assessment of the success of treatment.

The ringworm fungus breeds by budding off spores, which are very resistant to many disinfectants. It can be difficult to eliminate it from a house, and especially a cattery. Vacuuming is ideal with the contents and bag being burnt, and if surfaces can be wiped with bleach without any risk to the cat, this will kill the spores.

Solar Dermatitis

This is a precancerous skin problem brought on by sunlight in white cats or cats with white ear flaps and noses (*see* Chapter 11); it can, and does, also occur on white noses. It starts as a small sore, but gradually enlarges and erodes the skin. If caught early, your vet may remove it by cryosurgery (freezing the tissue) but if it is very advanced, surgery in nasal cases, even by this method, is not always successful.

Burns

Cats are very inquisitive and will knock over pans of boiling water. I have seen substantial scalded areas, especially over the backs of cats, where the only explanation is boiling water. With careful veterinary treatment, even large areas can heal, sometimes with skin transplants. Strangely, often the first sign is a hard, rough-feeling area of skin on the back, which is still complete with hair, and only a mildly disturbed cat.

Food Allergies

This type of allergy, although it does occur in cats from time to time, is very rare.

Signs. When it occurs, it may mimic flea allergy, in that the cat will be generally very itchy, or just have areas of skin that the cat cannot resist licking.

Diagnosis is usually by eliminating fleas as the cause, and then food testing. Occasionally your vet will need to administer anti-inflammatory treatment to prevent further damage by the cat itself.

Auto-Immune Skin Diseases

These are also uncommon but pemphigus and lupus have been seen. An auto-immune disease occurs when, for some unknown reason, the cat's own defence mechanisms start to attack his own tissue. This can occur in the skin, as well as other tissues. Changes usually occur around the mouth, nose, eyes or anus. The skin becomes very inflamed and blisters or ulcers may form.

Diagnosis. This can be difficult but a skin biopsy will often help.

Treatment. High levels of steroids are required to suppress the disease and it may be necessary to continue them for a prolonged period, even years.

Psychogenic Dermatitis

This is seen as a very itchy skin condition leading to widespread hair loss on the back and flanks of, especially, the foreign breeds of cat, including the Siamese, Burmese and Abyssinian. The cause is not known but thought to be due to stress. The signs are so similar to flea allergic dermatitis that it is thought in many cases to be due to that cause without a flea having been found.

Pemphigus lesions on the ears.

Treatment. Flea prevention is always advised, and anti-anxiety medications may be prescribed by your vet.

Facial Dermatitis

This is a poorly understood problem seen in Persian and Himalayan cats. The lesions slowly develop over months or years, and are mainly localized to the face, where a patchy,

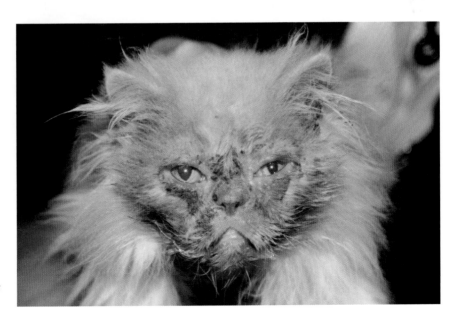

Severe facial dermatitis in a Persian cat.

waxy, exudate can matt the hair, especially on the chin.

Treatment. Cyclosporine, an anti-cancer drug, seems to control the disease, but it can recur. Secondary infections with bacteria and fungi can occur and need to be treated.

Feline Alopecia

This is a skin problem where the exact cause is not known. It used to be thought of as a hormonal problem but is now thought to be due to the cat over-grooming as a stereotypic behaviour, possibly related to psychogenic or allergic dermatitis.

Signs. The cat is not itchy, but develops hair loss symmetrically on both sides of the body because the cat over-grooms in this stereotypic way. I have seen it affecting both ear flaps, the backs of the hind legs, the abdomen, the front of both forelegs and, occasionally, elsewhere. The skin looks normal, is not swollen, discoloured or inflamed, but the hair is absent or thinning.

Treatment. Despite the fact that this resembles hypothyroidism in other species, thyroid levels are usually normal in these cats. However, supplementation by thyroid hormone and the use of steroid hormones sometimes bring about recovery in these cases.

Eosinophilic Granuloma Complex

This is not truly a disease, as such, but an extreme reaction to one or more of the allergies to which cats are prone.

Signs. Mainly due to the cat's rough tongue and determination to lick itself frequently and furiously, cats can and do convert minor skin irritations or lesions into bright red, swollen, bleeding sores within hours. This will often lead to ulcerating plaques called eosinophilic granulomas. They can occur anywhere, but mostly on the abdomen, inner thighs and lower back.

A peculiar version occurs on the cat's upper lip, and is called a rodent ulcer (after 'eroding', not the mouse family!).

Treatment. Antibiotics and corticosteroids are usually needed and, in extreme cases, surgical removal of the affected area is needed. This condition can be and often is recurrent.

Feline Acne

This condition, of unknown cause, is often seen on the chin of cats.

Signs. The area is very glandular and becomes swollen and discoloured but not necessarily irritant to the cat. On close examination, many blackhead-type areas will be seen, which may be due to food remaining on the chin; so once it has occurred, the chin should be kept clean after feeding.

Treatment. The chin should be bathed and the 'blackheads' gently squeezed out. Your vet may feel that an antibiotic ointment will help, if the area appears infected.

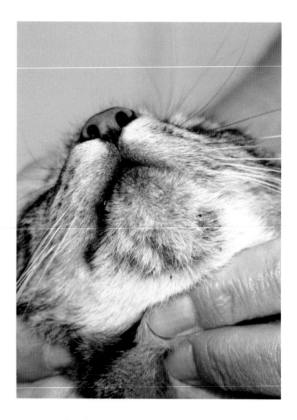

Acne on the chin.

Stud Tail

I have seen this mainly in breeding male tom cats, especially Siamese. The cat has an area on the dorsal aspect, at the base of the tail, which is very glandular; stud tail, as it is called by breeders, seems to occur due to this gland overproducing its secretion.

Signs. The area becomes very oily, matted and discoloured with some hair loss.

Treatment. The area should be treated as for acne; antibiotics may be needed if the area becomes infected.

TUMOURS AND CYSTS

Skin tumours are relatively uncommon in the cat but, when they occur, they are often cancerous. For this reason, any lump or mass appearing on the skin of your cat should result in a visit to your vet. In most cases, your vet will suggest either removal or biopsy of the lump to determine what it is. Apart from the squamous cell carcinomas of the nose and ear, already described, the commonest tumours seem to be fibrous tissue, glandular or mast cell tumours. Conversely, warts are very uncommon in the cat.

DISEASES OF THE ANAL AREA

Anal-Sac Problems: Impaction

This is not a very common problem in the cat but it does occur. Cats have a small scent 'gland' below and on each side of the anus, both of which empty just inside the anus.

Signs. If the anal-sac secretion accumulates in the gland, instead of being expressed during defecation, the impacted anal sac become itchy and sore, and the cat will usually lick himself a lot more than usual around the base of his tail.

Treatment. The full glands can be felt through the skin below the anus and are emptied by the vet using manual pressure. The anal-sac material is constantly being produced and the frequency

with which the glands refill is variable. In some cats, it can be as rapid as two weeks. In mild, infrequent cases, it is sufficient to empty the anal sacs when necessary. Where the problem is recurrent, surgical removal of the anal sacs may be necessary.

Anal-Sac Problems: Anal Abscess

Occasionally, an impacted gland will become infected to form an abscess. Usually, only one gland is affected, but the condition is painful and the cat will be reluctant to move and will be depressed. The abscess usually discharges through the skin over the area of the anal sac.

Treatment. The infected gland should be bathed and cleaned, and excess pus removed. A short course of antibiotics may be necessary, either given in tablet or injection form, or by ointment instilled into the gland. Very occasionally, repeat infections will affect the same sacs repeatedly and surgical excision will be necessary.

PROBLEMS OF THE CLAWS

The cat's claws, in pristine condition, are ultrasharp, lethal weapons, normally five on each front foot and four on each hind foot. Each is a specialization of normal skin, and is broader at the base but narrows down to a sharp point. The wider base contains the blood and nerve supply to the claw and is constantly growing, like our nails. Conversely, the outer shell of the claw is constantly being replaced and shed. Cats will attempt to keep their claws in first-class condition by using scratching posts, trees, sofas and so on, to remove the old outer sheath and to expose the new sharp tip. As explained earlier in the book, it is a good idea to provide a scratching post or to allow access to the garden for this purpose.

Broken or Damaged Claws

Cats break claws frequently during climbing, fighting or road accidents, and if the 'quick' is exposed, it can be very painful. Veterinary help is usually needed in these cases to prevent the claw

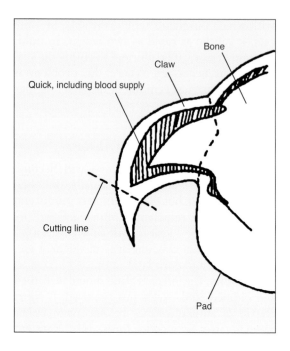

Fig 22 *A cat's claw and where to cut.*

Overgrown Claws

Clipping cats' claws should not be undertaken lightly or without tuition from your vet. As you can see from the figure opposite, the sensitive part or quick extends about half-way down the claw to where it rapidly narrows, so when clipping, only the very sharp point should be removed using a sharp pair of cat nail-clippers. In old cats, the claws don't shed so easily, perhaps because the cat itself doesn't use a scratching post so easily. They begin to look very thick and long, and will often impede walking, so it is essential to clip them for the cat and remove the old nail sheath. White claws are easier to clip, as the pink quick can be seen; the nail should be cut about 2mm nearer the tip than the quick. Black claws, however, are more difficult and should be left to the expert.

Occasionally, especially in older cats or on the dew claw, a claw will grow almost in a circle and penetrate the cat's pad, like a splinter. The pad will become infected and very painful. The answer is to clip the claw and bathe the sore in saline, and if the infection is severe, antibiotics may be needed. Once this has happened, you must be on the lookout for it, as it is almost certain to recur. In this case regular claw clipping must be carried out.

becoming infected. The broken tip may need to be removed, using a local or general anaesthetic. It is not uncommon for the whole claw to be removed and the foot dressed. In many cases, the claws will grow again, as do our nails.

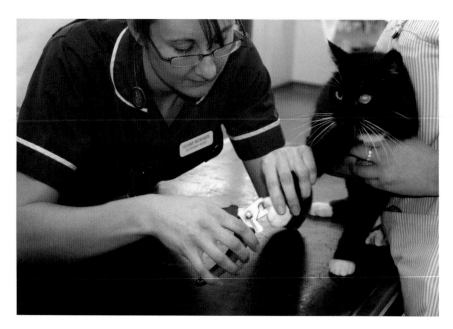

A veterinary nurse clipping claws.

Chapter 11
The Ear

Cats' ears have two separate functions:

- to receive sound waves and convert these into messages, which are passed to the brain;
- to appreciate movement and balance, so that the cat is aware of his position in relation to the ground.

NORMAL STRUCTURE AND FUNCTION

The only part of the ear easily visible is the pinna (ear flap) but there are three distinct sections to the ear, each of which has a different function.

The Outer Ear

This consists of the pinna, which leads into the ear canal and ends at the ear drum. The pinna itself is composed of a layer of cartilage covered on both sides by skin. Its function is to trap and direct sound waves into the ear canal. It is very mobile and the cat can flatten it, or rotate it, to locate the source of the sound. In the cat, its position is erect as distinct from many breeds of dog and thus cats have far fewer ear problems than dogs. In only one breed (the Scottish Fold) does the ear permanently fold over the entrance to the ear canal.

The ear canal is an L-shaped tube with a

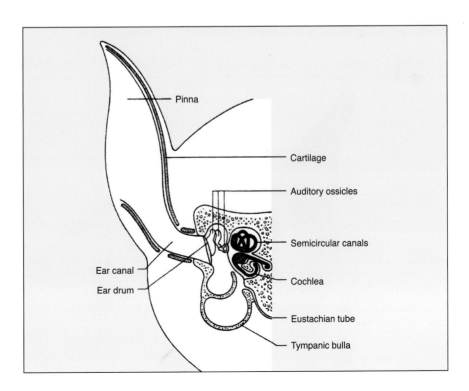

Fig 23 *Structure of the feline ear.*

Pinna

Cartilage

Auditory ossicles

Semicircular canals

Cochlea

Ear canal

Ear drum

Eustachian tube

Tympanic bulla

horizontal and a vertical section. It is mainly cartilaginous and covered by a modified skin containing wax-secreting glands and numerous microscopic hairs called cilia, which propel the wax and any debris up and out of the ear. The canal ends at the ear drum, which is a thin membrane across the canal and vibrates when stimulated by sound waves.

The Middle Ear

The middle ear is enclosed within a bony structure, the tympanic bulla, inside the base of the skull, and is an air-filled cavity, which is also connected to the throat by the Eustachian tube to equalize the pressure with the outer ear. The bulla protects the inner ear and also is thought to help in the transmission of sound waves. Sound waves are mainly transmitted from the ear drum across the middle ear by three small bones, the auditory ossicles (known by the wonderful names of incus, malleus and stapes), to another small membrane that separates the middle and inner ear.

The Inner Ear

The inner ear, also enclosed in the skull, is composed of a number of small fluid-filled tubes. One of these, the cochlea, converts the sound vibrations into messages that pass along the auditory nerve to the brain. The others are the semi-circular canals, which, because they are present in each ear on either side of the skull, detect any movement of the head, which sets up a disturbance in the fluid. This disturbance is monitored by little hair-like sensors at the end of the auditory nerve, which gives the cat its sense of balance and position – particularly important to the cat when actively climbing and jumping.

PROBLEMS OF THE PINNA

Haematoma

This is a leakage of blood between the skin and the central cartilage of the pinna and causes an obvious swelling as it presses the skin away from the cartilage. Unless infected it is not particularly painful to the touch. If untreated, the blood clots and the liquid portion (serum) is slowly reabsorbed, but the fibrous clot left causes shrinkage and deformity of the pinna, which can obscure the opening to the ear canal. This results in what is known in humans as a cauliflower ear! The correct term is an aural haematoma.

The cat's erect ears gather sound extremely well.

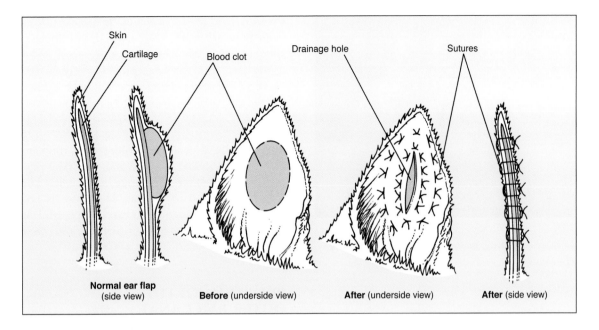

Fig 24 *Aural haematoma before and after repair.*

Causes:

- Ear mites (*see* page 115) cause severe irritation and the resultant shaking of the head and scratching of the ear can cause this haemorrhage. Check to see if the ear canal is sore or full of wax or discharge.
- Blows to the ear.
- Fight wounds. Check to see if there are any puncture wounds. If an ear pinna is bitten or scratched and the skin is punctured, haemorrhage and infection will often follow.

Treatment. In a non-infected case, your vet will drain the blood from the haematoma, usually under an anaesthetic. Sometimes this will be done via a hypodermic needle but usually using a scalpel blade to ensure the ear does not refill with blood. Because the skin has now become separated from the underlying cartilage, the vet will often need to place sutures through the pinna to prevent a repeat swelling. Sometimes an injection of an anti-inflammatory medication into the space left by the haematoma may be all that's needed to prevent a recurrence.

If the haematoma has been caused by a fight wound and become infected, antibiotics will be needed and, indeed, an abscess may develop.

Lacerations

Cat fights often result in lacerations to the pinna. These may bleed profusely and, if presented to your vet promptly, can be sutured successfully. Unfortunately most wounds are found in tom cats, which often do not arrive home in time for a successful operation and the wounds heal as deep rents in the pinna – the well-known tom's war wounds. Bathing in saline helps prevent infection but sometimes antibiotics are needed to prevent infection of the cartilage.

Abscess

The entry point of the tooth or claw should be located, and any scab gently removed by bathing and separating. Gentle pressure using cotton wool soaked in warm water should encourage the pus to drain from the wound. This can sometimes be carried out by the owner, but cat-bite abscesses are so painful that it is sensible to take the cat to your local surgery for an examination and antibiotic treatment, which is usually needed.

An early case of squamous cell carcinoma on ear of white cat.

Solar Dermatitis and Squamous Cell Carcinoma

This is quite a common and serious problem in white-coated cats or cats with white ears and nose. It is much more common in sunny climates but does occur in the UK with regularity.

Signs. The first indication that anything is wrong is the appearance on the tip or edge of the pinna of an area of crusting that just does not heal. This gradually extends and erodes down the pinna, and if left untreated will eventually involve the whole pinna. It usually occurs on both ears. The initial crusting is precancerous and sometimes called solar dermatitis but soon develops into the cancer called squamous cell carcinoma, which eventually can spread to other parts of the body. It is also common on the nose of white cats.

Treatment. Many treatments have been tried – cryosurgery (freezing the affected area is often the only method of choice where the nose is affected), diathermy (cautery), and ointments, but usually surgical removal is essential. Because the tumour cells infiltrate the normal tissues, radical removal of the whole pinna is usually the best approach, even in the early stages. Your cat may end up looking a bit like an owl but he will have no pain, usually no further recurrence and his hearing will be virtually unaffected.

Prevention. This problem is precancerous from the very start, so it's worth considering keeping cats with white ears and noses in on sunny days. Alternatively, applying a high-factor bland sun-block to these areas will help.

Hair Loss

Occasionally, especially in older cats, the ears can become quite hairless and the skin pigmented and leathery. This may be unsightly but it is not harmful to the cat. The cause is not known and any treatment is rarely successful. It seems to occur more often in Siamese and other oriental cats.

PROBLEMS OF THE OUTER EAR CANAL

Veterinary examination of the ear canal is by two main methods. Firstly, your vet will examine the ear flap and entrance to the ear with the naked eye, as many clues are picked up by just looking at, and smelling, any discharge that is present. Secondly, by using a torch-like instrument called an auriscope, your vet can look down and into the ear canal, as far as the ear drum. If the

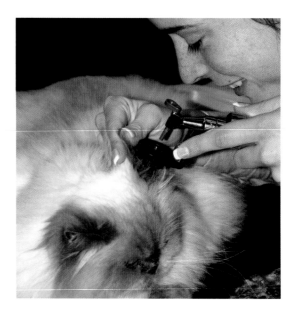

Examination of an ear using an auriscope.

diagnosis is not obvious by then, a sample can be taken on a swab for microscope examination or to culture to see if any bacteria or yeasts are involved.

Ear Mites

These are tiny parasitic members of the spider family that live and breed in the ear canals of cats and dogs. They graze on the lining of the ear canal and cause intense irritation. The ear produces a lot of wax in response, which can block the canal, and infection by bacteria and yeasts can set in.

Signs. It is a common problem, especially in kittens, usually in both ears, and in the early stages there may be little to see, apart from an increase in wax. If the problem is not treated, infection sets in and the ear begins to smell, the discharge increases and the cat shakes his head, scratches his ear or rubs it along the ground. The ear may become very painful and the cat will resent examination. If only one ear is affected, the cat may hold his head towards that side.

Vets are very aware of this condition and will usually check for and treat it when the kitten is first presented for his vaccinations and health examination, at about nine weeks of age. It is very contagious between cats, and to dogs (but not to humans), and the kittens have invariably caught it from their mother or from other cats in their immediate community. It is much more common in farm or feral cats, or other situations where a number of cats live together and are not closely examined or contacted frequently.

Diagnosis. Your vet will firstly examine the ears with the naked eye and then with an auriscope (an instrument for looking in ears). She will usually be able to see the tiny white mites moving about in the canal but if a lot of wax is present, may gently remove this with a cotton bud and examine it for mites under a microscope.

Treatment. If caught in the early stages this condition responds very well to treatment.

Cat's ear with severe ear mite infestation.

Firstly, a thorough cleaning of the canal with a wax solvent may be needed. Then it is necessary to use a parasiticide to kill the mites. Various methods are available. Your vet could supply you with parasiticide drops to instil into the ears until the problem is cleared, which will kill the mites and remove the waxy debris. Because the mites breed in the ears and lay eggs that are resistant to the drops, it's wise to continue treatment on an occasional basis for up to six weeks in some cases to ensure there is no recurrence. Spot-on treatments now also are available that will cure the condition and are applied to the skin of the scruff of the neck as with flea spot-ons.

If the condition has been unnoticed, untreated and allowed to progress, a secondary infection can invade the ear. If this progresses to the middle or inner ears, loss of balance and a head tilt may result. It may be necessary for your vet to clean out all the accumulated debris and wax from the ears under an anaesthetic before providing treatment. In very severe cases, surgery is needed to open up the ear canal.

Grass Seeds

The culprit is almost always the awn of the wild barley grass and the usual history is that the cat has had access to long grass and suddenly starts to shake his head or scratch his ear violently. The grass seed can only be seen with the auriscope

Kitten with a head tilt due to a severe ear mite infestation and secondary infection.

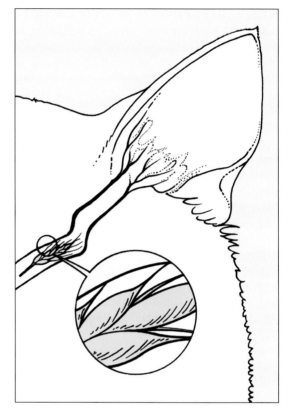

Fig 25 *Grass seed in ear canal.*

but, because of the discomfort, the vet may have to examine him under either sedation or a general anaesthetic.

The seed (*see* diagram opposite) has bristles emerging from a pointed end, like a miniature shuttlecock, so can only move one way – further into the ear.

Treatment. Using an auriscope to see the seed, it is then firmly grasped by the vet with a pair of long, thin forceps through the auriscope lens and gently removed from the ear. Occasionally, with a calm cat, if the seed can be seen with the auriscope, it can be removed in the consulting room without an anaesthetic, but usually one is needed. Sometimes soothing drops are prescribed afterwards.

Ear Polyps and Tumours

Polyps are fairly common in cats' ears, especially older cats. There are two main types:

• Multiple, blue polyps, which line the ear canal and the opening to the canal, so are often visible to the naked eye. The cause is not certain but is thought to be the result of a long-standing ear infection, possibly by mites, and the resulting secondary infection has led to the production of these polyps.
• Individual polyps or tumours in the canal.

Signs. Because of the presence of these polyps or tumours, the canal becomes partially or totally blocked, so normal ear wax cannot escape and builds up below the obstruction. This causes pain and irritation and often a secondary infection.

Diagnosis. All these cause the cat to shake his head or scratch his ears, so your vet will examine him with an auriscope whenever this occurs and will be able to diagnose the problem. In severe cases an anaesthetic may be needed.

Treatment. Surgical removal of individual tumours or polyps is possible but an operation may be needed to remove part or the entire wall of the ear canal for access. Where multiple, blue polyps are present, it is not always possible to remove them all but usually some can be removed to open up the canal again, or the entire canal may need to be removed surgically.

PROBLEMS OF THE MIDDLE EAR (BULLA)

A fairly common condition of the middle ear in cats is the development of inflammatory polyps in the bulla. However, the middle ear can also become infected usually from otitis externa through a damaged ear drum, but it can also reach the middle ear through the Eustachian tube. As inflammation of the middle ear (called otitis media) is nearly always associated with otitis externa, the symptoms are very similar – head shaking, rubbing the ear, head held to one side, pain and discharge.

Diagnosis. Middle-ear disease can be diagnosed by careful examination of the ear drum using the auriscope. If a polyp is the cause, it may be seen partially in the external ear canal. A torn ear drum may imply that infection has entered the middle ear. In long-standing cases, the air-filled spaces become full of pus and the surrounding bone thickened and irregular. An X-ray of the skull will usually reveal these changes and thus the cause.

Treatment. If the problem is an infected middle ear, the initial treatment is similar to that of disease of the external canal. The ear is gently syringed to remove all discharge and then an ear preparation containing antibiotics, fungicidal drugs and/or steroids is instilled. Usually your vet will prescribe antibiotics by mouth also. In severe cases of infection, an operation called a bulla osteotomy is needed, where the entire affected area is surgically removed. However, the most common condition requiring a bulla osteotomy is inflammatory polyps in cats.

PROBLEMS OF THE INNER EAR

The infection in middle-ear disease may spread directly to the inner ear.

Signs. The symptoms will be similar to those of otitis externa and otitis media but the cat may also be deaf. However, as the inner ear also controls balance, inflammation of the semi-circular canals will produce a disturbance in the cat's ability to walk or in his posture. This is shown by a head tilt, walking in circles or falling over, all to the affected side. A flicking movement of the eyes, known as nystagmus, will also frequently be present.

Treatment. The treatment is again similar to that for otitis externa, although antibiotic and steroid tablets are usually necessary in addition to ear drops or ointments. Although the infection may be eliminated, the cat may be left with a permanent head tilt.

DEAFNESS

There are no specific tests for deafness in the cat available to the general practitioner. To assess a cat's hearing it is necessary to study his response to noises of varying intensity. Total deafness in the younger cat is very uncommon and few kittens are born deaf. Hereditary deafness, however, is a major concern in white cats, and especially if one or both irises are blue in colour. Researchers at Cornell University Veterinary School found that only 17 to 22 per cent of white cats with non-blue eyes are born deaf. The percentage rises to 40 per cent if the cat has one blue eye (a so-called odd-eyed cat), while upwards of 65 to 85 per cent of all-white cats with both eyes blue are deaf. Some of these cats are deaf in only one ear. Interestingly, if a white cat with one blue eye is deaf in only one ear, that ear will invariably be on the same side of the head as the blue eye.

Severe infection of the ear canal with thickening of the canal walls, blockage of the canal with discharge or damage to the ear drum will reduce hearing. Normal hearing will usually return with prompt treatment of the infection. Infection of the middle or inner ear may cause severe impairment of hearing, which can be permanent despite treatment. The degree of loss of hearing will depend on the severity of the infection and whether one, or both, ears are affected. Senile deafness is, however, more common.

Chapter 12
The Eye

STRUCTURE AND FUNCTION

The eye receives and converts light images from the cat's surroundings, and passes them down the optic nerve to an area of the cat's brain, called the visual cortex.

In cats, the eyes are situated on the front of the face giving the cat the ability to detect and focus on prey. Both eyes point forwards but occasionally, especially in Siamese cats, they appear to squint. This is called strabismus, which, although not affecting the cat in any way, is an undesirable characteristic. Legend has it that this was so the cats in ancient times could see round the pillars in the temples they were guarding.

In a way, the eye works like a camera. Light rays pass through a clear window in the front of the eye, the cornea and then through the pupil, the dark centre part of the eye, where they are focused by the lens lying just behind the pupil, on to a light-sensitive layer at the back of the eye, the retina. The iris is the coloured area around the pupil and controls the amount of light entering the eye by constricting or dilating the pupil. The iris in each eye is normally the same colour, but in some cats called 'odd-eyed cats' they are different colours. In these cats, usually white cats, one eye is blue and the other either green, yellow or brown.

The retina is made up of two types of photo-receptor cells, the rods and cones, which perform different functions and are named according to their shape. The rods are very light-sensitive, so they are most abundant in

Close-up view of cat's eyes – note narrow vertical pupil when constricted in bright light.

Eyes partially dilated – pupils more open.

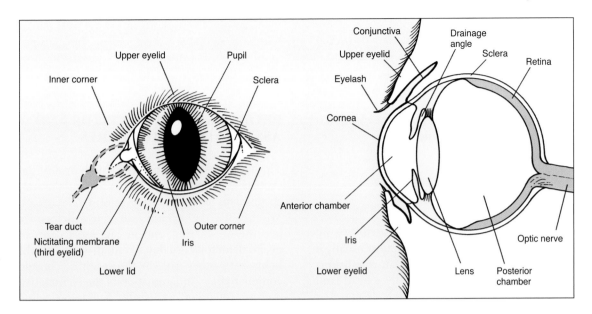

Fig 26 A cat's eye – front view and section.

nocturnal species such as the cat. The cones need bright light, and they are for sharp image formation and perception of colour. Cats have mostly rods, and are unable to distinguish colours well but can see well at night. The retina converts the light rays into nerve impulses, which pass to the brain along the optic nerve.

The part of the eye between the pupil and the cornea is the anterior chamber and is filled with a watery fluid, the aqueous humour, which is maintained at a constant pressure. This is produced by a small area just behind the iris called the ciliary body, from which fine fibres suspend and hold the lens in place. The posterior chamber behind the lens is filled with a clear jelly-like material, called the vitreous humour.

The eye is protected from behind, below and above to some degree by the skull, and in front by the upper and lower eyelids. The eyelids of cats open between ten and fourteen days of age, but if the eyelids open too early, tear production is not present and, unless kept lubricated with eye ointment, problems set in. Cats also have a third eyelid, the nictitating membrane, at the inner corner of each eye, which gives further protection. The eyelids are lined by a membrane, the conjunctiva, which continues on to the surface of the eyeball lining the white part

called the sclera, then leading on to the clear cornea. Each eye is moved around by small muscles behind it. The surface of the eye needs to remain moist at all times to function correctly, and this is supplied by tears from the tear glands. Any tears in excess are drained through two small tear ducts from the inner corner of the eyelids, which run along the inside of the nose and out through each nostril.

An odd-eyed cat.

Cats have exceptionally good eyesight and rely a lot on their vision for assessing their environment and prey, and are even able to hunt at night. There are few tests available to your vet for her to assess a cat's vision. Any loss of eyesight can only be deduced from the cat's behaviour and an examination of the changes to the various structures of the eye.

EXAMINATION OF THE EYE

All veterinary practices have one or more instruments with which to examine the eye and surrounding structures. The two most usually in use are a focal illuminator and an ophthalmoscope. The illuminator is basically a head lamp with magnifying lenses with which your vet can examine, hands free, the external parts of the eye. The ophthalmoscope is a torch-like instrument with a magnifying and focusing lens through which your vet looks into the cat's eye to examine the internal structures such as the lens and the retina. It is sometimes necessary to widen the pupil to allow a fuller examination and this is done by placing some drops on to the cornea, usually of a substance called

tropicamide. Consultants in eye referral clinics will have specialized variations on these instrument to allow a more detailed examination of the eye.

PROBLEMS OF THE EYELIDS AND ASSOCIATED STRUCTURES

The edge of the eyelid must sit snugly against the eyeball. If there is a gap, then tears and dirt can accumulate and this may lead to infection. Wounds to the eyelids can cause deformity because of scarring, and in cats most cases of eyelid deformity are due to either wounds from fights with other cats, or the result of chronic conjunctivitis – inflammation of the conjunctiva due to infection, especially following feline influenza.

Entropion

This in-rolling of the edge of the eyelid is rare in cats but, occasionally, inherited entropion of the lower lid is present in pure-bred cats that have short, round faces, such as the Persian. When it occurs, lashes and hairs on its outer surface rub

A general practitioner vet examining an eye using an ophthalmoscope.

against the surface of the eye producing irritation of the eyeball, so the cat is reluctant to open his eye, which is inflamed and produces excess tears. If the condition is not treated, the constant rubbing of the hairs against the surface of the eye will produce ulceration of the cornea. This is a very serious complication and requires immediate treatment. Occasionally a severe infection of an eye will lead to spasm of the eyelids, which then produces an in-rolling of the eyelid edge.

Treatment is essential. Your vet will surgically remove a small, crescent-shaped area of the outer surface of the skin of the eyelid and suture the edges together. This then pulls the rim of the eyelid back into its normal position.

Ectropion

Ectropion is the opposite of entropion, as in this case the eyelid rolls outward away from the eye. It is less serious than entropion but gives rise to an unsightly inflamed eye. It is very uncommon in cats, only really occurring due to scarring after injury to the eyelid. Surgery is the only treatment available.

Distichiasis

In this condition, in addition to the normal eyelashes, very fine hairs grow along the rim of the eyelid and rub against the cornea. This constant rubbing irritates the eye causing excessive tear production and a wet eye. To treat this condition, which is very uncommon in cats, an extremely delicate operation is necessary to remove the hair roots.

Blocked Tear (Lachrymal) Duct

Tears are the fluid produced by the body to ensure that the surface of the eye does not dry out. This tear film is essential to the normal function of the eye, and the tear duct is a tube that drains tears from the eyelids to the nose. When excess tears are produced, the nose 'runs', as it does in people when they cry or have a cold. If the eye is infected, the ducts then have to drain this discharge of pus and debris from

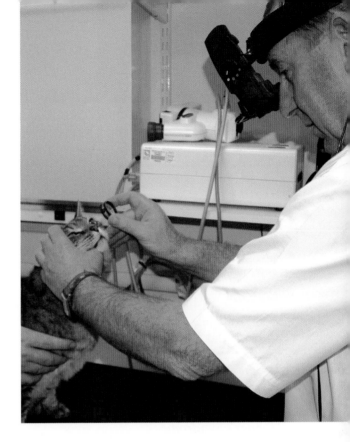

A consultant vet examining a cat's eye using an indirect ophthalmoscope.

the eye. As this duct is narrow, it can easily become blocked in one or both eyes, resulting in tears overflowing from the lower eyelid on to the face. This will stain the skin of the face where it runs down, but can also dry on the eyelids, stick them together and prevent the eye from opening.

Treatment. The affected eye should be bathed with warm water or saline, which should remove the overflow and enable the eye to be opened. Antibiotic eye drops applied several times daily may clear the infection and unblock the tear duct, but if not, it will be necessary for your vet to anaesthetize the cat, insert a small lachrymal canula into the entrance to the tear duct just in the corner of the eyelid and try to flush the debris through. If this is done early in the disease, it is usually successful, but if left, the inflammation and debris in the canal can permanently block the ducts leading to a permanent overflow of tears.

Infection

The skin of the eyelids is very thin and susceptible to infection. Most eyelid infections follow conjunctivitis and are due to the cat rubbing his eyes. The eyelids will be inflamed, painful and often moist with scab formation.

Treatment. The eyelids should be bathed with warm water and then a cream containing antibiotics applied on to the surface of the cornea and on the eyelids. Any underlying cause, such as entropion, must also be corrected.

Tumours

Small, wart-like growths are occasionally seen on the eyelid margin of old cats and can rub against the eyeball and cause irritation. Provided they are not allowed to grow too big, they can be surgically removed by your vet.

Horner's Syndrome

The symptoms of this disease generally include a sunken eye with a small pupil, a droopy upper eyelid and a prominent third eyelid. Usually occurring in one eye only, it is not uncommon in cats.

Horner's syndrome showing in the cat's right eye.

Horner's syndrome in cats is usually associated with damage to the sympathetic nerve supply to the eye and may occur anywhere along the course of the nerve route from the brain to the eye. Horner's syndrome may be caused by a brain tumour, spinal cord injury in the neck region, a chest tumour such as a lymphosarcoma, injury to the neck from fighting, collar injury, middle ear infection or other rarer causes.

Treatment. It is often very difficult to diagnose the cause, but if the cause is found, specific treatment can be tried. In many cases only time will cure the condition, unless the cause is a progressive one such as a tumour. Many cats are left with permanent symptoms.

Conjunctival Problems

Conjunctivitis

This is inflammation of the conjunctiva seen as a red, sore and discharging eye, and is common in the cat. It can vary from being mild to very severe. In mild conjunctivitis there may be very few signs, perhaps a slight redness and irritation, with increased tear production. However, in severe conjunctivitis the eye is very painful and red, the cat keeps his eye closed and there will be a lot of discharge varying from clear and watery to grey or yellow and thick. The cat will resent having the eye examined. Conjunctivitis can occur in one or both eyes, as an individual problem, or as a part of a more generalized disease.

Possible causes of conjunctivitis include viruses, especially cat flu, organisms such as *Chlamydia*, foreign bodies, other damage, chemicals and allergies. Your vet will examine the eye carefully using an ophthalmoscope to ascertain the cause. Usually, if only one eye is affected, the cause is local to that eye such as trauma or a foreign body, but if both eyes are affected, it is more likely to be caused by an infection. If your vet is in any doubt of the cause, she may take a sample of the discharge from the eye with a swab and have it analysed in a laboratory.

A longstanding conjunctivitis can lead to very sore eyelids, including the third eyelid, the nictitating membrane. They become red raw and then can try to heal together, forming adhesions between the eyelid and the third

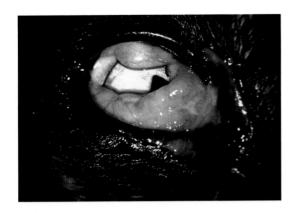

An eye with severe conjunctivitis.

eyelid. This is very serious and it is essential that these adhesions are broken down by your vet. This is sometimes possible under a local anaesthetic eye drop but sometimes needs a general anaesthetic. Prevention is much better, using a lubricating antibiotic eye ointment and frequent bathing.

Treatment. Generally, depending on the cause, the eyes must be bathed with warm sterile water and treated with antibiotic and/or anti-inflammatory drops. Most cases of conjunctivitis are easily treated but, as mentioned, laboratory tests may be necessary to ascertain the cause.

Foreign Bodies

Foreign bodies are not very commonly seen in cats' eyes but, when they do occur, they produce severe irritation and conjunctivitis. Usually, only one eye is affected, so any cat presented to the vet with severe inflammation of one eye will be closely examined for evidence of foreign material. Occasionally, grass seeds will lodge behind the nictitating membrane in the summer when the cat has been moving through long grass, and this foreign material must be removed as soon as possible, either under a local or general anaesthetic. The resulting irritation of the eye will often also need treatment.

Trauma

A severe knock to the eye will often rupture the small blood vessels under the conjunctiva and produce a haemorrhage, which can clearly be seen against the white part (sclera) of the eye. Trauma can also produce haemorrhage within the eye, ocular swelling and uveitis

Treatment required will depend on the degree of pain and other symptoms. Your vet will need to assess this thoroughly.

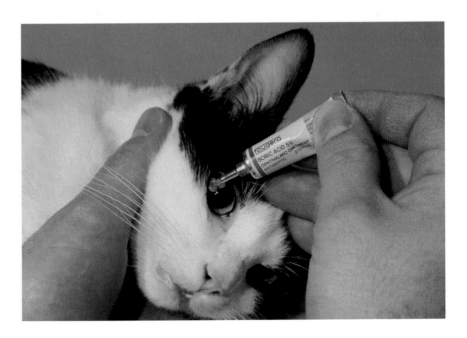

How to instill eye ointment.

PROBLEMS OF THE CORNEA

Keratitis

Inflammation of the cornea is called keratitis. In the early stages, the cornea appears bluish or whitish due to oedema, but as the condition progresses, blood vessels grow on to the cornea from the edge of the eye and darken it. In severe cases, the cat will become blind. Keratitis is often associated with conjunctivitis, the usual cause being an infection.

Treatment consists of cleaning the eyes with damp cotton wool and instilling drops or ointments containing an antibiotic and/or an anti-inflammatory medication as for conjunctivitis.

Corneal Scratches and Ulcers

Scratches and ulcers of the cornea are common in cats and are usually caused by claws during fights. It should always be regarded as potentially a serious problem because a scratch or ulcer can be so deep as to rupture the cornea and lead to possible loss of the eye. The flat-faced breeds, such as Persian cats, are more susceptible to non-healing ulcers because of their prominent eyes, but all types of cats can be susceptible to corneal damage from fighting or other trauma.

Both scratches and ulcers are very painful and usually cause eyelid spasm. Some scratches and ulcers can easily be seen by the naked eye but others can only be demonstrated by staining the eye with fluorescein drops, which highlight the damaged area as a green scratch or ulcer.

Treatment. Shallow scratches and small ulcers can be treated by cleansing the eye with warm, sterile water and instilling appropriate ointment. Steroid drops must not be used, as these will worsen the problem. More severe ulcers, or non-healing ulcers, may have to be debrided, which means surgically removing non-healing parts of the ulcer and, in some severe cases, the surface of the eye will have to be protected by suturing the nictitating membrane or a conjunctival flap across the eye for two to three weeks. Most ulcers will heal with treatment, although in some cases a faint transparent grey scar will remain on the cornea.

Sequestrum

A corneal sequestrum is a condition peculiar to the cat and occurs where death of part of the cornea occurs. The dead area turns black and, in most cases, is rejected by the body and detaches, leaving a corneal ulcer with a pigmented crater.

The cause is unknown but may be due to a primary corneal fault or secondary to anything that makes the cornea vulnerable. Sequestra are

A corneal ulcer outlined by fluorescein drops.

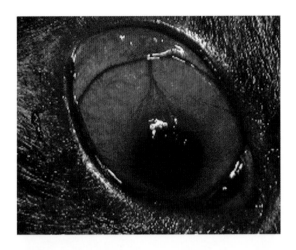

The black area on the cornea is a sequestrum.

seen in cats of both sexes and all ages except the new-born, but most tend to be young adults. There is a noticeable breed distribution in Persian, Siamese and Himalayan cats; the condition occurs less often in the domestic short-hair breeds.

Treatment. Some vets will adopt a conservative approach and allow the sequestrum to detach while treating with antibiotics and eye ointments. However, as this may take months to years, others prefer surgical removal of the sequestrum where possible, which shortens the course of the disease.

Foreign Bodies

Occasionally a fleck of dirt or paint will stick to the cornea, or a thorn, claw or grass seed may become embedded. The offending foreign body must be removed under a local or general anaesthetic, as leaving it in place will lead to pain and possibly permanent damage to, or even rupture of, the eye.

PROBLEMS OF THE EYEBALL

Nystagmus

This is seen as a rapid sideways flicking of the eyes caused by damage to the part of the brain and/or inner ear, which controls balance. Any

treatment depends on the cause but the condition is always serious, and usually associated with a loss of balance. Affected cats may fall over and walk in a circle or unbalanced fashion. It is important to contact your vet as soon as possible (*see* Chapter 14).

Exophthalmus

This occurs when the eyeball is forced out of its bony socket, and occurs usually in one of two ways:

- An abscess developing in the eye socket forces the eye forward and partially out of the eye socket. This would occur fairly rapidly as the abscess enlarged. If caught early, antibiotics may resolve the situation but, in severe cases, where the orbit is infected and destroyed, the eye may have to be removed surgically.
- A tumour in the orbit behind the eye will slowly enlarge gradually pushing the eye forwards, making it more prominent. The cat will increasingly have difficulty in closing its eyelids, and the surface of the cornea will become dry and ulcerated. This will be very painful in the later stages. Tumours in the orbit are not easy to treat. Surgical removal of the eye is often necessary to reach the tumour. Many tumours, however, are cancerous and not operable.

This eye has a tumour behind it and had to be removed.

PROBLEMS OF THE INTERIOR OF THE EYE

Infection

Occasionally, infection will gain entry into the chambers of the eye from a penetrating wound of the cornea or a ruptured ulcer. If the eye fills with pus, this can easily be seen through the cornea as a grey area. However, infection of the interior of the eye can occur as a result of general bacterial infection or toxoplasmosis, without pus necessarily being produced. The conjunctiva is very inflamed, the eye is very painful and the cat will almost certainly be blind.

Treatment with antibiotics is necessary in an attempt to save the eye but, although the eye may heal, sight cannot always be restored. If the eye remains blind and painful, it should be surgically removed.

Haemorrhage (Hyphaema)

A sharp blow to the eye or a penetrating wound can result in internal bleeding and the anterior chamber fills with blood, which colours the anterior chamber red. The eye will be at that stage blind, but may not appear to be particularly painful.

Treatment. There is often no treatment possible except to ensure that the cat is kept very quiet and rested. In some cases, the blood is slowly removed by the normal drainage system of the eye, leaving no damage to the eye.

Uveitis

This is a very painful inflammation of the iris and ciliary body. The pupil is small with a poor light reflex, and the iris is often discoloured. The cause of uveitis is not always known but it can result from trauma. In a case of uveitis, uneven pupil size can occur and the eye with the smaller pupil is likely to be the one affected.

Treatment. Uveitis is treated with anti-inflammatory medication and also drops to dilate the pupils, otherwise the iris may adhere to the lens.

Different sized pupils.

Uneven Pupils

Apart from uveitis, uneven pupil size can also occur for several other reasons. Corneal ulceration can cause the pupil in the affected eye to be smaller, Horner's syndrome (*see* page 122) makes the pupil of the affected eye smaller, feline leukemia can cause pupillary spasms, also resulting in a difference in size of the pupils. Central nervous system injury can lead to difference in pupil size and in this case, the eye with the larger pupil is often the affected one.

Glaucoma

This is an eye disease in which the normal fluid pressure inside the eyes slowly rises, leading to pain and loss of function. This fluid inside the eye is constantly being formed and drained from the eye; glaucoma occurs when this balanced mechanism is upset. It can be a primary glaucoma, where there are no other problems with the eye, or it can be secondary glaucoma, due to another problem in the eye. Glaucoma generally only affects one eye initially but, depending on the underlying cause, the other eye may be at risk for the future.

Signs. The cat may rub the eye and there is often excessive tear production. The pupil dilates and shows no light reflex. The cornea looks cloudy and later becomes invaded by blood vessels. The white of the eye shows distended blood vessels. As more fluid builds up inside the eye, it becomes enlarged, painful and eyesight fails. The affected eye looks larger than the other eye, and is painful to the touch.

- Primary glaucoma is usually inherited and develops with no underlying disease. It is very rare in the cat.
- Secondary glaucoma This type of glaucoma follows another eye problem.

Causes of secondary glaucoma include:

- Infection. Severe inflammation in the eye, often from a penetrating wound, is the commonest cause of glaucoma in the cat. This produces debris in the aqueous humour, which can block the drainage area outflow of fluid, allowing it to build up inside the eye.
- Uveitis. Drainage may also be blocked at the pupil if an inflamed iris adheres to the lens, which sits immediately behind it. In the cat, inflammation of the iris is one of the most common cause of glaucoma.
- Lens luxation – where the lens becomes dislocated and displaced into the anterior chamber of the eye. Lens luxation in the cat can be caused by trauma but is usually a side-effect of long-term inflammation of the iris called uveitis and it is this that leads to the glaucoma.
- Tumours inside the eye affecting the drainage area can prevent fluid from leaving the eye, causing a build-up of fluid and glaucoma.
- Trauma. Injury to an eye causing it to fill up with blood may block the drainage pathway as it clots and produces fibrin, which leads to adhesions. If so glaucoma can follow as the drainage of the eye is blocked.

Diagnosis of glaucoma is based on the clinical signs and confirmed by your vet, by measurement of the internal pressure of the eye using an instrument called a tonometer. Sometimes, if the eye is too cloudy to be examined, ultrasonography (ultrasound examination) of the eye can help identify the cause.

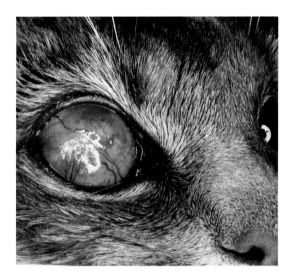

Glaucoma in the right eye.

Treatment is never straightforward and invariably surgical treatment is needed. It may be that your vet will refer the case to an ophthalmic veterinarian. The surgical correction usually used is to make a small hole under the conjunctiva, which allows fluid to drain out, but treatment is not always successful. In secondary glaucoma, if the cause can be found, then this should be corrected if possible, e.g. uveitis or tumour. If it is not possible to correct the glaucoma because of the continuing pain, it may be necessary to remove the diseased eyeball.

Tumours

Fortunately tumours inside the eye are very uncommon. When they occur, they normally affect only one eye but lymphosarcoma tumours can affect both eyes. The pupil will become grey and dull with loss of vision. The eye may become inflamed and painful. The only treatment possible is removal of the affected eyeball.

PROBLEMS OF THE LENS

Cataract

A cataract causes the normally clear lens to become opaque and can affect one or both eyes. In cats, however, cataracts are very uncommon.

The pupil, instead of appearing black, turns greyish and, in severe cases, the lens looks like a pearl. The process of cataract formation is usually slow and the degree of lens opacity will determine the effect on vision.

Most cataracts in the cat develop secondary to inflammation within the eye, from trauma or some other eye problem. Rarely, cataracts in the cat may be inherited, may arise with abnormal development of the lens or may occur in association with nutritional abnormalities in the young cat. In contrast to dogs, cataracts do not occur in cats with diabetes. Senile cataracts due to old age sometimes occur.

Diagnosis. If both eyes are affected, usually the owner notices that the cat is having difficulty seeing, but if only the one eye is affected, it may be the colour of the eye that alerts the owner. Often this condition is diagnosed by your vet during a routine examination, such as that for the annual vaccination. Your vet will confirm the diagnosis by using an ophthalmoscope to examine the eye.

Treatment. If only one eye is affected, it will rarely be necessary to do anything, as the cat will have normal vision through the other eye. If

A cataract in the left eye.

both eyes are affected, it may be necessary to operate on one or both eyes. The most successful method is phacoemulsification, where a very small incision is made into the cornea and the lens is converted in to a soft pulp using high-frequency sound waves and sucked out. Sometimes an artificial lens implantation can be performed in the cat but this technique is usually only performed in a specialist referral veterinary centre.

Lens Luxation (Dislocation)

Primary or congenital lens luxation is rare in cats, although it has been noted in the Siamese cat. Most cases of lens luxation in cats are secondary to chronic uveitis, cataract formation or glaucoma. The ligament suspending the lens breaks and the lens can either fall into the anterior or posterior chamber. Lens luxation can also be caused by a severe blow to the eye.

Diagnosis. Your vet will examine the eye with the ophthalmoscope and be able to see the lens in an odd position, either in the anterior or posterior chamber of the eye.

Treatment is surgical removal of the lens. In contrast to dogs, in which an anterior lens luxation quickly leads to secondary glaucoma, this sequel is less common in cats, only occurring if the iris becomes inflamed, but it is still important to seek veterinary help. A prolapsed lens in the posterior chamber will often cause little damage and may be difficult to diagnose. There may be some loss of sight and a dilated pupil. Removal from this site is extremely difficult, and is usually not necessary.

PROBLEMS OF THE RETINA

Diseases of the retina seriously impair vision and do occur in the cat, although not as frequently as in the dog.

Retinal Degeneration

Hereditary retinal degeneration in cats is similar to progressive retinal atrophy (PRA) in dogs but much less common. It has been diagnosed in young Abyssinian cats. Late onset PRA has also been seen in Abyssinian and Siamese cats, resulting in slowly progressive loss of vision and blindness by middle age or older. The signs of retinal degeneration are often not noticed by owners until late in the disease.

Feline central retinal degeneration is a variation of the above due to taurine deficiency, and is a disease unique to cats. Cats have a nutritional requirement for taurine, an amino-acid obtained from animal protein. All commercial cat foods have an adequate concentration of taurine for cats, so this disease is rare in cats that are fed a proper diet. However, it is still occasionally seen in cats that are on home-made diets, or cats fed on dog food. This disease is the main reason that cats cannot be turned into vegetarians!

Retinal Detachment

The retina separates from the back of the eye in one or both eyes and can cause complete and sudden blindness. It can be caused by a knock but often follows another problem and, in particular, hypertension or raised blood pressure. This is a very important problem of the older cat and may be associated with other syndromes, such as such as kidney, heart or thyroid disease. The resulting increase in blood pressure firstly causes haemorrhages in the retina and then detachment of the retina from the back of the eye. Your vet can see this using her ophthalmoscope. It is very important for older cats to have their blood pressure measured by the veterinary practice, usually one of the veterinary nurses, from time to time. There are occasional other causes of retinal detachment, such as a prolapsed lens or PRA (*see* Chapter 9).

Treatment. The immediate priority is to reduce the blood pressure and your vet will supply medication for this once she has diagnosed the underlying cause. Occasionally the retina will reattach, but only if caught in the early stages of disease.

Blindness

This is obviously a serious problem for the cat but many can live happily, provided it is not a painful blindness, such as in the case of glaucoma. Cats will usually adapt to going blind, particularly if the onset of blindness is gradual. Their other senses of hearing, touch and smell become more acute and help them enormously to navigate around familiar territory. It is not easy for owners to notice gradual onset blindness but the cat may become more vocal. An obvious sign is the fact that both pupils will be widely dilated (opened) and the cat will not blink or respond to movement near its eye.

There are many things the owner can do to ensure the blind cat has a good quality of life, and most of these involve ensuring the cat's environment is constant. Don't move the furniture around; keep the usual doors open; food and water bowls, and litter trays should remain in their usual place. Provided the garden or yard is familiar and contained, it may be safe to let the cat out into this area.

However, if a cat suffers especially rapid onset irreversible blindness, and becomes very miserable, it may be sensible to discuss with your vet as to whether it is kind to let him carry on – a long happy life is wonderful, but a long miserable confused existence isn't.

Chapter 13
The Locomotor System

NORMAL STRUCTURE AND FUNCTION

The locomotor system is the system concerned with the movement and support of the body, and to some extent its protection. The structures involved are the bones, joints, ligaments, tendons and muscles.

The bones are the solid framework of the body, and the ligaments, muscles and tendons are the so-called soft-tissue structures that link these. There are numerous separate bones in the cat of various different types. A typical long (leg) bone consists of the shaft (diaphysis) and two ends called the epiphyses. The shaft consists of an outer hard layer of bone called the cortex, and a central cavity that is filled with the marrow. In some bones this marrow produces some of the blood cells. The epiphyses have a thinner outer layer that is filled with a supporting framework of softer bone.

Bone is produced in areas called centres of

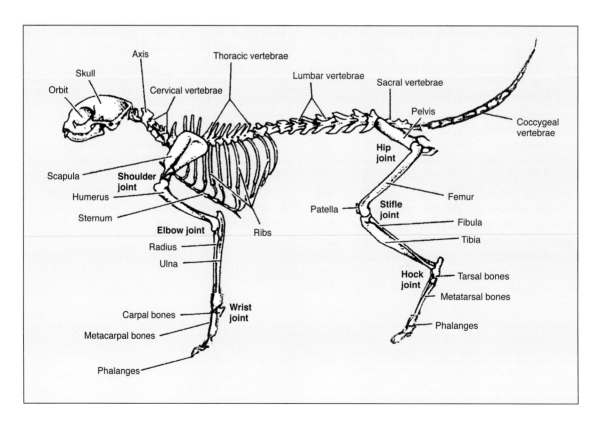

Fig 27 Skeleton of a cat.

ossification, during which the cartilage template of the young cat becomes calcified. For this process to take place, an adequate supply of calcium, phosphorus and vitamin D is needed. Bone calcification and growth is complicated: in the long bones, such as the femur, the bone grows from each end at a special cartilage layer, called the growth plate, which separates the shaft from the epiphysis; flat bones and small bones, however, develop from a single centre of ossification. Bone, although hard and resistant, is a living tissue and throughout life is still capable of slowly changing shape in response to stresses and strains that are put upon it, and of course to fractures.

To enable movement to occur, where two or more bones meet, a joint is needed. This enables the bones to move against – articulate with – one another. At the joint, the ends of the bones are covered by shiny, smooth cartilage, which allows them to slide over each other without friction or damage. This joint is enclosed by a joint capsule that produces a thick oily fluid called synovial fluid, which lubricates the joint. The structures holding the bones in place at the joints are called ligaments and are strands of a tough fibrous tissue.

The structures bringing about movement of the bones and joints are the muscles. These consist of bunches of small contractile filaments, which, when they all contract together, shorten the muscle and alter the position of the bones. At any time, even in a resting muscle, a few fibres are contracting and this gives a muscle 'tone'. Each muscle has its own blood and nerve supply and is attached at each end to bone, either directly or by a fibrous tissue structure called a tendon.

Tendons vary in shape from flat and wide to narrow and tubular, and can be long or short. The longest tendons are those moving the toes. The cat's body contains other muscles that have different functions to locomotion. For example, the heart muscle pumps blood around the body, and the intercostal muscles, between the ribs and the diaphragm muscle, enable the cat to breathe. In addition, contraction of the abdominal muscles also helps in bodily functions such as defecation, urination and birth.

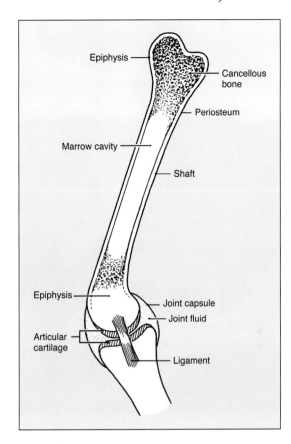

Fig 28 *Structure of a normal long bone and typical joint.*

Problems with the cat's musculoskeletal or locomotor system usually result in lameness, inability to move or stand, due to impaired movement or pain.

DIAGNOSIS OF LOCOMOTOR PROBLEMS

Because of the vastly different tissues involved in this system in the body, and the numerous ways in which they can be affected, it is useful to look at the various ways in which your vet can achieve a diagnosis as to the cause of a problem.

Clinical Examination and History Taking

This is the first and by far the most important method of trying to establish a diagnosis that

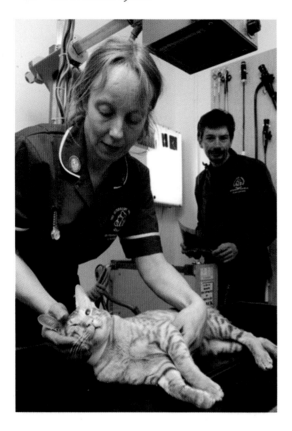

A cat about to have an X-ray.

which is why bones, for example, absorb far more X-rays than the surrounding muscles, so the bone can easily be seen as a white image on the darker surrounds of the X-ray film.

Vets are required by law to fulfil all the safety standards that are demanded for human radiography. For example, the vet or nurse must wear protective clothing with a monitor badge, and the X-ray equipment must be in a safe room from which X-rays cannot escape. Very few animals will lie still on an X-ray table, so it is common practice to take X-ray pictures under a short-acting anaesthetic or heavy sedation. This has several advantages: first, it is easier to position the cat because often he is in pain or frightened; second, because the cat is relaxed, it is easier to examine the part to be X-rayed; last, the safety of the human operator is paramount and, in most cases, he or she must be able to leave the room while the picture is taken. The law is quite specific as to the circumstances under which X-rays may be taken using manual restraint. Therefore, if your vet advises you that anaesthetic consent is necessary, you must be prepared to give it.

your vet will use. Some signs the cat is showing, however, will not have an obvious cause and your vet will have to resort to other aids to diagnosis in order to establish both the cause, the necessary treatment and the likely outcome (prognosis).

Radiography

Radiography is the taking of X-rays of the internal structures of the body and it is used more for diagnosis of disorders of the locomotor system than any other body system. A diagnostic X-ray picture is obtained when X-rays are projected from an X-ray machine through part of the body on to an X-ray film, which is then developed rather like a photographic film, or, often now, digitally. Where the X-rays are not obstructed, they turn the film black and where a high degree of obstruction occurs, the film remains white. Different tissues of the body absorb differing amounts of X-rays,

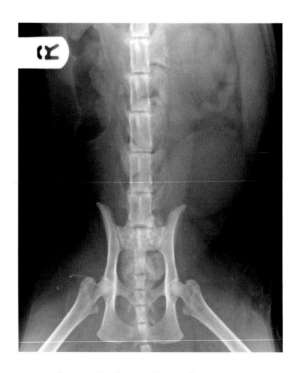

X-ray of normal pelvis and hips of a cat.

Experience

In many cases, your vet's knowledge and experience of the likely cause will help in establishing a diagnosis. For example, by far the commonest cause of lameness in the cat is trauma (damage) of some sort. Cats are territorial – tom cats have a wide territory, females and neutered cats have a smaller territory but all tend to guard their territory by fighting other cats, and due to the cat's tendency to patrol their territory, road traffic accidents, fights with dogs and airgun pellet wounds occur. Your vet will almost certainly try to rule one of these causes out before searching for another cause of the lameness. Damage may have been done to any or all of the structures – muscle, tendons and ligaments of bones. It may be so mild that it is difficult to detect which leg is lame or it may affect a leg so severely that the cat cannot put any weight on the leg. Lameness may affect one leg only or it may affect two or more.

Joint problems, such as sprains, are far less common in cats than dogs because of their size and ability to jump and land expertly.

BONE PROBLEMS AND THEIR TREATMENT

Fractures

Any break or crack in a bone is called a fracture, and fractures are by far the most frequent bone problem seen in veterinary practice. There are six types of fracture:

- Fissure fracture. The bone is only cracked and there is no displacement of the parts.
- Green stick fracture. Almost always seen in kittens. The break in the bone is incomplete, as the bone is not yet fully ossified. The bone may bend but part of the fractured bone remains intact, exactly as a green, new twig of a tree would break.
- Simple fracture. The bone is completely broken at one site into two separate pieces.
- Comminuted fracture. The bone is broken into several pieces.
- Compound fracture. A broken end of bone penetrates the skin.
- Folding fracture. The bone is so weak that it just collapses or bends.

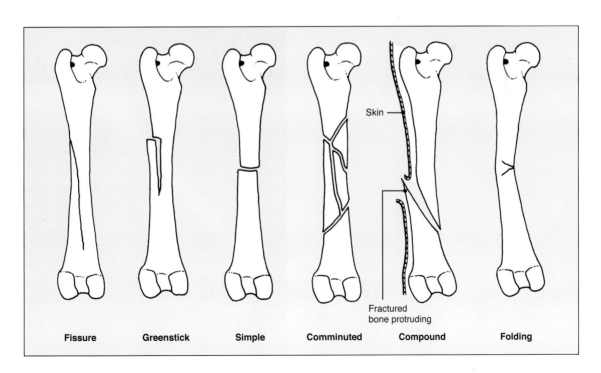

Fissure **Greenstick** **Simple** **Comminuted** **Compound** **Folding**

Fig 29 Types of bone fractures.

Bones, especially the long bones of the legs, require a substantial force to break them and the most common causes are road traffic accidents, attacks by dogs or kittens being accidentally trodden on. The bones that are most commonly fractured are the femur, pelvis, humerus, spine, radius and ulna, tibia and fibula and the lower jaw.

Pain is a feature of all fractures and even a minor fracture will cause the animal to be lame. In addition, both heat and swelling are usually present over the fracture site. If the bone is completely broken, the leg below the fracture will be 'floppy' and not able to bear weight. Sometimes fractures may cause severe injury to other organs, as in the case of a rib puncturing a lung or a fractured vertebra compressing the spinal cord to produce paralysis. The jagged end of a fractured leg bone may sever nerves or blood vessels.

Diagnosis. In most cases this is straightforward as the cat will usually have other injuries, skin or claw wounds, be bleeding and in pain and shock. The vet, presented with a lame cat with a history of an accident, may be able to palpate the fracture, but some fractures are more difficult to diagnose. If the cat is in pain, sedation or anaesthesia may be necessary to carry out a full examination, but the priority after severe trauma is to keep the cat alive and free of pain, so an accurate diagnosis of a fracture may not be deemed necessary or safe at this early stage. If a fracture is suspected, radiography will be needed at a later stage to confirm this and locate the site.

Also, except for compound fractures, where the bone is exposed with the danger of infection, it is not necessary to repair fractures immediately. Other more serious problems such as shock, haemorrhage or damage to internal organs, which are more life-threatening, must be treated first. Only when the cat is in a stable condition will an anaesthetic be administered and the fracture repaired. However, a temporary splint will often be used to support the fractured bone and keep the cat comfortable until surgery is possible, and where certain bones, such as the pelvis are fractured, close confinement in a hospital kennel gives relief from discomfort.

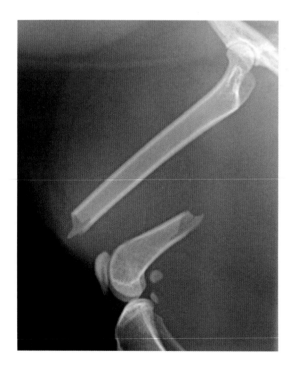 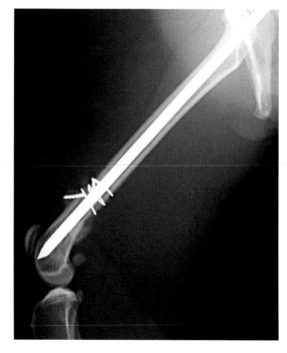

(LEFT) A fractured femur; (RIGHT) The same fracture repaired with an intra-medullary pin.

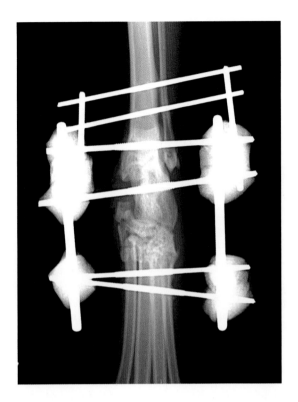 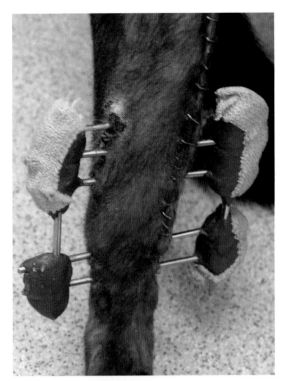

(LEFT) An X-ray of an external fixation of a hock fracture; (RIGHT) external fixation of the fracture.

Treatment. In repairing a fracture, the aim is to restore the fractured ends of bone into their normal position as closely as possible, and then immobilize the bone for approximately four to six weeks. Depending on the fracture site, methods of achieving this are: cage rest, external casts or surgery to perform internal fixation.

Cage rest is suitable for fractured bones that have little displacement and are well supported by muscle. Many pelvic fractures can be treated in this way.

External casts are only really suitable for simple or green stick fractures, where there is little or no displacement of the fractured segments of the bone. It is used mainly in fractures of the lower legs, such as those involving the radius/ulna, tibia/fibula and fractures of the feet. For a cast to be effective, it must 'fit' closely to the limb without being too tight and it must immobilize the joints above and below the fracture. An external cast can be a problem for various reasons: a cat may chew through it, it may get wet and crumble, although modern casting materials are waterproof, and because the cat may be too active or the leg may swell, rub or pressure sores may develop under it. The cast is normally applied for a minimum of four weeks, ideally six, but sometimes it may be necessary to replace it periodically especially on growing kittens.

Fractures that cannot be accurately or easily stabilized with external casts will require surgery to fix the broken fragments in close apposition. The most common methods of internal fixation are intramedullary pins, bone plates and screws, small pins and wire, and single screws.

Intramedullary pins can be used in the larger straight bones, such as the femur and humerus. The pin is inserted into the fractured bone in one of two ways. One way is through the broken upper end and then pushed out through the top of the bone; the fractured ends are then replaced into the correct position and the pin pushed into the lower fractured section to secure it. The other method is to insert the pin from the top end of the bone and down through the fracture

This still agile cat lost his left hind leg in a road accident 11 years before this photograph was taken.

site into the lower fractured portion of bone – this is better as it avoids disturbing the fracture site but is more difficult.

In more complicated fractures, or if the bone is one without a marrow cavity, your vet may choose to use plates and screws. The bone plate is applied on the outside of the bone and is fixed to either side of the fracture by screws. The holes are drilled in the bone using a sterile drill.

Another method of immobilizing bones to allow a fracture to heal is by external fixation. This consists of placing pins or screws into the bone on both sides of the fracture. These are then secured together outside the skin with clamps and rods. Advantages of external fixation are that it is quickly and easily applied, and also that the risk of infection at the site of the fracture is minimized.

Small, displaced fragments of bone can be re-attached using small steel pins, stainless steel wire or single screws. Such fractures usually occur near the ends of bones.

In most fractures, the pin, plate or screw is left in place, even after the fracture has healed. Occasionally a cat will reject the metal, and this may need to be replaced; a procedure that is not always straightforward.

Most fractures will be fully healed after about six weeks, and if the bones have been immobilized in the normal alignment, and not disturbed, the cat will walk perfectly normally again. However, despite correct immobilization, some fractures fail to heal for various reasons, such as infection, or because the fractured ends are non-viable as a result of the accident.

Amputation

In very rare cases, fractures will never heal and it may be necessary to amputate the leg. Although this is a last resort, cats manage very well on three legs, regardless as to whether it is a front or hind leg that has to be removed. If a leg is amputated, it is usually removed high up the leg to avoid any risk of the cat damaging the remaining part of the leg. The photograph above shows a twelve-year-old cat, Gripper, who had his leg amputated after a severe road accident at 6 months of age.

Fractures of the Jaw

Fractures of the jaw, especially of the lower jaw (mandible), are particularly common in cats. There seem to be two main types of accidents that cause this: a road traffic accident, where presumably the cat turns to look at the approaching car at the last minute, and a fall from a height, where the cat's jaw impacts on the ground. The common break is in the midline of the jaw resulting in one side of the lower jaw being displaced relative to the other half. If the damage to the jaw is limited to this midline area, repair is relatively straightforward using surgical wire applied round the lower canine teeth, or perhaps more commonly now, dental acrylic being used to stabilize both sides of the jaw. These fractures usually heal well, and the support can usually be removed within three weeks or so.

During the first week or so, it is often necessary to feed the cat through a tube – usually a nasogastric tube fed down to the stomach via the nose. These are tolerated well by most patients.

Infections

Bone infection (osteomyelitis) is caused when bacteria invade the bone. Most cases of osteomyelitis follow trauma, such as a bite, or the protrusion of the end of a broken bone through the skin. In the toe, infection can affect

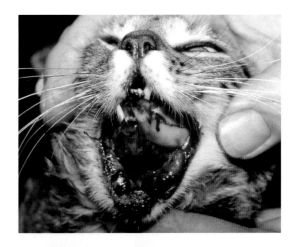

(TOP) Severe jaw fracture following a road accident; (MIDDLE) repair of the jaw using dental acrylic and skin and gum sutures; (BOTTOM) full recovery four weeks later.

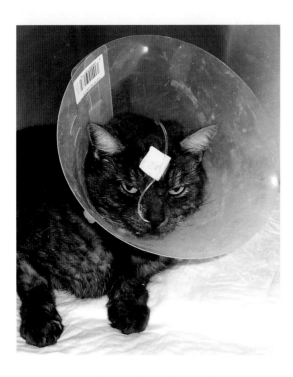

A nasogastric tube and Elizabethan collar in place.

the bone by gaining access through a damaged nail bed, or a bite from another cat.

Usually the first indication of osteomyelitis is pain, accompanied by heat and swelling over the site of the infection in the bone. If a limb bone is affected, there can be severe lameness. As the disease progresses, the cat will become lethargic, off his food and may have a temperature.

Diagnosis. In most cases an X-ray will be needed to confirm the diagnosis, when osteomyelitis will show as an irregular pattern of thinning in the bone.

Treatment. Large doses of the appropriate antibiotic for several weeks are essential, but sometimes it will be necessary to remove the diseased portion of bone surgically. Severe osteomyelitis of the small bones of a toe, arising from a nail-bed infection, may require amputation of the toe.

Tumours

Tumours do occur in the bones of cats, especially the humerus and femur, but less commonly than in dogs. The most serious tumour is the osteosarcoma, which is a malignant tumour, often, but not always, spreading elsewhere in the body. This tumour is much less aggressive in cats than dogs.

Symptoms. Usually seen in older cats, the first signs are a lame cat with pain and swelling over the affected bone.

Diagnosis. The bone swelling is suggestive of a tumour in the older cat and the diagnosis is confirmed by X-ray.

Treatment. Before any treatment is considered, an X-ray of the chest should be taken, as if there is spread to the lungs, the prognosis

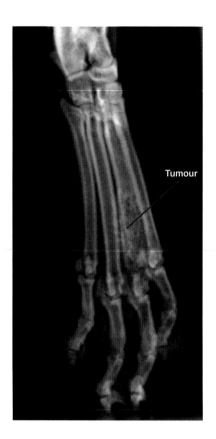
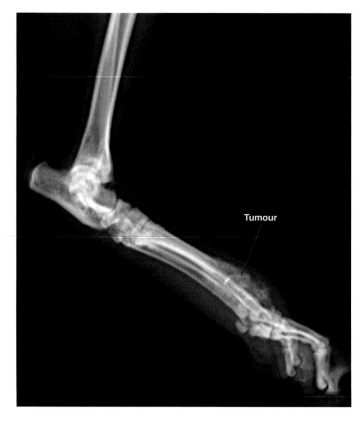

Two x-ray views of an osteosarcoma in a metatarsal bone.

is hopeless and the cat would normally be painlessly euthanased.

Other types of tumours are seen elsewhere in the body – in the nasal chambers, jaw bones and toes. Treatment, if indeed possible, will depend on the site and type of tumour.

JOINT PROBLEMS

Sprains

A sprain is an inflammation of a joint and it is caused when the joint is over-stretched; for example, by an awkward fall. They are sudden in onset and occur when the ligaments and capsule surrounding and holding the joint in place are stretched by the accident, resulting in a hot, swollen, painful joint and some degree of lameness. As stated earlier, because of the cat's extraordinary ability to land well from a fall, sprains are rare in this species.

Treatment. Rest and, perhaps, mild painkilling drugs, such as non-steroidal anti-inflammatory medication, will usually cause the symptoms to disappear within a few days.

Note: It can be very dangerous to treat cats with human medications, such as aspirin and paracetamol.

Dislocations

Dislocations (also called luxations) occur when there is total rupture of the ligaments and joint capsule of a joint, allowing the bones involved in the joint to separate. These are also normally sudden in onset and usually affect a single leg. The cause is usually a severe blow or twist, usually sustained in a road accident. In cats, the joint most often dislocated is the hip, but dislocations of the hock (ankle) joint are not uncommon due to rupture of the ligaments. Dislocations are characterized by severe pain and lameness of sudden onset following trauma.

Treatment. The joint must be restored to its normal state by replacing the dislocated bone or bones into the normal position as soon as

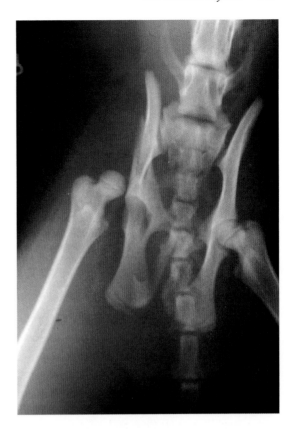

X-ray of a dislocated right hip.

possible after the injury, before tissue swelling, haemorrhage and muscle contraction make the reduction more difficult or impossible. This cannot always be immediately, as life-saving measures must be the priority; it may have to wait until the cat is stable enough for the procedure. Reduction of a dislocated joint is carried out under a general anaesthetic and, afterwards, the hip joint may need support for several days. If the damage to the tissues around the joint is severe, surgery is often necessary in order to stabilize the joint, using a technique known as toggling. Dislocation of the hock joint will need support for longer.

Dislocating Patella

Dislocation of the patella or kneecap is an example of a partial dislocation of a joint. The femur and tibia usually remain in place, while the patella moves out of its groove. It can be a deformity of the stifle joint, which results in the patella slipping to either side of the joint, instead of remaining centrally in the trochlea groove at the lower end of the femur. This is regarded as an hereditary disease. However, a patella can also dislocate if its supporting ligaments are torn during an accident.

Some cats show little or no lameness, except for a slightly crouching gait, whereas in other cases, the patella slips in and out of position intermittently causing the cat to hold the leg raised for a short time until the patella is replaced. In a severe case following an accident, the joint will be painful. In a conscious cat, it is not possible for the vet to push a normal patella out of position, so if this is possible on examining a patient, the joint is abnormal.

Treatment. Surgical correction is necessary in recurrent or painful cases and several techniques are available, depending on the severity of the condition. Mild cases respond well to surgery to shorten the stretched ligament on the opposite side of the joint to which the patella dislocates, but more serious or frequent dislocations indicate that the trochlea groove on the femur may be too shallow and require surgery to deepen it.

Note: Lameness, of course, is not always due to damage to the locomotor system itself. A bite or thorn in the pad or leg can cause a very acute lameness and, therefore, a detailed examination and radiography of an affected leg may be necessary.

Ruptured Cruciate Ligament

This is a very specific problem of sudden onset that occurs to the knee (stifle) joint usually after a fall or accident. It is not, however, a common injury in the cat. The anterior and posterior cruciate ligaments are present in the stifle or knee to prevent the bones of the joint from moving forwards and backwards in relation to each other. When they rupture, as a result of a severe sprain, the joint is destabilized and the cat becomes totally lame on that leg. This most commonly occurs in middle-aged, overweight cats, whose excess weight gives added momentum to a sprain and ruptures the ligament.

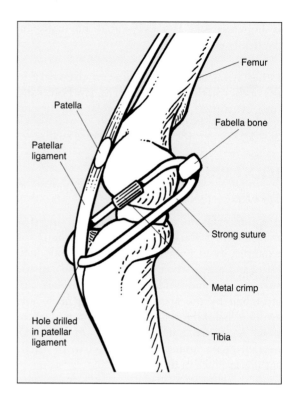

Fig 30 Surgical repair of ruptured cruciate ligament in stifle.

Diagnosis. The injury will be diagnosed by your vet, who will note the excessive movement of the joint, which results from rupture of this ligament – the so-called 'cranial draw movement'.

Treatment. In the cat, strict rest or confinement for four to six weeks is often sufficient to allow the joint capsule to fibrose and stabilize the joint. However, in a few cases, if no improvement is seen after a short time, it will be necessary to replace the ligament surgically.

Infection (Septic Arthritis)

Joint infections are rare in cats and when they occur, they are usually caused by penetrating wounds, such as a bite from another cat. The clinical signs are severe pain, heat and swelling of a joint, a wound is often present and the cat is lame. Usually only one joint is involved, and toe joints seem to be most susceptible. In severe cases, the cat will be lethargic, lame and off his food.

Diagnosis. An X-ray will show the characteristic changes, and the withdrawal of a small sample of joint fluid by the vet for laboratory testing will confirm the diagnosis. In severe infections, the damage to the joint will result in severe lameness and a chronic arthritis.

Treatment. Antibiotic sensitivity testing of the joint fluid will identify the drug of choice and this will normally be used in high doses for a prolonged course.

Osteoarthritis

Osteoarthritis is a chronic degeneration of a joint, which results in erosion of the joint cartilage, formation of new bone around the edges of the joint and thickening of the capsule. The joint swells, is painful and has a reduced range of movement. In cats, this type of arthritis usually results from earlier damage to a joint, such as infection, a sprain or cruciate ligament damage, but cats can also occasionally develop osteoarthritis secondary to dysplasia. In the elbow and stifle, arthritis will often occur in both joints.

Symptoms. There is usually a gradual onset of signs of lameness or stiffness, and the cat will find previously easy heights increasingly difficult to scale. Osteoarthritis tends to be a disease of the older cat and, for obvious reasons, is more of a problem to the overweight cat. The joints most commonly affected are the hips, shoulders, stifles and elbows. If arthritis is present in a single joint, the cat will be lame on that leg, the degree of lameness reflecting the severity of the arthritis. If more than one joint is affected, the cat will have difficulty in moving and jumping, and he will be generally slow. As the arthritis progresses, the cat will spend more time lying down and he will be more stiff and lame after he has rested. Once he has moved around a little, he seems to be able to move more freely.

Treatment. There is often no cure for arthritis and treatment is aimed at alleviating the pain with anti-inflammatory medications. Disease-modifying drugs, such as cartrophen and glucosamine, are also thought to be helpful. Arthritic, or indeed any older cats, should not be allowed to become overweight, and great attention should be paid to diet. As osteoarthritis is made worse by cold and wet weather, undue exposure to this should also be avoided.

Prevention. It is important to try to eliminate the causes of arthritis, as once it has occurred it is impossible to cure. Prompt attention should be paid to all types of lameness, sprains and joint infections, and attention to diet to ensure the cat does not become overweight, especially as middle age approaches.

PROBLEMS OF THE SPINE

Spondylosis

This can be regarded as arthritis of the spine. This condition used to be more commonly seen in middle-aged cats due to an excess of vitamin A in the diet. This led to the formation of excess bone in the ligaments and tendons in the spine, causing lameness, stiffness and pain. The cause was usually an all-liver diet, as liver is rich in vitamin A. Now, with most cats being fed a balanced proprietary diet, this disease is very uncommon.

Diagnosis. The bony lesions show up well on X-ray and the diagnosis is confirmed by the cat's diet.

Treatment. Feeding liver should be stopped and the cat fed on a balanced diet. However, the bony lesions are permanent, so help may be needed from safe anti-inflammatory medication.

Spinal Fracture or Dislocation

When this occurs in the cervical (neck), thoracic (chest) or lumbar (back) spine, this problem is a severe and fatal sequel to many a road traffic accident. The cat will be in severe pain and paralysed to a greater or lesser

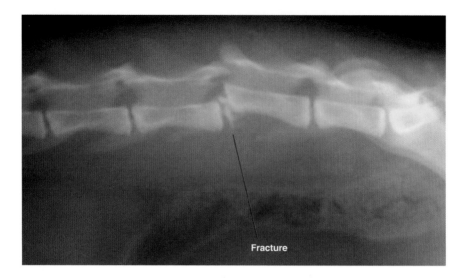

Fracture

A fractured lumbar spine with disruption of the spinal cord.

degree. Once diagnosed by X-ray, or even by a veterinary clinical examination, the cat should be painlessly euthanased.

Dislocation at the Base of the Tail

This seems to be a fairly frequent sequel to a road or other type of accident. The tail has somehow been trapped or pulled with considerable force, or had an impact at the base, where it leaves the pelvis. This results in a paralysed tail and the cat is unable to move his tail, which is just dragged along the ground.

This problem can be temporary or permanent, depending on the cause and damage. If the impact on the base of the tail was relatively minor, with no separation of the bones, use may begin to return to the tail within a week or two. If, however, there has been separation of the bones, there will be a permanent paralysis of the tail. A complication is that sometimes the nerves to the bladder and rectum in the same area can be damaged by the accident, resulting in an incontinent cat – again temporarily or permanent.

Diagnosis. An X-ray will usually be undertaken to assess the seriousness of the damage and separation or otherwise of the bones of the tail.

Treatment. If the area shows no separation, pain relief, using safe anti-inflammatory medication, will be given until the pain subsides or the tail use is restored. If the tail has not returned to function within, say, two or three weeks, the paralysis will be permanent and the tail would normally be surgically removed. If the blood supply has also been affected and the tail left on, death (necrosis) of the tail usually sets in and it may just drop off after a long period. Meanwhile the cat cannot position its tail to defecate or urinate and can become very soiled around the rear end, thus it is much kinder to amputate the useless tail.

Fracture of Tail Vertebrae

The tail can be damaged along its length resulting in paralysis of the part of the tail beyond the damaged area. If the damage is permanent, the affected length must be amputated or gangrene and death of the tissue will set in.

PROBLEMS OF MUSCLES AND TENDONS

Strains

A strain is a tear in either a muscle or a tendon and it is usually caused by over-exertion. A strained muscle is swollen, hot and painful, and there is some degree of lameness. Most cats with mild strains will recover with rest alone, but the treatment of more severe strains may also involve the use of anti-inflammatory drugs. Cats very rarely tear muscles severely enough to require surgery.

Trauma

Muscles and tendons, especially those of the lower legs and feet, are frequently damaged by trauma, such as road accidents, cuts and bites. The resulting degree of lameness depends on the muscle affected and the depth of the injury. However, even very shallow wounds in the feet may completely sever the small tendons to the toes, resulting in loss of function of one or more toes, unless the severed ends are located and repaired immediately. The most severe tendon injury we see is the complete rupture of the Achilles tendon of the hock. This results in the sudden, complete loss of function of that leg and the whole of the lower part of the leg from the hock will lie flat on the ground. This injury is usually caused by the Achilles tendon pulling away from the bone in the hock to which it is attached, or being severed close to the hock joint.

Treatment. Torn muscles may need no other treatment apart from cage rest for a week or two but if severely damaged, may need surgical repair. Damaged tendons usually require surgical repair to restore full function to the muscle affected, but they heal slowly as they have a very poor blood supply. It is, therefore, necessary for the cat to be completely rested after surgery and if a large tendon, such as the Achilles tendon, is involved, the leg is usually supported in a cast. Tendon repair is normally achieved using stainless steel or nylon sutures. There is a small tendon under and above each toe and either is easily severed during fights or accidents. Depending which one is damaged, the toe will either be pulled up or down by the remaining intact tendon. The cat will adapt without surgery but if the severed ends are located and re-attached as soon as possible, full function should be restored to that toe.

Infections

Muscle infection, called myositis, usually arises from a penetrating wound – usually a cat bite or air gun pellet injury. The muscle becomes hot and painful, and if the infection is severe, the cat may be depressed and off his food. An abscess may form and discharge pus through the skin at the site of the original injury.

Diagnosis. If a cat fight has been heard or seen, that is often sufficient for a diagnosis. However, your vet will search diligently for an entry wound, and if the wound does not heal, or if it is large and circular, like an air gun pellet wound, an X-ray may be indicated and will often reveal a foreign body.

Treatment. Any foreign body should be removed surgically and the wound bathed with sterile saline. Antibiotics may be needed and if so, prescribed by the vet. In severe cases, it may be necessary to remove any diseased tissue surgically and a drainage tube inserted to allow mechanical drainage of pus from the wound.

Muscle Atrophy

Muscles atrophy or waste if they are not used or if the nerve supply is damaged. Physiotherapy helps to prevent atrophy by encouraging movement of the muscles. The commonest cause of muscle atrophy in the cat occurs after a road traffic accident, if the radial nerve supplying the front leg is damaged. If the damage is permanent, treatment is ineffective, the leg is paralysed and useless, and amputation is necessary (*see* Chapter 14).

INHERITED AND CONGENITAL DEFECTS OF THE MUSCULO-SKELETAL SYSTEM

Tail Kinks

A kink is often seen in the tails of cats, especially those of the foreign or exotic types, such as Siamese and Burmese. It is of no consequence or harm to the cat, no treatment is necessary but naturally a kink is frowned upon in the cat showing and breeding world.

Polydactyl Feet

Cats normally have four toes on each hind foot and five on each front foot, the fifth being the

A Manx cat.

equivalent of the human thumb and called the dew claw. It is, however, not uncommon to see cats with extra toes on all four feet, and this condition is called polydactylia. The extra toes have claws, may be large or small, and often will cause no problem. Sometimes, however, the claws will grow too long, curl in and impinge on other toes. In this case, it is necessary to clip the claws short from time to time, and even in some cases to amputate the supernumerary toes.

Manx Cat

This tail-less breed of cat is due to an inherited trait. It is a dominant gene and many pure Manx cats die in the womb due to excessive shortening of the spine during development. However, where the shortening is purely restricted to the tail itself, Manx cats are happy, normal cats with a tail length varying from no tail at all to a stumpy tail.

Maxillo-Facial Compression

Exaggerated shortening of the face by selective breeding in some breeds, such as the Persian, has led to respiratory, throat and eye problems in some cases. The so-called 'Peke Face', where the nose may be level with, or even higher up, the face than the eyes, constricts the tear duct, which conveys tears from the eyes to the nose, resulting in tears constantly overflowing the eyelids and running down the face. Breathing difficulties also can occur due to the shortening of the nose and throat.

Sternum Abnormality

A deformity is sometimes seen where the sternum, which is the base bone of the chest, develops too far up into the chest and reduces the available chest space. It is sometimes possible to correct this surgically.

Chapter 14
The Nervous System

NORMAL STRUCTURE AND FUNCTION

The function of the nervous system is to help control other systems in the body and to receive information about the outside world, which is relayed to the brain. The brain then analyses this information and decides which, or if any, action needs to be taken. Messages are then relayed back along nerves to organs that will carry out that function. The nervous system is the most complicated system in the body.

The nervous system consists of two distinct parts.

- The central nervous system (CNS), which is the brain and the spinal cord, which runs through the vertebral canal in the vertebral column. The brain has three main parts: the cerebrum, the cerebellum and the brain

stem. There are, in addition, other parts to the brain including the temporal lobe, the frontal lobe, the thalamus, the hypothalamus, the pituitary gland, the medulla oblongata, the occipital lobe and others. All are essential to life, despite their differing sizes – for instance, the medulla oblongata keeps the heart beating and it keeps the cat breathing, blinking and swallowing.
- The peripheral nervous system, which consists of all the nerves that connect the CNS to all the rest of the body.

The basic units of the nervous system are the millions of tiny nerve cells, each of which consists of a cell body from which arises a long process called the axon. The ends of the axons make contact with cell bodies of other nerve cells via fine processes called dendrites that protrude from the cell bodies. These junctions

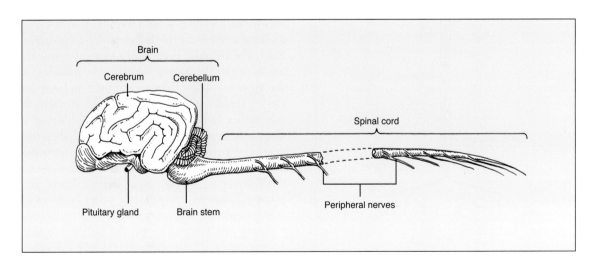

Fig 31 The central nervous system.

between different nerve cells are called synapses. When a nerve cell 'fires', an electrical impulse passes down the axon to the synapse where a chemical is released, which passes across the synapse to the next nerve, which it activates. Nerve tissue is very soft and any pressure on a nerve axon will reduce the ability of that nerve to pass an impulse. Complete compression of the axon will render that nerve completely functionless, causing paralysis of the structures beyond the damaged area.

There are two main types of nerve in the nervous system: sensory and motor nerves. Sensory nerves pass messages to the brain from sensory organs, such as the eye and skin, whereas motor nerves pass messages from the brain to the receiving organs, such as the muscles. In the central nervous system the motor and sensory nerves follow different pathways but once they reach the peripheral nerves they run side by side.

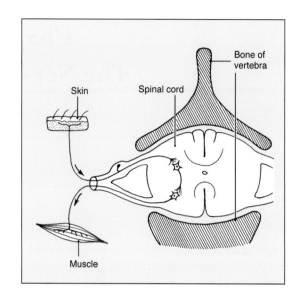

Fig 33 A nervous reflex.

A nerve reflex is an automatic response to a certain stimulus; it enables the CNS to carry out many functions without conscious thought. The understanding of reflexes is very important, as much clinical information about the proper functioning of the nervous system can be gained from the study of nervous reflexes. A reflex simply consists of a sensory nerve arising from a sensor, which passes to a specific area of the CNS, a connecting nerve, and then a motor nerve to a muscle. An example would be a cat's reflex when standing on a sharp object. The sensors in the pad 'fire' and an impulse passes along a sensory nerve to the lower part of the spinal cord. The impulse then passes along a connecting nerve to the motor nerve to the muscles of the leg stimulating them to contract and to take the leg rapidly away from the painful stimulus. If this reflex fails, when, for instance, during a diagnosis, a pad is touched by a needle, then the vet knows that there is damage to either the nerves from the foot to the spine, or damage to the lower part of the spinal nerves. There are many reflexes in almost every part of the nervous system.

Some small nerves supply the internal organs of the body. These are called the autonomic nerves and control such organs as the eye, the heart and the digestive system.

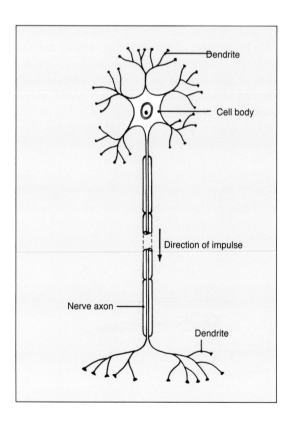

Fig 32 A typical nerve cell (neurone) greatly magnified.

NEUROLOGICAL EXAMINATION

A logical approach to the examination of a cat with a suspected problem of the nervous system should be carried out. Your vet will probably adopt the following approach, but this will vary depending on the signs the cat is showing:

- A general assessment of the cat from a distance as to its behaviour, alertness, movement, posture, balance and so on.
- Can the cat walk properly, placing its feet normally?
- Test the tendon reflexes – patellar (knee) and Achilles tendon.
- Test for pain perception – can the cat feel a sharp needle on the skin in various areas, or pressure on a claw?
- Test whether the cat can right itself when turned on its side, or replace a limb that is moved away from its normal position, place the foot when knuckled over and so on.
- Test the cranial nerves, which are the nerves that supply various structures of the head such as the eyes, facial muscles and skin.
- If the problem is spinal, X-rays may be of great help, as may the examination of the cerebrospinal fluid that bathes the central nervous system. X-rays of the spinal anatomy using a contrast medium may also be carried out in order to outline a lesion.
- MRI and scanning is now available in some veterinary practices, and especially in veterinary referral centres, for an accurate examination and assessment of the brain and spinal cord. This might be used in cases, for example, where a tumour is suspected.

PROBLEMS OF THE CNS: BRAIN

Diseases and problems of the brain can produce symptoms in any area of the body, depending on which area of the brain is affected. Signs can vary from seizures to paralysis, blindness to deafness, or dullness to hyperexcitability an so on.

Hydrocephalus

This is an uncommon congenital disease in which there is excessive accumulation of cerebrospinal fluid (CSF) within the brain. In normal animals, this bathes, protects and circulates through parts of the brain, but in hydrocephalus-affected kittens it sometimes leads to an open area on the top of the skull, and often a domed head. Such kittens are usually very wobbly and can be blind, and usually die very early in life. Occasionally treatment might be possible, which involves drugs to reduce CSF production or surgery to improve CSF drainage, which would usually only be done at a referral neurosurgery hospital.

Trauma (Damage)

In the cat, the brain is fairly well protected from damage by the skull. However, damage to the brain can occur in two ways:

- Localized. A small part of the brain may be damaged by a skull fracture from a localized blow; for example, during a road accident. The symptoms shown by the cat will depend on the part of the brain affected and the severity of the damage. Symptoms may vary from partial paralysis, to difficulties in movement or to change of personality.
- Generalized. The brain is very soft and encased in a rigid 'box', the skull, so any impact or damage to the skull is likely to result in swelling of the brain called oedema. This swollen brain has no room for expansion in the skull and the resulting pressure can result in loss of consciousness and other severe neurological symptoms. Haemorrhage within the skull will also apply pressure to the soft brain tissue. Less severe damage will render the cat dull and weak, and the cat will have difficulty in moving and will not be interested in food and water. The pupils may be widely dilated and the cat may develop seizures. Total paralysis, loss of consciousness and even death may result.

Diagnosis. There is usually a known history of trauma, such as a road traffic accident, or the accompanying injuries, such as skin wounds or scuffed claws, will point to this. Your vet, in examining the head, may detect a

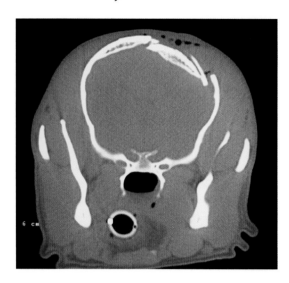

A CT scan showing a skull fracture.

fractured skull, especially if the bone has been depressed. If any doubt exists, X-rays can show up fractures.

Treatment. This must be instigated immediately to prevent permanent damage, and usually medications to reduce any oedema and swelling will be used. The cat must be kept quiet and medications given to prevent seizures or struggling. Effective pain relief is also needed. Depressed fractures need to be surgically repaired, if possible, but recovery from brain damage can take a long time. After the initial examination it is often very difficult for the vet to say whether the cat will recover and, if so, how long it will take and how complete the recovery will be.

Seizures or Fits

A seizure is not a disease in itself but a symptom, and occurs when abnormal brain cells 'fire' spontaneously sending out electrical impulses that spread quickly through the surrounding cerebrum part of the brain. A fit that is localized to one part of the brain is called a partial seizure, or if it affects the whole brain, a generalized seizure. Seizures are not very commonly seen in cats but when they occur, the partial seizure is the commoner form. In partial seizures, unusual

behaviour such as crying out for no reason or twitching of the face or legs, can be seen. In generalized seizures, the cat falls on to his side, the legs 'paddle', becoming intermittently rigid and then relaxed, the eyes remain open and the lips are drawn back. There is champing of the jaws with excessive salivation. The cat may also defecate and urinate. Most fits last for no more than one to two minutes. Afterwards the cat will be unsteady and confused but within half an hour is usually back to normal. Occasionally a fit will become continuous, a condition known as status epilepticus. This can be life-threatening if not treated.

In such cases, the owner need take no immediate action except to reduce any unnecessary noise, reduce the light intensity and prevent the cat from damaging himself. If, however, the seizure activity continues for more than ten minutes, a veterinary surgeon should be contacted immediately.

Causes. There are numerous causes of seizures, including a primary brain problem, such as epilepsy, or secondary problems, including a brain tumour, brain damage, poisoning or as a result of some other disease process in the body.

- Idiopathic (primary) epilepsy has no known cause, and is usually diagnosed based upon the clinical signs of a fit or fits occurring for no obvious reason. Investigation requires the vet to rule out other known causes of seizures through neurological and laboratory tests and, if necessary and affordable, special imaging techniques, such as computed tomography (CT) scans and magnetic resonance imaging (MRI) scans to examine the skull and brain. If the fits occur on a very occasional basis, it may not be necessary to treat epilepsy, but if the fits are frequent, an anti-epileptic medication, usually phenobarbitone is used. This is available in either tablet or liquid form and in cats the liquid form may be better as sometimes it is easier to give, and also the dose can be adjusted more easily. Once treatment has started, it must not be stopped without advice from your vet or a fit may be precipitated. Long-term treatment with phenobarbitone can adversely affect the liver, so your vet will probably advise a blood test once a year to ensure that the liver function is normal and also that the level of phenobarbitone in the blood is within the therapeutic range.

- Any infection that damages the brain cells can produce epilepsy.
- Trauma may cause epilepsy by damaging brain cells. Diagnosis is based on the history of trauma to the head and the elimination of other diseases. Treatment is as above.
- Small tumours will sometimes produce epilepsy but in most cases as the tumour grows other neurological signs will develop.
- Metabolic disease. Diseases of other organs may alter the blood levels of substances, which will affect the brain, and therefore the cat's behaviour. Certain liver and kidney diseases can increase the level of toxic substances in the blood. Diseases of the pancreas can reduce blood sugar, and complications of diabetes can cause a variety of neurological problems including fits. Severe respiratory disease can produce very low blood oxygen, affecting brain function. Low blood calcium (hypocalcaemia) can result from disease or damage of the parathyroid glands. These causes of seizures are diagnosed by laboratory testing of blood samples. Low blood potassium (hypokalaemia) can cause weakness, stiffness of hind legs making the cat very wobbly. The common causes of this are kidney disease, vomiting or diarrhoea. In most cases, if the underlying metabolic disease can be successfully treated, then the fits and other symptoms will disappear.
- Poisoning by slug bait, which contains a substance attractive to cats called metaldehyde. This can cause loss of consciousness and convulsions in extreme cases (*see* Poisons, page 150).

Infections

There are a few diseases of cats that can produce nervous signs in addition to other effects they have on the body. These include: viral infections, such as rabies and feline infectious peritonitis; bacterial infections, including very rarely tetanus; fungus infections, such as *Cryptococcus* and *Aspergillus*, both of which are also rare; and the protozoan infection of *Toxoplasma*.

Diagnosis is possible on clinical signs but often a thorough neurological assessment and laboratory testing will be necessary to identify the cause, and therefore the treatment.

These important diseases are described in Chapter 5.

Tetanus

This is caused by the toxins released by the tetanus bacteria, which grow in dirty wounds. These toxins travel along the nerves to the CNS and when the toxins reach this they affect nerves of the central nervous system, causing spasm of the muscles. Cats are normally very resistant to tetanus, but when it occurs, there may simply be stiffness of a leg or tail, difficulty in rising from lying down or muscle spasms.

Diagnosis. Tetanus is diagnosed from the clinical signs.

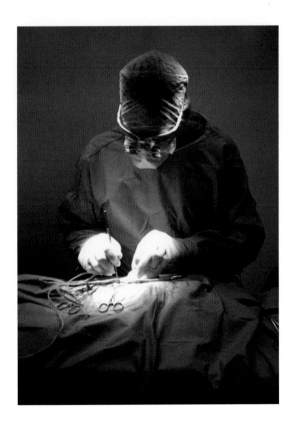

A surgical operation on the spine.

Treatment. Affected cats must be kept very quiet and treated with antitoxins, antibiotics and sedative drugs. The disease is so uncommon in cats that it is not necessary to vaccinate, as in humans or horses.

Vestibular Syndrome

This is a fairly common condition of cats, and affects that part of the brain that controls balance on one side. The onset is sudden, affected cats showing a head tilt to the affected side, and the cat may repeatedly fall over or walk in circles to that side. There is also a rapid sideways flicking of the eyes, called nystagmus. Symptoms vary greatly – some cats are unable to stand and constantly roll to the affected side, while others are hardly affected. Most cases are due to middle or internal ear disease, which must be treated as described in Chapter 11 (*see* page 117). With treatment and good nursing, many cats will recover slowly in about five days, but this condition will often recur and may be more severe the next time.

A congenital form of vestibular disease can occur in kittens. It has been seen in Siamese, Burmese, Birman and some British breeds. The signs are as described above – varying degrees of head tilt, circling and ataxia.

A cat with a head tilt due to vestibular syndrome.

Poisons

Poisons that affect the CNS are not seen very commonly but the most serious are listed below.

Insecticides

The commonest poisonings seen in cats are caused by owners applying insecticides designed for other species, especially dogs, to their cat. You should *never* use a flea treatment designed for dogs on your cat. The usual culprits are the organophosphates, organochlorines and carbamates. These are found especially in spray-on insecticides and in flea collars, and it is essential to ensure that you use the ones designed for cats. It is not fully known whether the problem is due to the cat's particular sensitivity to these drugs or due to their much more concentrated grooming activity.

Symptoms. The effects these toxic insecticides have on the body vary but nervous signs are most likely. These may be just excess salivation, or dullness, vomiting, restlessness, excitability, twitching, seizures, paralysis and death.

Treatment. Contact your vet immediately if you suspect poisoning. If a flea collar is worn, this should be removed. Depending on the symptoms and the content of the insecticide, treatment can include anticonvulsant sedatives, atropine and intravenous fluids as supportive treatment.

Slug bait

This contains a substance called metaldehyde, which seems very attractive to cats. If a cat eats enough slug bait pellets, then central nervous system disturbances will occur. The cat initially appears 'drunk', and this incoordination can progress to inability to stand, loss of consciousness and convulsions in extreme cases.

Treatment. There is no specific antidote to metaldehyde poisoning, but if it is known that the cat has just eaten it, the cat can be given an emetic (a medication to make the cat vomit) to empty the stomach. If severe neurological signs develop, the cat will require an anticonvulsant sedative. Some cats do not eat enough to cause death, but do still need treatment with sedation and intravenous fluids, when recovery usually takes about twenty-four hours.

Alphachloralose (Mouse Poison)

Cats will usually take this in by eating a mouse or bird that has been poisoned. This substance can cause either severe depression or, less commonly, excitation with fits. Again there is no specific antidote, but warmth is a very important part of the treatment. The vast majority of cats recover.

Aspirin

This should not be given to cats on a regular basis, as it can be poisonous. Occasionally it is used therapeutically by vets at very low dose rates, when a blood clot (thrombus) has formed in a major vessel.

Symptoms. Diarrhoea with haemorrhage, vomiting, depression and seizures.

Treatment. If the aspirin has been given very recently, stomach washing is helpful, along with intravenous fluids and gastroprotectants.

Antifreeze

This has a very sweet taste and appears to be attractive to cats.

Symptoms. Signs usually begin about twenty-four hours after drinking the antifreeze. Ataxia, coma and death are common, and are mainly due to kidney failure

Treatment. This must be started as soon as possible and your vet will try injecting a substance called ethanol, which slows the absorption of the antifreeze. As in all poisonings, intravenous fluids would also normally be given, but recovery is by no means certain.

Feline Spongiform Encephalopathy (FSE)

A rare fatal disease of the brain allied to BSE (the so-called mad cow disease), which only occurred in a few cats but was a great worry until it became obvious this was not to be a major problem. Affected cats became ataxic, dull and progressively weaker and died. There

was no treatment available. It has not been diagnosed in cats for many years now.

Taurine Deficiency

Taurine is an amino acid that is an essential constituent of a cat's diet. Deficiencies used to be seen in the early days of complete diets or when a vegetarian diet is attempted, but this problem is rarely seen now if cats are fed balanced, complete diets.

PROBLEMS OF THE SPINAL CORD

Disease of the spinal cord mostly shows as a weakness and incoordination of the limbs, especially the hind legs, or paralysis. If the damage is in the neck, all four legs are usually affected. If the damage occurs between front and rear legs, then only the rear legs and tail are affected.

Congenital Spinal Abnormalities

These are only commonly seen in Manx cats, whose lack of normal tail is due to a condition called sacrocaudal (spinal) dysgenesis. This condition is hereditary and the tail can be of varying lengths described as stumpy (several tail vertebrae and often kinked), rumpy riser (a few fused vertebrae and an upright tail) and rumpy (no tail). They are included in this nervous system chapter because the rumpies particularly may have a deficient nerve supply at the base of the spine and may suffer from paralysis of the hind legs and urinary incontinence.

Trauma

By far the commonest problem of the spinal cord in cats is damage following a road traffic accident. Damage to the spinal cord will affect either two or four legs depending on the level of injury. There are two different forms of damage to the cord which cannot initially always be easily differentiated, complete rupture of the spinal cord and bruising of the spinal cord. A related and fairly common injury, not strictly a spinal cord problem as the cord does not carry into the tail, is paralysis of the cat's tail.

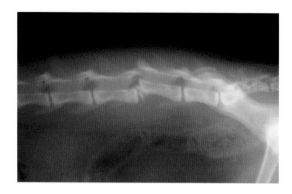

The lumbar spine is fractured. This cat was paralysed.

Disruption of the Spinal Cord

If the spinal cord is completely severed, there can be no nerve transmission across the break. The limbs behind the lesion will be completely paralysed and there can be no recovery. This type of injury, caused by a broken spine, is nearly always the result of a road accident and most injuries occur between the fore and hind legs. The cat will be in a lot of pain and unable to move the affected legs. Nearly always the fractured spine can be seen on X-ray. Repair by a neurosurgical specialist may be possible if there is still movement and feeling in the legs. However, if there is no movement or feeling, it is usually advisable to put the cat to sleep immediately to save further suffering.

Bruising of the Spinal Cord

Even a mild impact can cause bruising of the cord, which results in oedema and swelling. In addition, the spinal cord has a large blood supply and it is possible, in less severe accidents or severe spinal sprains, to rupture the spinal blood vessels. Because the cord is enclosed in a bony tunnel through the vertebrae, the swelling caused by either of these eventualities leads to pressure on the nerve tissue of the cord and loss of function. The clinical signs depend on the degree of swelling or haemorrhage, and range from weakness to paralysis. There is far less pain than in a spinal fracture. An X-ray of the spinal cord will differentiate between a broken back and spinal bruising. Surgery to reduce the pressure and remove the blood clot is very rarely attempted, but drugs are administered to reduce this pressure on the nerves caused by haemorrhage or oedema. The cat must be kept quiet, preferably in a small cage, to prevent further damage. The bladder may be temporarily paralysed and need draining twice daily by the vet. The outcome of these lesser injuries is very difficult to predict but, in general, the more severe the clinical signs, the less favourable the outcome.

Tail Paralysis

Due to severe bruising, fracture or dislocation at the base of the tail; this is also covered in Chapter 13.

This seems to be a fairly frequent sequel to a road or other type of accident. The tail has somehow been trapped or pulled with considerable force, or had an impact at the base where it leaves the pelvis. This results in damaged nerves and a paralysed tail, so that the cat is unable to move its tail, which is just dragged along the ground.

This problem can be temporary or permanent, depending on the cause and damage. If the impact on the base of the tail was relatively minor, with no separation of the bones, use may begin to return to the tail within a week or two. If, however, there has been separation of the bones, there may be a permanent paralysis of the tail. A complication is that sometimes the nerves to the bladder and rectum in the same area can be damaged by the accident resulting in an incontinent cat – again temporarily or permanent.

Diagnosis. An X-ray will usually be undertaken to assess the seriousness of the damage and separation or otherwise of the bones of the tail.

Treatment. If the area shows no separation, pain relief using safe anti-inflammatory medication will be given until the pain subsides or the tail use is restored. If the tail has not returned to function within, say, two or three weeks, the paralysis will be permanent and the tail would normally be surgically removed. Meanwhile the cat cannot position its tail to defecate or urinate and can become very soiled around the rear end, thus it is much kinder to amputate the useless tail.

Fracture of Tail Vertebrae

The tail can be damaged along its length result-ing in paralysis of the part of the tail beyond the damaged area. If the damage is permanent, it is usually better to amputate the affected part.

Intervertebral Disc Problems

Older cats do show degenerative problems of the discs between the vertebrae on X-ray but rarely seem to suffer any signs from these. One exception is the ankylosis or fusing of the verte-brae when cats are fed a diet too high in vitamin A – usually an exclusive liver diet. This is much less commonly seen now that commercial com-plete diets are so available and palatable.

Tumours

Tumours of the spinal cord are rare but do occur. The symptoms shown by the cat are caused by the tumour applying pressure on the spinal cord, which produces incoordination and weakness affecting one or more legs, depending on the site of the tumour. There may also be pain caused. These tumours can sometimes be seen on an X-ray, but often require myelography or advanced imaging, such as MRI, to be seen. Some spinal tumours are amenable to surgery but many are untreatable.

Contented cat with partial tail amputation.

PROBLEMS OF THE PERIPHERAL NERVES

Trauma leading to impact on the nerve is again the commonest cause of peripheral nerve dam-age. Damage to any of these nerves will cause a loss of reflexes, paralysis of any affected limb and loss of feeling. In the vast majority of cases, the damage and, therefore, signs shown by the cat will be one-sided – if the cat is affected on both sides, the problem is likely to be in the spinal cord itself.

Trauma

Most peripheral nerves are rarely damaged by trauma, which is surprising considering the number of broken bones vets see, but there are three particular areas where peripheral nerve damage occurs more often:

- Radial nerve injury. This nerve runs around the shoulder and down the front leg. If it is damaged by a blow to the shoulder area, the leg will hang loosely from the shoulder at the cat's side, and the cat will drag the leg when it walks. There may be no feeling in the leg and no pain. If it is damaged lower down the leg, the elbow may still function but the lower leg will be paralysed, being dragged along or flicked forward awkwardly by the cat.
- Brachial plexus injury. This complex group of nerves is situated on each side in the axilla (armpit) of the cat's front leg, and is quite often damaged, usually by being torn in a road traffic accident. It supplies various areas of the body, and damage to it produces a vari-ety of signs, depending on which nerves are affected. Paralysis of the leg invariably occurs and the cat cannot bear weight on the leg. Damage to this plexus can also be one of the causes of Horner's syndrome.
- Sciatic nerve injury. The sciatic nerve is the main nerve supplying the hind leg and is often damaged when the cat has pelvic injuries following a road traffic accident. When this nerve is damaged, the cat knuck-les over at the paw, and drops the lower part of the leg.

Treatment. There is no specific treatment for any of these nerve injuries but drugs that reduce inflammation and swelling, such as corticosteroids, may be appropriate in certain cases. Unfortunately, there is no easy way of assessing the degree of damage and only time will tell if nerve function will return. If the leg remains paralysed, there will be severe muscle wastage and shrinking of the useless leg. Sores will develop on those parts of the leg that drag on the ground, and usually your vet has no alternative, where the leg is permanently paralysed, but to amputate the leg.

Horner's Syndrome

This condition occurs when the small nerves that supply the eyes and eyelids are damaged anywhere along their route from the brain, down the spinal cord, along the neck, past the ear along to the eye. There are several causes, in addition to brachial plexus damage, such as ear infection, tumour or trauma, which can damage these small nerves as they leave the spinal cord in the chest, runs up the neck, past the inner ear to the eye. In many cases the cause remains a mystery.

Signs. The symptoms, which are sudden in onset, usually affect one eye only. They include a small pupil, sunken eye, dropped upper lid and prominence of the third eyelid. There is no apparent effect on eyesight. Many cases recover spontaneously, although some persist.

Myasthenia Gravis

This is a rare condition that affects the junction between nerves and muscle. The affected cat has a very low exercise tolerance and after a short period of exercise, collapses. After a little rest, it continues its exercise only to collapse again.

Diagnosis. The disease is diagnosed using a trial injection of a drug that aids transmission between nerve and muscle, and so increases the length of time the cat can be exercised.

Horner's syndrome showing in the right eye.

Treatment. If this test proves positive, myasthenia gravis can be treated with a similar drug in tablet form, although sometimes, serious complications mean that treatment is not always successful.

Key–Gaskell Syndrome

This disease of the nerve ganglia appeared from nowhere in 1981, was seen widely in veterinary practices for about a decade, and now suddenly appears to be far less common! It is a disease of the autonomic nervous system and the symptoms appear over a few days. The cause remains a mystery.

Symptoms. The signs of the disease vary but include some or all of the following: the pupils of the eyes dilate, with no pupil reflex, the cat is depressed, dehydrated, can't eat or swallow easily, retches, is constipated and the bladder ceases to function. This can lead to urine and faecal incontinence.

Treatment. Supportive treatment to prevent dehydration and starvation, laxatives and sometimes manual emptying of the bladder can help but the prognosis is poor. Luckily this disease is now extremely rare – the cause was never discovered or proven.

Chapter 15
The Urinary System

The function of the urinary system is to maintain the correct composition of the fluids in the body and to control the elimination of waste products from the body. These waste products are formed mainly from the breakdown of food but also from the natural breakdown of body tissues, such as muscle. The urinary system consists of: two kidneys; two ureters, which link the kidneys with the single bladder; the bladder; and the single urethra, which allows the urine to pass out from the body in both sexes.

NORMAL STRUCTURE AND FUNCTION

The kidneys are situated in the upper part of the abdomen, one on either side, below the back muscles. The right kidney lies slightly in front of the left; both can normally be felt by the vet in a cat that is not overweight. Each kidney is composed of numerous tiny tubes called nephrons, which filter waste products and impurities out of the blood passing through the kidneys and then concentrate this fluid by reabsorbing water to produce urine. This process of filtration is controlled by hormones produced in, and released from, the brain and requires the kidneys to have a large blood supply. Urine consists of waste products, mainly urea and other waste substances, excess body water and minerals. The kidney itself also produces hormones, which affect blood pressure and red blood cell production. After filtration from the blood, the resulting urine collects in an area of each kidney called the renal pelvis, where it leaves the kidney and enters the fine tube called the ureter, which runs through the abdomen to enter into the bladder, one on each side.

The bladder is a muscular sac lying on

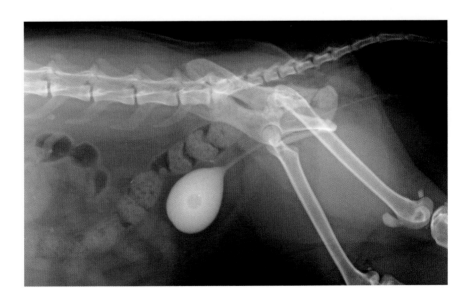

X-ray of bladder and urethra containing contrast medium.

the floor of the abdomen, just in front of the pelvis. It gradually fills with urine through the urethras and expands as it does so, being composed of an elastic type of muscle. Urine is expelled from the bladder into the urethra by contraction of the bladder, along with the cat's abdominal muscles. The control of this is via small nerves that arise from the spinal cord at the level of the pelvis and run through the pelvic canal to the bladder wall. These nerves are easily damaged, and either temporary or permanent loss of bladder control can follow road traffic accidents due to damage in this area.

The urethra is a narrow, muscular tube through which urine is expelled from the bladder. In the female cat, the urethra is short but fairly wide and runs through the pelvis, under the rectum, to enter the vulva behind the vagina. However, in the male cat the urethra is much narrower but longer, and runs backwards through the pelvis and then out of the body through the penis.

Correct functioning of the urinary system, especially the kidneys, is necessary for the maintenance of life and, therefore, any disease affecting this system is potentially life-threatening. Human medicine has made great advances in the treatment of kidney disease in recent years, with the development of artificial kidneys and kidney transplants. Kidney transplants have been carried out in small numbers of cats in the USA, but both the operation and aftercare is very complicated, not always successful, and is very expensive. In addition, the ethics of transplants are not straightforward, especially concerning the cat whose kidney is being used for the transplant. In fact, the latest information is that cats do just as well on medical treatment, such as rehydration through a fixed oesophageal feeding tube, so even the USA is beginning to realize that transplants are neither kind nor necessary. So far, storage of organs has not been possible, so donors (or more accurately 'source cats' as they do not decide to donate!) are needed. Whether it is ethical to remove a kidney from a normal cat to give another one an extended life is a debate that is just starting in the UK! Therefore, in general practice, treatment is aimed at curing kidney disease, if possible, and encouraging failing kidneys to function, if a cure is not possible.

VETERINARY EXAMINATION OF THE URINARY SYSTEM

The examination of this complex system will depend on which part of it the vet suspects is not functioning well.

- The kidneys and ureters. In cats it is possible to palpate (feel) at least one of the kidneys through the abdominal wall and this can reveal changes in shape, feel and response of the cat to pressure here. Tumours, fibrosed or cystic, and inflamed kidneys can be suspected by this examination. X-rays and scans are often helpful. Plain X-rays will not always reveal the cause of a problem and contrast X-rays may be needed – some contrast media are given by mouth, and others by catheter into the urethra and bladder. Blood tests can reveal kidney disfunction, and urine tests are also useful.
- The bladder and urethra. Again palpation can be very helpful in diagnosing bladder obstructions, cystitis and some tumours, but X-rays can also be very useful in diagnosing bladder tumours or stones. Again, a contrast medium inserted into the bladder by a catheter can be necessary. Urine samples are particularly useful in bladder problems, and are the only way to diagnose crystals in the urine.

DISEASES OF THE KIDNEY

Polycystic Kidney Disease

This is a congenital condition in which cysts form in the kidneys and decrease kidney function. It is uncommon but, when seen, occurs mostly in Persian and other breeds, such as the British shorthair, which are born with small cysts in their kidneys. These increase in size and compromise the surrounding normal kidney tissue, which leads to kidney failure. Although this is a condition that is present from birth in affected cats, signs of it may not be evident until later in life, when too little functioning kidney tissue remains.

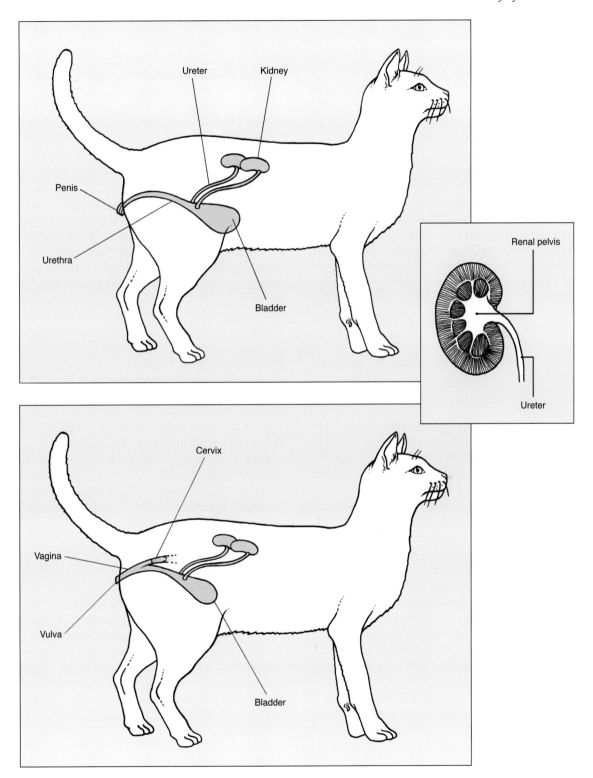

Fig 34 *(TOP) The urinary system of male cat; (BOTTOM) the urinary system of the female cat; (INSET) section through a kidney.*

Acute Nephritis

Acute nephritis is an inflammation of the kidney and can lead to failure of filtration by the kidney of waste products in the blood and failure of urine production. Acute nephritis will rapidly produce a sick cat.

Signs. The important clinical signs are: lethargy, loss of appetite, abdominal pain and vomiting. In the early stages of acute nephritis, little urine is produced because swelling of the nephrons prevents the filtration process, but as damage to the nephrons continues, large quantities of dilute urine are produced because the filtration process is faulty. Therefore, during the first few days of acute kidney failure, there is little change in the cat's drinking habits, but the thirst increases when the damage to the nephrons has been established.

Causes of acute nephritis include are discussed below.

Infection
Diagnosis of acute nephritis is usually made on the clinical signs, as above, but blood tests can help. The infective causal organism can also be isolated sometimes from a urine sample in the laboratory.

Treatment. If the cause is bacterial, nephritis usually responds to treatment with antibiotics and, if the disease is treated in the early stages, there will often be a complete recovery with little residual damage to the kidneys. However, a prolonged infection, or repeated bouts of acute nephritis, will produce severe kidney damage and lead to chronic kidney failure, called chronic interstitial nephritis. As the kidneys filter out mainly breakdown products of the protein that the cat eats, a light diet of high-quality protein or reduced protein will help recovery. Prescription kidney diets are available from your vet.

Pyelonephritis
Pyelonephritis is a particular type of kidney infection characterized by the formation of pus within the kidney. The infection usually reaches the kidney via the renal pelvis by ascending the ureter from the bladder.

Signs. These are similar to those of acute nephritis, i.e. a raised temperature, poor appetite, abdominal pain and vomiting. However, blood and pus may also be seen in the urine.

Diagnosis of pyelonephritis is based on the signs and confirmed by laboratory testing of blood and often urine also. A prolonged course of the appropriate antibiotic is needed to treat this condition but the kidneys may be permanently damaged and chronic renal failure is a possible sequel. Attention to diet is important to avoid stressing the kidneys and a light diet, or prescription diet from your vet, should be fed. The cat should be encouraged to drink as much water as possible to flush the infection through.

Failure of Urine Flow
Acute kidney failure will develop if there is a complete blockage of urine flow, which causes a back pressure on the nephrons in the kidney. One of the most common causes is blockage of the urinary tract in the urethra with crystals or even a bladder or urethral stone. Another is paralysis of the bladder following loss of nerve function, which usually follows a road accident involving a fractured pelvis or tailbase damage.

Shock
Shock can cause acute kidney failure because the blood pressure falls to such a low level that the filtration process in the nephrons ceases. The main causes of shock are severe accidents, especially road accidents, profuse haemorrhage and fluid-losing diseases, such as feline enteritis. Blood pressure can also fall during a major operation and affect the kidney, which is one of the main reasons cats are given intravenous fluid therapy during major operations. Kidney failure may only become apparent several days after the initial injury.

Toxins and Poisons
If cats have access to, and drink, poisons such as paraquat (weed killer) and antifreeze, these can rapidly damage the kidney and produce the

typical signs of acute kidney failure. As most of these poisons have no specific antidote, treatment is directed at flushing out the poison by intravenous fluid therapy and supporting kidney function with drugs and special low-protein diets, as before.

Plant Poisons. An unexpected group of poisons are all the plants in the lily family, where cats can be poisoned during self-grooming by licking off pollen from their coats or chewing the leaves. Also grapes and their derivatives, such as sultanas and currants, are poisonous to cats if somehow combined into their food. All these cause kidney failure.

Toxins released from bacteria involved in severe infections, such as large abscesses, gastro-enteritis and uterine infections, can cause acute kidney failure. In such cases, it is important to treat the underlying disease; in the case of an abscess this should be treated and drained or a very toxic uterus with pyometra removed surgically, as soon as possible. In most cases, kidney function will return to normal once the toxic cause is eliminated.

Chronic Nephritis or Kidney Failure

This is a common condition of the older cat but can occur occasionally in younger animals that have had their kidneys damaged by previous bouts of acute nephritis. Chronic kidney failure occurs when persistent or recurrent damage to the kidney reduces the number of functional nephrons to a level at which the kidney cannot perform its proper function. This allows toxic substances, such as urea, to accumulate in the circulation. When urea is present in significant quantities in the blood to make the cat feel sick, then the cat is said to uraemic.

It is worth mentioning that cats, like humans, can live very well on much less functioning kidney tissue than they are born with. For instance, one kidney can be removed with no noticeable effect on the cat (or human!). In fact, about 75 per cent of kidney tissue can be destroyed before any signs of kidney failure appear. However, if this residual kidney tissue is suddenly stressed by, for example, a road accident or an infection,

kidney function may completely fail. The result is a very ill cat, showing all the typical signs of acute kidney failure, including lethargy, a poor appetite and vomiting. Treatment of such a patient is often unsuccessful because the kidney reserves have already been destroyed. The cat will require intensive treatment from the vet, including intravenous fluid therapy and hospitalization; but despite all this, he is unlikely to recover.

Signs. A cat with chronic kidney failure usually begins to drink a lot more water than previously, and passes urine in greater quantities and more often. There is always a gradual weight loss, and as the disease progresses and the level of urea in the blood rises, the cat becomes toxic, lethargic and his appetite starts to fail. There is often an unpleasant smell to the breath, like ammonia, due to the uraemia and also due to gum and mouth ulcers, which often develop. The cat will become anaemic, which makes him more lethargic. In the final stages of the disease there is a complete loss of appetite, persistent vomiting and extreme weakness, followed by convulsions, coma and death.

Diagnosis. The above signs in an old cat, especially where the characteristic mouth odour occurs, are usually diagnostic, but it is confirmed by a blood test, which will show that the blood urea levels are very much higher than normal.

If your cat is drinking more than usual, seek veterinary attention.

Treatment. The prognosis is poor, as, in many cases, chronic renal failure is irreversible. However, any treatment is aimed at maximizing the function of any remaining kidney tissue, which, as mentioned above, may be only a small amount. Water must be available at all times and, where a patient is dehydrated, it may be necessary to replace fluid by intravenous therapy. Rest is important but the cat will be quiet. Stress should be avoided and special diets rich in energy and low in protein must be fed. Ideal canned, sachet or dry prescription diets are available from your vet. Anabolic steroids may be prescribed that can help by improving the metabolic rate and help to prevent weight loss.

Tumours

Tumours of the kidneys are rare and if both kidneys are affected, kidney failure will result. The most common tumour to develop in kidneys in the cat is a malignant lymphosarcoma, and the disease pattern will be similar to that of chronic renal failure, usually including abdominal enlargement and discomfort. There is no curative treatment if both kidneys are affected, but chemotherapy may give temporary remission for up to nine months.

Diagnosis is by palpation and radiography, when the affected kidney will be seen to be enlarged.

Treatment. If a single kidney is affected by a non-cancerous tumour, surgical removal of the kidney, in an operation called a nephrectomy, will invariably be successful, as the cat should recover well and function normally on his remaining kidney.

DISEASES OF THE BLADDER AND URETHRA: FELINE LOWER URINARY TRACT DISEASE (FLUTD)

Cat bladder and urethra problems are very commonly seen in veterinary practice and can be very difficult to treat, depending on the cause. The term FLUTD encompasses all problems of this area of the body, as the initial signs of bladder and urethral problems, whatever the cause, are very similar and not easy, without laboratory testing, to distinguish from one another. FLUTD would include cystitis, urethritis, bladder crystals or stones, tumours or polyps. In addition, cats that are fed on dry food exclusively, and either have restricted access to, water or just don't drink enough, can develop FLUTD. The answer is to feed both wet and dry food to cats, and to ensure water is always available. All cases involve an increased frequency of urination, some degree of straining to urinate and, usually, a blood-stained urine. In male cats, due to their extremely narrow urethra, the added complication of blockage of the urethra can occur, so it is important that any cat showing signs of bladder problems should be presented to the vet as soon as possible.

It is now known that stress is a major factor in the development of FLUTD. Stress can occur for various reasons – when living with another cat with which the affected cat is in conflict (i.e. cats belonging to different social groups; *see* Chapters 2 and 19); abrupt changes in diet, environment or weather; overcrowding; owner stress; or the addition of new pets or people to the household. Social stress particularly occurs in cats living in multi-cat households, but can occur in single-cat homes, if there is evidence of tension with other cats in the neighbourhood.

Urine samples are of paramount importance in the diagnosis of most bladder problems in cats, so if you suspect that your cat may have a bladder problem, it is most helpful if you can take a urine sample along with you when you take your cat to the vet's. However, collecting urine samples from cats can be very difficult. If your cat can be persuaded to urinate in an empty, clean litter tray, this is a good start. You should then tip the urine into a clean small container, such as a pill container, and label it. Washed fishtank gravel is also useful, as it allows the urine through it cleanly. Your vet will also be able to supply a commercial non-absorbent cat litter to put into the litter tray specifically for collecting urine samples.

Cystitis

Cystitis is inflammation of the bladder and can have several causes. It can be caused by

A special cat litter is available for collecting a urine sample.

an infection that enters the bladder from the urethra, although it can also be a blood-borne infection. As mentioned above, stress can cause cystitis, as can reduction or failure of urine flow due to lack of water intake. If a cat is on a dry diet, it is very important to ensure fresh water is always available – remember rain or mineral water may be preferred to tap water, which contains chlorine.

Signs. The clinical signs are those described above – increased frequency of urination, straining and a bloody urine. In all other respects, the cat usually appears healthy.

Diagnosis. A diagnosis can often be made on clinical signs alone and, by palpating the cat's abdomen, your vet may be able to feel that the bladder wall is thickened. Urine tests are helpful and your vet may be able to detect protein or blood in the urine. In addition, the bacteria causing the infection may be able to be identified and so the appropriate antibiotic can be prescribed.

Treatment. Bacterial cystitis usually responds to a short course of antibiotics but it has a tendency to recur at frequent intervals in some cats, which may require repeated courses of antibiotics. Any cat that does not respond rapidly and permanently to treatment for cystitis may well have an underlying cause of this inflammation, which will need further investigation.

Struvite Crystals

It is a fact that crystals of some form (either struvite or oxylate) are seen in almost 100 per cent of normal healthy cats fed a dry diet – simply because their urine is super-saturated; something else also has to be occurring for them to cause a problem.

Cats normally produce an acid urine but, if this is not the case and the urine is alkaline, crystals can form in the urine. These are minute but sharp crystals composed of a chemical called struvite and they scratch and irritate the lining of the bladder. This is uncomfortable for the cat, which feels the need to urinate frequently. The inflamed lining of the bladder may become infected but crystals tend to be seen most in very concentrated urine in which bacteria cannot grow. The signs are similar to those of cystitis – straining to urinate frequently and blood stained urine.

Diagnosis. Examination of a urine sample by your veterinary practice will reveal the presence of these crystals in the urine. The urine sample will be spun in a centrifuge to concentrate the crystals and make them easier to locate.

Treatment. Sometimes antibiotics may be needed initially, especially after, but not during, any catheterization, to clear the secondary cystitis, which may occur; but the cat must be encouraged to take in more fluid and to produce acid urine. This latter is achieved by feeding a specific prescription diet from your vet, initially for a few weeks, to dissolve any crystals and restrict further formation until repeated urine samples are clear of struvite crystals. At this stage, the cat is then put on to a different diet, which is effective at preventing the urine becoming alkaline and producing crystals, but

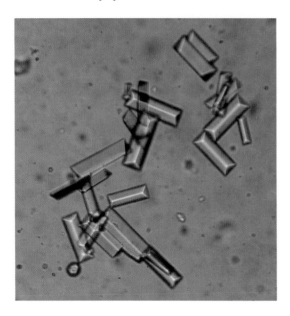

Struvite crystals seen in a urine sample through the microscope.

not as acidic as that required for treatment. However, affected cats should not be fed this diet for life, as these low-magnesium, acidifying diets in older cats can increase the risk of renal failure.

Urethral Obstruction

This is an acute, painful problem of the male cat and is potentially fatal if untreated. The struvite crystals when passed through the narrow male urethra scratch and inflame it, which causes the lining to swell and narrow the urethra even further. Very rapidly, the struvite crystals and other debris block the urethra and the cat cannot empty his bladder. This continues to fill, as the kidneys continue to produce urine, and very soon becomes very painful.

Signs. The cat will initially be trying to urinate continuously but unproductively, and will rapidly become depressed, restless and will almost certainly be crying out. If this continues, back pressure of urine up the ureters to the kidneys will lead to kidney failure. You must contact your vet immediately if you suspect this is the problem.

Diagnosis. On examining your cat and feeling his abdomen, your vet will recognize the hard swollen bladder necessitating immediate action.

Treatment. The bladder must be relieved of pressure immediately, either by gently inserting a needle through the skin into the bladder and drawing urine out, or by an immediate operation to unblock the urethra.

Under a general anaesthetic, your vet will use an instrument or catheter and a special solution possibly to try and dissolve and flush the crystals out. The male cat's urethra is not very long, perhaps about 5–8cm (2–3in) on average, and can be partially blocked at the penis or more fully blocked, so although this operation is usually successful, it is not always possible to remove the obstruction. Once the obstruction is cleared, a catheter is passed into the bladder to ensure the urethra is clear and this is usually left and sutured in place for a few days, draining into a bag, depending on the severity of the problem. Antibiotics and the crystal-dissolving food are needed, as for the less serious struvite crystal problem described above.

If the obstruction is impossible to clear, a very radical operation must be undertaken to bypass the obstructed portion of the urethra. This is called a urethrostomy, which is a permanent opening formed in the perineum (the area between the rectum and scrotum) and the procedure is termed 'perineal urethrostomy'.

Bladder Stones (Calculi)

True bladder stones are less common in the cat than the dog, but are seen and are usually formed of oxalate. A single stone can grow from tiny beginnings to fill the bladder, or there may be multiple smaller stones. Surgical removal is usually necessary but, depending on the chemical analysis of the stone, a prescription diet alone may change the acidity of the urine and cause it to dissolve.

Bladder Tumours

Tumours of the bladder are uncommon, but when they occur, they can affect the cat in one of two ways.

*An in-dwelling
urinary catheter in
male cat.*

Signs. As in cystitis, there may be frequent straining and bloody urine due to the tumour eroding the inner lining of the bladder, or the tumour may cause such damage to the bladder wall that it is unable to contract and empty normally. This will cause the bladder to leak urine involuntarily, which is called incontinence.

Diagnosis. In the early stages, the tumour may be very small and difficult to detect by your vet feeling the bladder through the abdominal wall, but larger ones may be diagnosed this way. If the diagnosis is not certain, X-rays may reveal the presence of a tumour, but it will often be necessary to use a contrast medium to reveal the tumour. This is a radio-opaque substance, such as a barium-type solution or even just air, introduced into the bladder through the urethra, which shows up on X-ray and will reveal if there is a mass in the bladder or its wall.

Treatment. Some bladder tumours can be treated using medical therapy with meloxicam and others by surgical removal; but some are not amenable to treatment.

Urinary Incontinence

Incontinence is the unconscious and uncontrolled leakage of urine from the urethra and is very uncommon in the cat. It usually shows as small puddles of urine whenever the cat lies down for any length of time or even when the cat walks. The hind legs become urine-stained

and an offensive smell develops, which is caused by the urine-soaked hair and infection of the urine-scalded skin. When it occurs, it is usually the result of a road traffic accident, where there has been damage to the lower spine in the area of nerve supply to the bladder. It can be temporary or permanent.

Treatment. In all cases, the bladder must be emptied manually by gentle pressure to prevent overfilling, which would lead to cystitis and kidney problems. Owners can be taught to do this by the practice nurse or vet, and if there is a chance the problem is temporary, it is worth progressing.

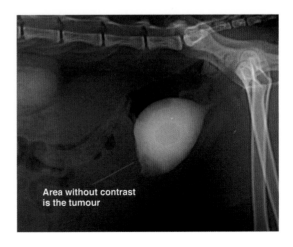

Area without contrast
is the tumour

*X-ray of a bladder with the tumour shown up using
contrast medium.*

Chapter 16
The Endocrine System

The endocrine system is the name given to the various glands in the body that produce, or control, the hormones. Most of these glands are small but the impact on the body of malfunction can be enormous. Fortunately, most potential dysfunctions of the endocrine glands in the cat are uncommon but two – diabetes mellitus and hyperthyroidism – are quite frequently diagnosed by vets in practice.

THE PANCREAS

The pancreas is a very important organ in the body and has two different functions. First, it is an 'endocrine' organ and produces hormones that regulate body functions, especially the hormone insulin, which regulates blood sugar levels. It is also an 'exocrine' organ and produces enzymes that are involved in the digestion of food. The signs of pancreatic disease depend on which function of the organ is malfunctioning; the exocrine function and disorders are covered in Chapter 7.

If the endocrine part is malfunctioning, production of the hormone insulin is affected. The most likely problem would be diabetes mellitus in which the pancreas produces insufficient quantities of insulin to control the blood sugar levels.

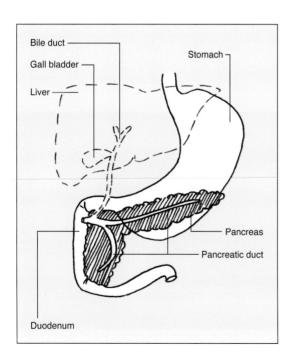

Fig 43 The pancreas and its duct.

Diabetes Mellitus

This is one of the most common glandular disorders in cats, affecting about 1 in every 200 cats, usually of seven years or older. Cats, like humans, can develop two types of diabetes: types 1 and 2. In type-1 diabetes, the pancreas fails to produce adequate amounts of insulin, whereas in type-2 diabetes, the commonest form in cats, the pancreas produces insulin, but the cat's body does not respond properly to the insulin. Overweight cats, especially males, are twice as likely as normal cats to develop type-2 diabetes, as are humans also.

Burmese are four times more likely than other breeds to develop type-2 diabetes.

In a cat with diabetes then, the pancreas either fails to produce enough insulin to control the level of glucose in the blood, or the cat cannot use the insulin, so the blood sugar rises.

Signs. The disease usually has a gradual onset over a few weeks, which may remain unnoticed until the first obvious signs appear. These are: weight loss or gain, excessive drinking and urination, whereas the appetite is suddenly either ravenous or the cat is off his food. If untreated, toxic substances build up in the bloodstream, which will cause the legs to become weak, followed by collapse and death of the cat.

Diagnosis. Only when the sugar reaches a certain level in the bloodstream, is glucose filtered out by the kidney and passed into the urine. So, glucose detected in the urine shows that the cat has diabetes, although urine samples are not always so easy to obtain in the cat. An even more useful test is to take a blood sample to test for the glucose level, and this can also show whether there is any damage to any of the internal organs due to the diabetes. This is done quite easily through an instrument called a glucometer, which painlessly punches a tiny opening in the skin and the glucose level can be ascertained from the resulting bleb of blood.

Treatment. Before treatment is started, the owner must realize that a certain amount of time must be spent each day in testing urine and injecting insulin. The syringes and needles will be supplied by your vet and are disposable, being used once only. The needles are very fine and sharp, and the cat genuinely will hardly feel them at all. Your veterinary practice will show you how to use these and it will rapidly become second nature to you and your cat. Once the blood glucose is stabilized, many cats live quite happily on their daily injections, with only the need for much less regular urine tests.

Diet. As the body obtains its sugar from the diet, it is important that the cat's diet is carefully worked out, and that a measured amount of a particular diet is fed each day to ensure that the insulin dose is easily and reliably calculated. Your vet and nurses in the practice will be able to advise on this.

Diabetic Comas. If the diabetes is unstabilized, a coma can occur. These are of two types:

- Hypoglycaemic coma is caused by too much insulin, which lowers the blood sugar too

The insulin injection is given just before feeding.

much. The immediate first-aid treatment is to give the cat a teaspoonful of glucose by mouth, which should fairly rapidly bring him round.
- Hyperglycaemic coma is caused by too little insulin which allows the blood sugar to rise. The immediate action is to give an insulin dose.

In both cases after this emergency treatment, the vet should be contacted for further advice.

THE THYROID GLAND

Cats have two thyroid glands, one situated on each side of the neck under the skin, alongside the trachea and just below the larynx. Each is tiny and almost impossible to feel in a normal cat. These glands produce the thyroid hormone that controls the normal metabolic rate of the cat, i.e. the rate at which many of the cat's bodily function take place. If too little thyroid hormone is produced, the cat will become lethargic, overweight and very lazy. This is called

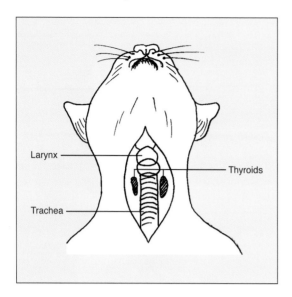

Fig 44 The position of the thyroid glands.

hypothyroidism and is extremely rare in cats. If too much thyroid hormone is produced, the metabolic rate increases and the body goes into overdrive. This is called hyperthyroidism and is quite common in older cats.

Hyperthyroidism

This over-production of thyroid hormone is usually caused by a tumour in one or both thyroid glands. The cause of the tumour is not known and this growth may be very small indeed and impossible to feel in the early stages.

Signs. Usually occurring in the older cat, in the initial stages this disease is often regarded as just old age by many owners. Affected cats just begin to look and behave old! They lose weight but their appetite often stays good or may even increase; they may begin to drink more but soon start to look thin and their coat begins to deteriorate and look uncared for.

Diagnosis. In an older cat, the above clinical signs will lead to your vet considering hyperthyroidism as a distinct possibility, but all or some of these same signs are also found in a number of other conditions, such as kidney or liver failure, and bowel tumours. A clinical examination by your vet may reveal an enlarged thyroid gland but not always, so a blood test is essential. This is a simple procedure, where a small volume of blood is taken through a fine needle from your cat's jugular vein and examined in a laboratory for thyroid hormone levels. It is, however, quite routine to look for other levels in the bloodstream in case the problem is not hyperthyroidism.

A normal cat's thyroid hormone level would be below 50 units, whereas in a cat suffering from hyperthyroidism, the level may be very much higher which is highly diagnostic.

Treatment. There are two main approaches to treatment depending on many factors, including the owner's opinion or ability to give tablets, finance, and age and condition of cat:

- surgical removal; or
- medical treatment.

Surgical removal of the affected gland(s) is usually very successful in curing the condition. Some vets prefer to treat the cat with a thyrotoxic drug called methimazole first to help the cat into a better condition to face surgery but others feel it is better to press on and remove the thyroid, especially if the cat is difficult to dose with tablets. One complication is that another important but even tinier gland, the parathyroid gland, which controls calcium levels in the body, is situated on the surface of the thyroid and should not be removed at the same time. Surgery should only be undertaken if the cat's kidneys are functioning well.

If only one thyroid is removed, post-operative treatment is straightforward, as the normal thyroid will compensate. If both are removed, it may be necessary to inject or give by mouth a calcium and vitamin D supplement to prevent hypocalcaemia. Also, if both are removed, the thyroid hormone level may drop too much, necessitating thyroid hormone supplementation. Oddly this is not always the case, as the thyroid tumour may have been in so-called ectopic (out of place) thyroid tissue.

If surgery is not possible or desired, for whatever reason, medical treatment, using the same medication as pre-operatively, can be very successful in controlling the disease. The methimazole tablets are given one or two times daily and the results can be very satisfactory. Affected cats gain weight, eat and drink less, and their coat and behaviour will often return to a more normal state. If enlarged thyroid glands could be felt, these will usually reduce in size. This is not curative but cats can, and must, remain on treatment permanently, unless surgery is eventually undertaken.

THE PARATHYROID GLAND

The two parathyroid glands, each sitting on the surface of each thyroid gland, produce the parathyroid hormone, which controls the calcium metabolism in the body. Problems with this gland are very rare in the cat.

Hypoparathyroidism will occur rarely, when a cat has had both thyroid glands removed and the parathyroid glands have been damaged, either by a thyroid tumour or inadvertently during the surgery. In this rare condition, affected cats will twitch, be wobbly and may have convulsions. Calcium supplementation will be urgently and continuously required.

Hyperparathyroidism is also very uncommon and when it does occur, it is usually secondary to another condition, such as a nutritional problem or kidney failure.

THE PITUITARY GLAND

This gland is situated in the brain and has a major effect on all or most of the hormone systems of the body. Fortunately problems of the pituitary gland are also rare in the cat.

Diabetes Insipidus

This is a rare problem in the cat, causing an excessive thirst and excessive urination. Affected cats may drink up to a litre of water a day! The urine is very dilute compared to normal cat urine, which may suggest that the cat has this condition, but there are few diagnostic tests; the most reliable being to eliminate all other possible causes.

Treatment. It may not be necessary to treat the cat if the excess urination is not a problem to the family but if so, a diuretic tablet, ironically normally used to increase urine output, may be helpful.

Pituitary Dwarfism

This is an even rarer condition caused by low levels of growth hormone due to pituitary dysfunction. Affected cats remain small, develop very slowly and even retain their temporary teeth until two years old or more.

An old, depressed cat with hyperthyroidism.

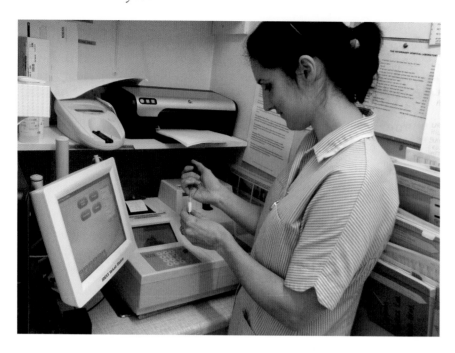

A student veterinary nurse testing a blood sample for thyroid hormone levels.

ADRENAL GLANDS

The two adrenal glands are situated, one on each side of the body, in the abdomen close to each kidney. Very small in size, they do, however, produce hormones that have important functions in the body. The central part of each adrenal produces adrenaline, which is involved in the fight-or-flight syndrome, and the outer part produces steroid and sex hormones. However, diseases of the adrenals are again rare in the cat and I can't recall ever seeing one during my forty years in veterinary practice. However, there is one condition, called Cushing's Syndrome, which occasionally occurs.

Cushing's Syndrome

This disease is caused when a tumour in an adrenal gland (or the controlling pituitary gland) leads to an excessive production of steroid hormones by the body. It is very rare in the cat, compared to the dog, where it is quite often diagnosed.

Signs. Affected cats drink and urinate excessively, have an increased appetite and become very lethargic. Their abdomens become bloated, the skin appears thinner and darker in colour, the coat thins and there is often a symmetrical hair loss on the cat's flanks.

Diagnosis. The clinical signs are very suggestive of the problem but it is confirmed by the so-called ACTH stimulation test, whereby a blood test is taken for steroid levels, then a hormone is injected and a second blood test taken two hours later, to test the response.

Treatment. Unfortunately, treatment is not usually successful, even after surgical removal of an affected adrenal gland.

Chapter 17
The Reproductive System

THE MALE CAT

The male reproductive system has two main functions: the production of semen and its introduction into the female cat's vagina via the penis; and also the production of testosterone, the male hormone, in the testes (testicles). The components of the male reproductive system are a pair of testicles, each of which is connected by the epididymis and the tubular vas deferens and the urethra, to the penis with its protective sheath, the prepuce. The single prostate gland provides the fluid to suspend and feed the semen.

Normal Structure and Function

The cat's penis consists mostly of erectile tissue and is contained in, and protected by, the prepuce. On its surface are tiny projections that point backwards and are thought to cause ovulation by stimulating the female vagina during mating. They cause some pain on withdrawal and females often cry out and are aggressive towards the male as mating finishes. Except when mating, the penis points backwards and is mostly enclosed within the body. The testes are oval in shape and lie below the anus and above the penis, firmly enclosed in a sac, the scrotum. This

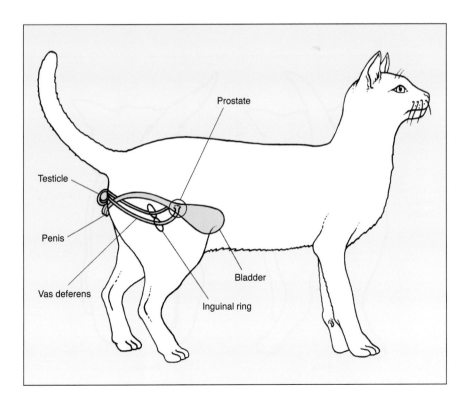

Prostate

Testicle

Penis

Bladder

Vas deferens

Inguinal ring

Fig 35 The male reproductive system.

ensures they are at a slightly lower temperature than normal body temperature, which is essential for their normal function. The testes produce sperm and testosterone, the male hormone. This hormone determines male characteristics and behaviour. In the foetus, the testicles are situated just behind the kidneys but, as the young kitten develops, they gradually move towards the rear of the abdomen and finally come to lie outside in the scrotum.

The sperm leave each testicle through the vas deferens and enter the epididymis where they are stored. From here, on ejaculation when mating, they enter the female's vagina.

The prostate is a small gland that surrounds the male urethra just behind the bladder in the pelvic canal. It produces a secretion that helps in the feeding and transport of the sperm.

Diseases of the Testicles

Retained Testicle (Cryptorchidism)

Occasionally during development, one or both testicles may fail to descend into the scrotum and can be retained somewhere along their developmental path. However, as they can take a long time to descend, a definite diagnosis should be delayed until the cat is about four months old. Such a testicle is usually retained in one of two positions: either in the abdomen just inside the inguinal ring, or just outside the inguinal ring in the groin, and is infertile. In my experience, medical treatment to further the descent of these testicles into the scrotum is not successful. As the condition is considered to be hereditary, surgical correction is unethical as it may lead to future generations of male cats with the same condition. For the same reason, because the normal testis is fertile, cats that have one retained testicle should not be used for breeding.

Treatment. As any retained testicle will be at a higher temperature than normally positioned ones, it will be infertile, as normal sperm formation is not possible in that testicle. However, as mentioned above, if only one testicle is retained, the other one will be fertile but mating should not be allowed, as the gene for cryptorchidism may be passed on. In addition, retained testicles are more susceptible to disease, especially cancerous change, and most vets will suggest castration, involving the surgical removal of both testicles.

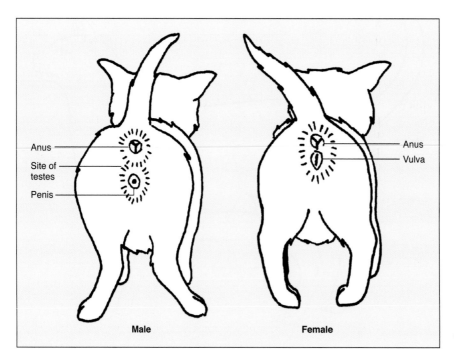

Fig 36 *Male and female external genitalia.*

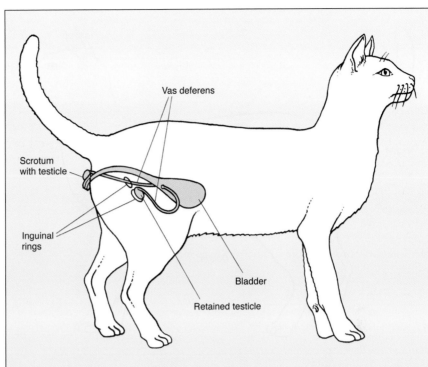

Vas deferens

Scrotum
with testicle

Inguinal
rings

Bladder

Retained testicle

Fig 37 *One testis*
retained in the abdomen.

Infection (Orchitis)

Infection is very rare but can be caused by bites or scratches in that area.

Signs. When present, one or both testicles become very painful and swollen. An affected cat will usually have a raised temperature, refuse food and be reluctant to move.

Treatment. Orchitis quickly responds to antibiotic therapy, but occasionally an abscess may result, which is much more resistant to treatment. In some cases, surgical removal of the affected testicle may be necessary.

Diseases of the Prostate Gland

Because by far the majority of male cats are castrated, prostate problems are extremely rare. I cannot recall ever diagnosing this problem in a cat.

Diseases of the Penis and Prepuce

Infection of the penis is not very common and, as with the testes, usually only occurs following a fight wound.

Signs. An affected cat will lick his penis frequently, and the area will look sore and may have a discharge.

Treatment consists of bathing the area with an antiseptic solution but if the infection has penetrated the skin, antibiotics are needed orally or by injection.

Blockage. In the male cat, obstruction of the penis by struvite crystals formed in the bladder is relatively common. It occurs when the cat produces alkaline urine instead of the more usual acid urine. This condition is covered fully in Chapter 15 under Urethral obstruction (*see* page 162).

Castration

Adult male cats (toms) have a large territory, which they patrol regularly. In a city situation this means that their chances of a road traffic accident are high. In addition, once mature, at about nine months old, their urine has a very strong and unpleasant smell and they will often

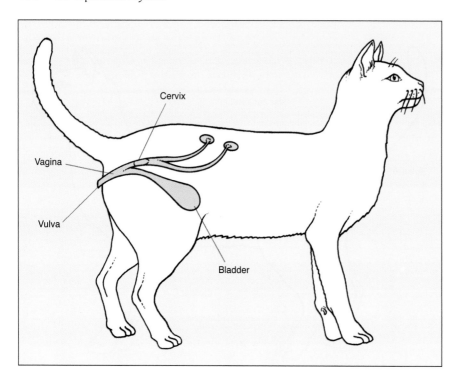

Cervix

Vagina

Vulva

Bladder

Fig 38 The female reproductive system.

mark their territory including their (your!) house. Castration (the surgical removal of both testes) stands the best chance of preventing all of this and is the commonest operation carried out on male cats. It also, of course, prevents unwanted litters. If carried out at the ideal age of about five months, by removing the testes, the testosterone they produce is eliminated, and the undesirable traits of wandering and inappropriate urinating are minimized, and also the urine does not develop the strong unpleasant odour. Stud cats used for breeding are invariably housed in outdoor runs for these very reasons. Most pet cats are castrated at about five months of age, but cats can be castrated at any age, although the most successful results concerning wandering and urine smell are achieved by castrating them before they are mature.

Under a general anaesthetic, the hair from around the scrotum is shaved or plucked, and the skin disinfected. Using surgically sterile instruments, the skin of the scrotum is incised over a testis, the testis firmly grasped, removed and the blood vessels tied off. In young kittens, rarely is any ligature needed, nor does the skin need suturing, as the opening being very small

heals naturally within a few days. With modern anaesthetics and pain relief, the cat will usually be demanding his supper that evening when he arrives home.

THE FEMALE CAT (QUEEN)

The function of the female reproductive system is to produce eggs in the ovaries, to produce hormones that stimulate the queen to mate with the male, conception and development of the fertilized eggs into foetal kittens in the uterus and the rearing of these kittens until weaning. The reproductive system consists of two ovaries from which a Y-shaped uterus leads through the cervix to the vagina. In addition, the five paired mammary glands produce milk to rear the young.

Normal Structure and Function

The ovaries are small, glandular structures situated one behind each kidney in a little pouch called the ovarian bursa, which is connected to the uterus by a short fine tube, the Fallopian tube. Eggs are produced in the ovary and, when released, pass across the bursa and enter the uterus along these Fallopian tubes. The ovaries also produce hormones, which are released into the bloodstream, to prepare the uterus for mating and pregnancy, and also help to maintain the resulting pregnancy.

The uterus in the cat is a long, narrow, Y-shaped organ. The so-called horns of the uterus join together to form a short uterine body, which is normally sealed from the vagina by the muscular cervix.

The cervix relaxes during each heat period to allow the introduction of sperm and during parturition (birth) so the foetuses can be expelled. The vagina connects the cervix to the vestibule, which is the common opening for the reproductive and urinary systems. The vulva is the external visible entrance to the vestibule.

The mammary glands, of which there are usually five pairs, are situated on the underside of the chest and belly as a continuous strip from the axilla to the groin. They begin to develop during pregnancy, begin to produce milk and lactate at birth, initially with the colostrum, and reach maximum production and size two to three weeks later.

Puberty varies from five or six months of age in shorthair and Oriental cats, such as Siamese, and up to one-year-old in some longhair breeds.

The cat is seasonally polyoestrous, which means she comes into oestrus or 'calls' frequently, governed by day length at certain times of the year. In outdoor cats living normal lives, this is usually between January and August, but cats kept indoors or under artificial light may call on and off all year.

The length of oestrus varies between breeds: longhair cats may only call twice a year with oestrus lasting just a few days, while shorthair cats may call for up to ten days with a gap of only a week or so between oestruses. My own Siamese cats seemed to be permanently on call at certain times of the year until mated! Mating in cats induces the queen to ovulate (release eggs from the ovaries) and this ends that oestrus and stops them calling. When a female cat is calling, she adopts peculiar postures, often rolling over and crying out. She will crouch and hold her tail to one side, especially when a male cat is around. This odd behaviour is often interpreted by new cat owners as meaning the cat is in pain, but it is completely normal.

Pregnancy in cats lasts for about nine weeks, usually sixty-three to sixty-five days.

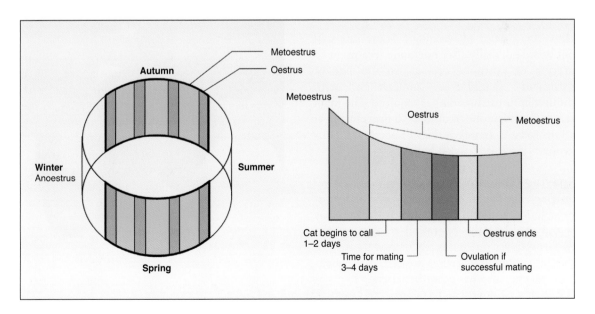

Fig 39 Female cat oestrus cycle.

Birth Control

Hormone Therapy

- Oral method. In cats intended for breeding in the future, oestrus can be prevented or postponed by giving tablets of a hormone preparation called megestrol acetate. Your vet will advise on an appropriate dose regime for your cat. However, the timing of the next oestrus following treatment may be variable and the next one after a prevention course given during the breeding season will probably occur a few days later than normally expected – on average about four weeks after the last dose is given. Queens given a correctly timed postponement course will not call whilst they are receiving the tablets.
- Injectable method. An injection is available that can be used for the permanent or temporary postponement of oestrus, or for suppressing oestrus once it has started in a cats. It contains a hormone, proligestone, which has a formulation that makes it possible to administer it to a cat at any stage of the oestrous cycle with little risk of undesirable effects on the uterus. Again, the timing of the next oestrus following treatment may be variable, so it is essential to discuss what is best for your cat with your vet.

However, a word of warning – some cats will not breed normally after hormone treatment to prevent or postpone oestrus, so this line of treatment should be undertaken with caution, if future breeding is required. The main reason for hormone treatment to prevent a heat seems to be to ensure it doesn't occur at inconvenient times, such as on holiday.

Spaying (Ovariohysterectomy)

Spaying is by far the commonest, best and most reliable method of birth control in cats. A spay is the name of the operation to remove the uterus and ovaries, and is performed to prevent the cat calling and having unwanted pregnancies. Spaying also has other beneficial effects as it prevents pyometra and, if performed early in life, reduces the chance of the queen suffering from mammary tumours and mastitis. It can be carried out on kittens or on cats at any age within reason.

In kittens the operation is usually carried out at about five months of age. A small incision is made under a general anaesthetic in a shaved and disinfected area, usually on the cat's flank, and the uterus and ovaries located and removed. Recovery is very rapid and most kittens will return home the same day, having had a dose of analgesia (pain relief), and will demand their evening meal! In most cases they will be back to normal behaviour within days and will be difficult to keep quiet. The sutures will be removed seven to ten days later, unless your vet has used dissolving sutures. Because the ovaries have also been removed, the cat will never undergo oestrus and will not attract the attention of passing tom cats.

Adult cats (usually pedigree ones) that have reached the end of their breeding life are also often spayed, and this again is by far the best way of making the rest of their life trouble-free and comfortable. There is some evidence that spayed cats find it easier to gain weight but if they are kept on their normal diet in normal amounts, this is easy to control.

Rapid recovery of five-month-old kitten almost immediately after spay operation.

Diseases of the Ovaries

Cystic Ovaries

Ovarian cysts are very uncommon in the cat but do occasionally occur. Several different types of cysts can form in the cat's ovaries, but most are small and lead to no signs of illness or reproductive abnormalities.

Signs. Some grow large, causing mild abdominal pain. One type of cyst, called the follicular cyst, is more of a problem and can lead to oestrous cycles without allowing the male to mate, or an altered calling pattern, or even failure to call on a regular basis.

Diagnosis. The signs described above, along with hormone analysis and the laboratory examination of cysts discovered at surgery.

Treatment. Surgical removal of the affected ovary or a total ovariohysterectomy.

Ovarian Tumours

These tumours are very rare in the cat. An exploratory operation carried out by your vet may identify the problem and the affected ovary will be surgically removed, unless there is evidence of spread to other organs.

Diseases of the Uterus

Pyometra

This is a probably the most common disease of the older unspayed cat and is a very serious condition. Due to hormonal and uterine changes that occur in the older cat, an infection can start in the uterus and lead to death due to sepsis or organ failure, if not treated properly.

There is a slow build-up of pus – an affected uterus can be so full of pus that it approaches the size of a normal full-term pregnant uterus. The queen slowly becomes poisoned by the release of toxins from the infection into her bloodstream.

Signs. Initially, there will be distension of the abdomen, loss of appetite and an excess thirst due to the toxicity and kidney damage. If untreated, vomiting often occurs and the queen

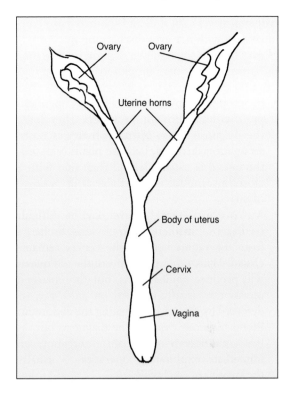

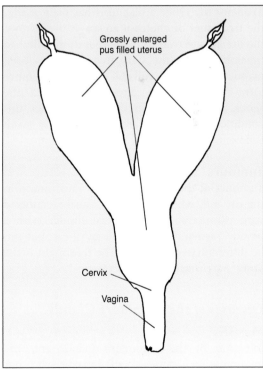

Fig 40 (TOP) A normal cat ovaries and uterus; (BOTTOM) a pus-filled uterus affected by pyometra.

will appear very ill, dull and she may have conjunctivitis with her eyes discharging pus.

Any further signs shown depend on whether the pyometra is 'open' or 'closed':

- In an open pyometra, the cervix is open and pus can drain through the vagina. Therefore, the diagnosis of an open pyometra is more straightforward and, because pus is released, the queen is usually less ill than one with a closed pyometra, where there is no leakage of pus.
- A closed pyometra, however, can be difficult to diagnose, as there is no obvious discharge from the vagina because the cervix remains closed. Many other problems of the old queen will produce similar signs, but the enlarged uterus can usually be seen on an X-ray, or detected by the vet by palpating the abdomen. Blood tests can confirm the diagnosis but, as the condition is often an emergency, an immediate exploratory operation is usually the treatment of choice.

Treatment. Once a diagnosis has been made, the treatment of choice is to surgically remove the uterus and ovaries in an operation called an ovariohysterectomy. Cats that have a closed pyometra can be very ill and will usually require intravenous fluid therapy to counteract the shock and dehydration that accompanies this condition. Antibiotics are also normally given following the operation.

Tumours
Tumours of the uterus are very uncommon in the cat and, when they occur, can be confused with pyometra. The signs are similar with a bloody vaginal discharge and an ill cat, but can be differentiated on X-ray. The treatment is the same – an ovariohysterectomy.

Diseases of the Mammary Glands
Mastitis
Infection of the mammary glands and the inflammation it causes is called mastitis. It is not common but is occasionally seen in lactating queens. The infection enters the gland via the teat and is most likely to happen where all the milk is not drawn off due to an excess production for the number of kittens, or where the kittens are not feeding well or have died.

Signs. The affected glands become swollen, hot and hard, and the queen may have a raised temperature. She will be very depressed, off her food and dehydrated, and she will be reluctant to feed the kittens, as the condition is painful. Any milk produced will become blood-tinged or discoloured, and in severe cases an abscess may form.

Treatment. This type of mastitis usually responds to antibiotic therapy, provided treatment is instigated early in the course of the disease. Bathing helps and the kittens must be removed from her and fed by hand.

Mammary Tumours
Mammary tumours are quite common in the older unspayed female cat, and most of them are malignant (cancerous). Any, or several, glands can be affected, and they can grow very rapidly and spread to other organs, especially the lungs.

Signs. One or more lumps will be felt in the mammary glands along the chest or abdomen but, initially, the cat will not be at all ill. If a tumour is left untreated, it increases in size, which causes the skin to overstretch and ulcerate; this produces a septic, sore, discharging area that does not respond to medical treatment.

Treatment. Early surgical removal of any lump discovered in the mammary glands is advisable because of the danger of malignancy. In the case of multiple or extensive tumours, it will be necessary to remove several glands and, in some cases, all the mammary tissue. This latter operation, known as a mammary strip, is very well-tolerated by the cat and an ideal way to remove multiple tumours. However, before deciding on surgery, your vet will X-ray the cat's chest to ensure that no spread has occurred to the lungs. If so, surgery on the mammary glands would be pointless.

Chapter 18
Breeding and Associated Problems

NORMAL REPRODUCTION

The cat is seasonally polyoestrous, which means she comes into oestrus ('calls') frequently at certain times of the year. In outdoor cats living normal lives, this is usually between January and August, but cats kept indoors or under artificial light may call on and off all year. Puberty varies from five or six months of age in shorthair and Oriental cats, such as Siamese, and up to one-year-old in some longhair breeds. The length of oestrus also varies between breeds;

Longhair cats may only call twice a year, with oestrus lasting just a few days; while shorthair types may call for up to ten days, with a gap of only a week or so between oestruses. My own Siamese cats seemed to be permanently on call at certain times of the year until mated. This mating induces the queen to ovulate (release eggs from the ovaries) and stops them calling.

When a female cat is calling, she adopts peculiar postures, often rolling over and crying out. She will crouch and hold her tail up and to one side, especially when a male cat is around. This odd behaviour is often interpreted by new cat owners as meaning the cat is in pain, but it is completely normal.

When the queen accepts the male, she will hold her tail up and to one side, and the tom will grasp the scruff of her neck and mount her. Coitus itself is very short, lasting less than a minute. The queen usually cries out at mating, as explained in Chapter 17 and appears angry with the tom. In arranged mating when breeding, it is advisable to let them mate several times to

Cats about to mate Note raised position of tail of female on the right.

increase the chances of a pregnancy. Most reputable breeders will have tested and vaccinated their stud cat against feline leukaemia virus and will expect the visiting queen to have been tested for, and vaccinated against, this disease, as well as feline enteritis and feline influenza.

If pregnancy does not result from the mating, the queen may have a period of a false or pseudo-pregnancy for about six weeks. Pregnancy itself lasts for about nine weeks, usually sixty-three to sixty-five days. Longhaired cats tend to have small litters of perhaps two to three kittens, most Moggies seem to have litters of about four to five kittens, while Orientals, such as Siamese, can have even larger litters.

PROBLEMS AT MATING

Reproductive failure can arise at a number of different stages throughout the reproductive process. A queen may never call or display oestrus and, even if she does call, she may refuse to mate. Failure of ovulation, fertilization and pregnancy may all occur, and finally there may be difficulty at the time of kittening. In addition, problems may occur in either queens or toms.

Failure to Call

If the queen has reached puberty, which, as mentioned above, varies with the breed, and if she is in good physical condition, it is very unlikely that she will fail to come into oestrus. Some pet cats kept alone and isolated from other cats more frequently fail to call but can be induced to call if kept with other queens for a while. It may be possible for your vet to induce her to call by using a specific gonadotrophin hormone, but the response is variable.

Mismating

If an unwanted mating has, or is thought to have, occurred, there is currently no hormone product licensed to prevent fertiliztion. If the cat is not intended for breeding, spaying some three weeks after mating will solve the problem. If she is to breed in the future, it is better to let her have the litter; this will not affect the pedigree or purity of the next planned mating.

Failure to Mate

It is unusual for cats to refuse to mate but in the case of pedigree cats, which are taken to the stud cat on his premises, it can happen. This is

Stud cat in his premises.

probably due to the stress of the journey and unfamiliar surroundings with a strange cat. From my own experience of breeding Siamese cats, mating is more likely to take place successfully if the cats have time to get to know each other a little first. So leave the queen with the stud cat for a few days, even if this is a few days before she is expected to start calling.

NORMAL PREGNANCY

In the cat, the gestation period or length of pregnancy is normally around sixty-three days. For the first three weeks there is little noticeable change in either the behaviour or the appearance of the queen, but you may notice that the teats begin to enlarge. At about three and a half to four and a half weeks after mating, your vet may be able to tell you if she is pregnant by gently palpating her abdomen. In a pregnant cat, the uterus swells around each developing kitten and can often be felt as a small, tense, spherical swelling at this stage. Later, each swelling becomes larger and softer and difficult to distinguish from bowel until about the seventh week when the kittens themselves are substantial enough to be detected by palpation. If the examination is inconclusive, and it is important to know whether she is pregnant or not, ultrasound scanning or blood tests are available.

From about six weeks pregnant onwards, the queen begins to show a more obvious increase in size of the abdomen and the teats and mammary glands begin to enlarge. She will usually slow down a bit but her appetite remains good. At this stage, food intake should be increased and it is advisable to change her diet gradually to one formulated for kittens, as this diet contains the correct proportion of calcium and vitamin D, which she needs to pass on to the developing kittens, and to produce her milk.

A few days before she is due to give birth (kitten), milk may start to ooze from the teats and she will begin to seek out a private place to kitten. Unless it is a highly inconvenient place, it is best to let her choose where to have the kittens, or to supply a suitable comfortable box for her a few days before in a safe, secure area of the house away from children and dogs.

PROBLEMS DURING PREGNANCY

Cats rarely have problems during pregnancy. The most likely are:

- Failure to conceive. It is not always possible to observe cats mating, so you cannot always be sure that they have. Also, the tom may be sterile unless he is a proven stud. If no kittens result, try again, but if unsuccessful after two matings, use a different stud cat.
- Resorption of foetuses. This is the commonest cause of failure to produce kittens and explains why an early positive pregnancy diagnosis by palpation or ultrasound is not always followed by live kittens. It is an uncommon happening but can occur if the queen is out of condition, has a uterine problem such as metritis, or is suffering from feline leukaemia virus.
- Abortion. This is also uncommon, and can be due to the same causes as resorption. In my experience, once a miscarriage has started to occur, there is little that can be done to halt it, but occasionally an injection of progesterone, the hormone responsible for maintaining pregnancy, will enable the queen to hold on to her kittens. If the abortion continues, veterinary supervision is essential to ensure all is well.

PARTURITION (BIRTH OR KITTENING)

It is essential that a kittening box, cage or cosy area has been prepared for the queen and, as there will be some fluid discharge during the birth, it is a good idea to pad the box with several layers of newspaper, which can be removed gradually as they become soiled. Her kittening box, cage or area should be made of material that can be suitably disinfected or discarded after use. If a cosy box is provided, her body heat should ensure that the temperature of the nesting environment is adequate, but I would recommend an infra-red heat source directly over the kittening area for the first week or so, even in summer. If she is to kitten in cold weather, this heat source should remain in place for much

A kittening cage.

longer, as it helps to prevent the kittens developing hypothermia. However, most queens have very strong maternal instincts and make good, attentive mothers, but it is important that the queen is settled in the kittening box; if not she may constantly be moving the kittens, which can lead to chilling.

Birth is very quick and without fuss in most cats, and the classic three stages of labour merge into one usually. First-stage labour is characterized by a gradually developing restlessness on the part of the queen, who appears uneasy, often 'bed-making', such as tearing up newspaper in her box. This stage occurs as the cervix is widening to allow passage of the kittens and as the first kitten is being moved towards the cervix; it may only last for an hour or two. Shortly, contractions begin to develop that increase in

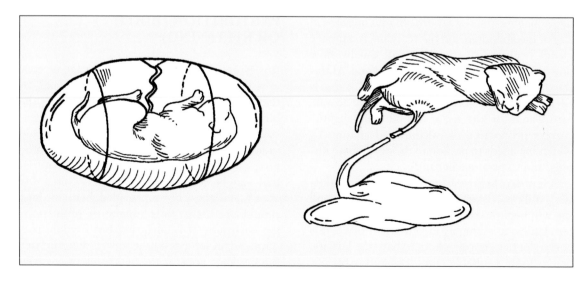

Fig 41 *(LEFT) Foetus just before birth; (RIGHT) newborn kitten showing where to cut the umbilical cord.*

frequency until her abdomen is contracting several times each minute. This is the second-stage labour during which the kittens are born. A 'water bag' appears at the vulva and a kitten is usually born within twenty minutes of the onset of her strong contractions. After the first kitten, the interval between kittens varies enormously, but the litter is usually complete within three to four hours.

Each kitten is contained in a fluid-filled membrane bag in the uterus and has its own placenta attached to the uterine lining. It may be born enclosed in the bag or may have ruptured it during birth. By licking the kitten immediately on birth, the queen will usually rupture the bag and revive the kitten who will very shortly begin to cry as he fills his lungs for the first time. If the queen ignores the kitten or seems confused, the owner must gently but firmly tear the bag from around it, hold the kitten in a towel, wipe out the mouth and gently but vigorously rub the kitten within the towel to stimulate breathing. If the placenta is still attached to the kitten, the umbilical cord should be tied with cotton about two and a half centimetres (one inch) from the kitten and then carefully cut with scissors beyond this. In experienced hands, the cord can be carefully shredded with finger nails, which will prevent any loss of blood. The kitten should then be placed gently in the kittening box on to

a teat, when it will normally begin suckling. The placenta (afterbirth) is usually passed immediately after the kitten and still attached to it by the umbilical cord – this is the third-stage labour. Very often, however, the placenta becomes detached as the umbilical cord ruptures, due to the vigour of birth, and remains inside the uterus. This is perfectly normal and any retained placentae will slowly disintegrate and be expelled from the uterus as a darkish discharge over the next few weeks. If the placenta is expelled at birth, it will often be eaten by the queen and this should be encouraged.

The queen will pay nominal attention to each kitten when it is born but will not normally be very interested in the litter until kittening is complete. You should supervise the kittening but not so intensively that you disturb the queen continuously; as long as everything is progressing well, check on her every twenty minutes or so from a reasonable distance. It is advisable to have a separate box nearby, which is heated by a hot water bottle, well-covered in a blanket, in which to place each kitten as it is born, to keep it dry and warm. If the queen is concerned about this, place the strongest kitten in with her to placate her. When kittening is complete, a change in her attitude is usually obvious: she will brighten up, clean herself thoroughly and begin to look after the kittens in earnest.

A queen and contented litter.

PROBLEMS AT PARTURITION

There are basically two categories into which birth problems fit:

- Problems associated with the queen.
- Problems associated with the kittens.

Problems Associated with the Queen – Maternal Dystocia

Primary Inertia

This is very uncommon in cats but is a condition whereby the queen simply fails to start second-stage labour. She has no contractions at all, despite showing all the signs of first-stage labour, including a dilated cervix. If kittening does not follow within twenty-four hours of the queen becoming restless, or if the pregnancy has lasted more than sixty-five days, or if a vaginal discharge is noticed, the queen should be examined by a vet in case inertia is present.

Treatment. An injection of a hormone, oxytocin, may stimulate contractions, and your vet may decide to try this if it can be detected that the cervix is open. A Caesarean section may be the course of action decided on by your vet. The queen is anaesthetized, an incision made into the abdomen and then the uterus, and the kittens are surgically removed and revived in the operating theatre. This operation and modern anaesthetics are well-tolerated by queen and kittens alike, and within twenty-four hours the queen will seem fully recovered and will be suckling the kittens well. Sometimes, however, the kittens may be dead in the uterus, and the vet may have to prescribe hormones to cause reabsorption of the milk and prevent mastitis in the absence of any kittens.

Secondary Inertia

This can occur where the cat has been contracting but, due to an obstruction, birth cannot take place and she becomes exhausted. This can be caused by an abnormal or abnormally-positioned foetus (foetal dystocia) (*see* opposite) or by a uterine obstruction (maternal dystocia). The term dystocia, simply means a difficult birth.

Maternal dystocia must be suspected where the queen has been contracting unproductively for over two hours. The possible causes are:

- An old pelvic fracture. This causes a narrowing of the birth canal and is invariably the result of a previous road accident. A queen that suffers a pelvic fracture should by spayed to eliminate the possibility of this occurrence.
- Uterine twist. This can occur in a queen that is heavily pregnant with a large number of kittens present in the uterus, and is thought to be due to rotation of this heavy organ within the abdomen, responding to an awkward movement of the queen.
- Rupture of the uterus can occur spontaneously or be due to trauma or follow a twist of the uterus. The queen would show signs of pain or profound depression.

Treatment. All of these conditions necessitate a Caesarean section to save the life of both the queen and kittens. In most cases it would be sensible to also remove the ovaries and uterus at the same time, due to severe damage to the uterus.

Problems Associated with the Kittens – Foetal Dystocia

Overlarge Kitten

This can be a genuine oversized kitten, especially in single-kitten litters, or relative oversize due to a small birth canal. Invariably if this problem arises, it is the first kitten that moves into the birth canal that causes the problem and, if successfully delivered, the rest usually follow.

Malpresentation

In a normal birth, kittens should be born with either head and forelegs first (anterior presentation) or tail and back legs first (posterior presentation). Both presentations are completely normal and the kittens are usually easily delivered. Any variations on this, however, can cause a foetal dystocia. Three common examples are:

- Breech presentation. This is where the tail is presenting first but the hind legs are tucked up and forwards under the kitten's abdomen, as in a sitting position. This greatly enlarges the buttocks of the kitten and causes an obstruction.

- Head first with forelegs pointing backwards along the kitten's chest. This grossly enlarges the shoulders and prevents delivery.
- Head and neck deflected down or to one side, so that the neck is the nearest part of the body to the birth canal – an impossible situation for a normal birth.

Treatment. Sometimes manipulation from outside the abdomen by your vet can correct a malposture, such as a deflected head. However, due to the small size of the queen's vagina, it is almost always impossible to help her deliver a kitten in any of these abnormal positions, and a Caesarean section is invariably needed.

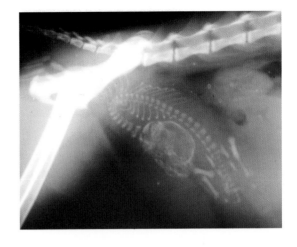

X-ray of malpresenting kitten with the head and neck twisted backwards.

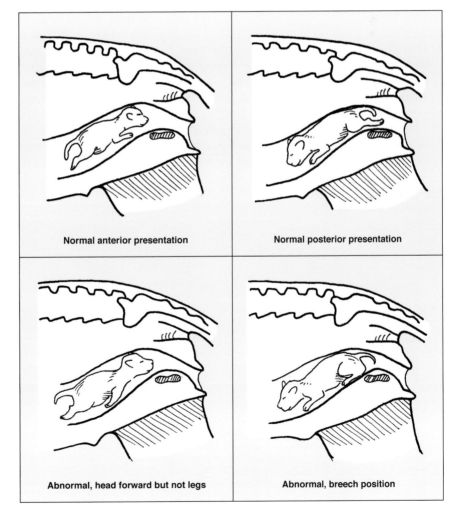

Normal anterior presentation

Normal posterior presentation

Abnormal, head forward but not legs

Abnormal, breech position

Fig 42 The main four possible kitten positions at birth.

Congenital Abnormalities

These can result in malformed kittens, which may be difficult or impossible for the queen to deliver. These are usually only diagnosed on X-ray or during a Caesarean section. Most do not survive and, indeed, if a severe abnormality exists, euthanasia at birth may be the kindest course of action.

THE FIRST FEW WEEKS AFTER THE BIRTH

The Kittens

Days 1 and 2

The kittens are born blind with their eyes closed. Check them all to ensure there are no obvious congenital abnormalities present. If in doubt, the vet should be asked to attend. Things to look for are:

- Hare lip, where the area between the nose and mouth does not unite fully leaving an open area from the mouth to the nose. If extreme, euthanasia is kinder but it may be possible to repair minor defects.
- Cleft palate, where the roof of the mouth fails to join during development leaving a gap between the nose and mouth. When the kitten suckles, milk will be seen running down the nose. Again, if extreme, euthanasia is kinder but it may be possible to repair minor defects.
- Atresia ani (absence of an anus) – I have seen this on occasion. Sometimes if the defect is slight, a new anus can be constructed but if a large segment of the colon is missing, euthanasia is essential.
- Undershot/overshot jaws – exaggerated examples may be detected at this stage. An undershot jaw is where the lower jaw is longer than the upper jaw (commoner in Persian type cats) and overshot is where the upper jaw is longer than the lower jaw. Correction is not possible.

Any disruption during development of the foetus can lead to congenital abnormalities of a variety of types. Thus defects in the limbs, head or spine can all be seen, I have even seen a two-headed kitten, but all are uncommon.

The queen will normally settle down contentedly with the kittens but it is essential to ensure that the kittens all suckle the queen on the first day. This is important as her antibody-rich first milk (colostrum) is only produced for a day or two. The kittens can also only absorb these maternal antibodies for two days at the most, so it is essential they receive a good supply

A litter of newborn Birman kittens. Note the eyes are not open at birth.

at this stage to enable them to withstand infections during their first six to twelve weeks of life. They will obtain antibodies to most diseases to which their mother is immune. If the queen is unsure of what to do, hold the kittens on to a teat to encourage them and her.

Make sure that the kittens are having enough to drink. A quiet litter is usually a happy, well-fed litter. It's advisable to weigh the kittens at birth and every few days to ensure they are gaining weight. If any kittens are weaker or not gaining weight, it may be necessary to supplement them with synthetic queen's milk obtainable from your vet or a pet shop, using a foster feeder bottle.

Days 5–21

Contented kittens spend around 90 per cent of their time sleeping for the first few weeks of life and their eyes begin to open seven to ten days after birth. From around three weeks of age they become more adventurous, emerge from the nest box and begin to feed themselves, often sharing some of the queen's solid food before they learn to lap fluids. This is the stage at which to begin to wean them. It is very important at this stage to begin to, and continue to, handle and socialize them within the family if they are to become happy and interactive members of their future families.

Weeks 3–10

By twenty-eight days they should have progressed on to four or five small meals a day and can be fed on palatable mini-kibble-type food, which have a soft texture ideally suited to the milk teeth of young kittens, or on moistened queen's food. In this way a kitten can successfully be weaned from milk to solids.

To control roundworms, the BSAVA recommends that worming of kittens should start at six weeks of age, as infection is acquired after birth, and then repeated according to the manufacturers' recommendations until kittens are twelve to fourteen weeks of age – consult your vet, as several products are available but it is important to use a safe one at the correct dose.

Thereafter, worming should be carried out at six months of age and then two to four times a year for the rest of their lives.

Problems in the First Few Weeks: Fading Kitten Syndrome

This is not a disease as such, but a description of what can happen. As the name implies, the kittens begin to fade and die for no apparent reason. A better term is neonatal mortality and covers any death around the time of birth (perinatal mortality) and death during the first few weeks of life, when the kittens are still highly dependent on their mother. The problem is multifactoral, i.e. several possible causes, singly or together. It is essential the vet is consulted. The cause may be hypothermia, infection, lack of food, lack of colostrum, trauma from the queen, roundworms or any stress. Stressed queens will sometimes even kill and eat their own kittens.

Diagnosis. Your vet will need to examine the queen and the litter of kittens and, sadly, it will be helpful if she has a dead kitten on which she can perform a post-mortem examination. It may be necessary to visit the house and check the conditions under which the kittens were born and raised. In case the queen has passed on an infection, blood and other tests may be helpful.

Treatment will depend on the diagnosis, but in all cases it is better to try and prevent any problems by approaching the impending birth and litter-raising fully informed about the likely process and how to handle it.

The Queen

It is important to ensure that the queen is fed an adequate diet during pregnancy and lactation. The best for her is one formulated for kittens, as this contains more than adequate levels of calcium and, indeed, all the other essential nutrients for her to make the milk. Roundworm larvae are passed to the kittens via the milk while they are suckling and this can be minimized by giving a single dose to the queen, during pregnancy, of a wormer containing fenbendazole, which kills the roundworm larvae. Your vet should be consulted for details of dose and timing. As specified above, the kittens should be wormed at six weeks of age and the queen should also be dosed at this time in an attempt to prevent the build-up of a roundworm burden within the litter and its environment.

Post-Kittening Problems

Vaginal Discharge. A mild, greenish-brown discharge is normal for the first few days and may continue for several weeks. Provided the queen is otherwise well, there should be no cause for worry.

Failure of Milk. Sometimes the queen fails to produce milk and the mammary glands dry up. The kittens fail to thrive and cry continuously. It is essential to supplement the kittens by feeding with a foster feeding bottle and synthetic milk.

Mastitis. This can occur in over-enlarged mammary glands. Check daily that no breasts are sore or very hard or hot. If this occurs, the vet must be contacted immediately. (For further details see Chapter 17).

Anxious Behaviour to the Kittens. This can occur in the first day or two and is usually due to stress, or constant moving of the kittens because she is not happy with the kittening site. It is very important to ensure she is in a quiet, secure place before and after she kittens.

Eclampsia. This is an uncommon condition in the cat but, if it occurs, is a serious and potentially fatal condition for the queen. It occurs if the blood calcium level of the queen becomes too low, either due to excessive demands of the kittens through her milk, such as a very large litter, or lack of calcium due to an inadequate diet for the queen during lactation. She begins to show some odd signs – to start with she may just look a little odd, walk stiffly, twitch or shiver and appear unsteady. If left untreated, this progresses to obvious staggering, a wide-eyed frightened expression and possibly convulsions. It is essential that the vet is contacted immediately, as an injection of calcium, usually directly into a vein, is essential to save the life of the queen. The response is dramatic and within a few minutes she is able to stand and walk normally again.

However, once the blood calcium has been this low, the kittens should be weaned from her to ensure the eclampsia does not recur. The time of onset varies but it is usually seen when the kittens are about three weeks old and making maximum demands on her.

Prevention is usually possible by ensuring an adequate diet during pregnancy and lactation. As specified on page 185, the best diet to feed the queen is one formulated for kittens, as this contains more than adequate levels of calcium and all the other essential nutrients for her to make the milk.

THE KITTENS' NEW HOMES

The best age for the kitten to adapt to a new family is between nine and twelve weeks of age, so this is the age at which you should aim to part with them. Remember, the kitten will make a better pet if you and your family have been gently playing with it and handling it. Before parting with a kitten you should:

- Interview the prospective purchasers to ensure they will give him a caring home and that their life-style will suit the kitten as he grows.
- Ensure he is fit and well.
- Prepare a diet sheet to give to the new owners.
- Hand out the vaccination certificate, if the first vaccination has been carried out.
- Write down when the kitten has been wormed and with which wormer.
- Prepare and give to the new owners the pedigree form, if applicable.
- Take out a temporary pet health insurance policy on the kitten, which should last for four to six weeks. This relieves both you and the new owner of the worry of any unforeseen illness or problem in the first few weeks following purchase. The new owner should be advised to continue the insurance, as it is a sensible approach to the medical care of this new family member. Pet insurance is usually reasonable value for money and your vet should be able to discuss the type of insurance that is best for your kitten.

Chapter 19
Feline Behaviour Problems

Caroline Bower

A behaviour problem can spoil the relationship between cat and owner or between pets in the same household. It may also be a sign that your cat is unhappy or stressed, and that there is something wrong with his environment or management. It is, therefore, important that behavioural problems and changes are noticed and treated humanely and effectively without delay. A clear understanding of the normal behaviour and needs of the species will help to prevent many behaviour problems from occurring in the first place (*see* Chapter 2).

Any cat showing a behaviour problem should be thoroughly physically assessed by a veterinary surgeon before any further behavioural investigation takes place. This is an extremely important principle and cannot be too strongly emphasized, because many behaviour problems in the cat are associated with physical disease. In some cases there is concurrent disease, in others the behaviour problem *results* from a clinical condition and continues, even following effective veterinary treatment. Examples will be given throughout this chapter. Also note that, conversely, physical illness can be a *sign* of stress in some (though not all) cats. Examples include recurrent cystitis, inflammatory bowel disease (IBD), asthma and dermatitis.

We will examine the most commonly reported feline behaviour problems here and identify potential causes and remedies. In all behaviour cases, it is important to diagnose the underlying cause of the behaviour and not just treat the signs. Behaviour problems should only be treated by a vet with behavioural expertise or a qualified non-veterinary behaviourist to whom your vet has referred you. In the latter case, your vet should be kept fully informed of the diagnosis and behavioural treatment recommendations, and will be solely responsible should any prescription medication be required.

HOUSE SOILING

This includes any form of urination or defecation in the wrong place within the house. It is one of the most commonly reported cat behaviour problems for obvious reasons, and it can be complex to find the true cause or causes in order to establish an effective treatment programme.

First, it is vital to establish whether or not there is an associated medical condition (*see* Tables overleaf).

Diagnosis of any of the conditions specified in the tables opposite will require a full physical examination by a vet and, in many cases, further tests, such as urine or faeces analysis, radiology and blood tests.

Clearly, these clinical conditions, if present, must be identified by your vet and treated effectively. However, in certain cases, the house soiling may continue after treatment due to the fact that the cat has established new places to toilet, has deposited an associated scent there and may even find the new locations more comfortable and peaceful, thus becoming a behavioural problem.

House soiling may be broadly divided into two categories: inappropriate toileting and marking.

Inappropriate Toileting

This describes voiding of faeces or urine in various locations within the house, and not within the provided litter tray or trays. Some outdoor

Some medical conditions that may cause inappropriate urination

Causes of increased thirst.	Diabetes, kidney disease, and hyperthyroidism.
Causes of increased frequency of urination.	Lower urinary tract disease problems (including bladder stones and cystitis).
Causes of incontinence.	Neurological conditions following spinal or pelvic damage, e.g. arising from a road accident.
Causes affecting locomotion and positioning.	Arthritis, spinal disease, muscle wasting or weakness
Causes of CNS dysfunction.	Brain tumours, senile changes.

Some medical conditions that may cause inappropriate defecation

Causes of increased frequency or diarrhoea.	Colitis or inflammatory bowel disease, constipation, anal gland disease and others causes of pain or difficulty in defecation.
Causes of incontinence.	Neurological conditions following spinal or pelvic damage.
Causes affecting locomotion.	Neurological disorders, arthritis, spinal disease, muscle wasting and weakness.
Causes of CNS dysfunction.	Brain tumours and senile changes.

cats do not have, or use, litter trays at all, as they always toilet outdoors, but may still start to soil the house for a number of reasons. This section assumes that a medical problem has already been ruled out by your vet.

If the cat starts urinating and defecating outside the litter tray, both at the same time, it is likely that there is something about the tray that the cat dislikes. Examples include change of litter, use of a litter type that your cat finds unacceptable, change of litter tray location, soiled litter or disinfectant smell. The tray may be in a location where there is too much traffic of other pets or people. Cats will quickly develop an aversion to using the litter tray if they associate it with a negative experience; for example,

being punished or frightened near the tray or being medicated whilst in the tray.

Some cats will just find a place and substrate they like better!

Outdoor cats who normally toilet in the garden may start soiling in the house for a number of reasons. A common cause is bad weather; cats are not great lovers of wind, rain and stormy weather, and if they avoid such conditions and have no litter tray provided, accidents are inevitable. Another possible cause is intimidation or attack by a neighbouring cat, or some other fear-inducing stimulus, such as building and road works nearby.

If the cat urinates in the tray and defecates elsewhere, or vice versa, be very suspicious initially of an underlying medical problem or, alternatively, marking behaviour (*see* overleaf). In the latter case, observe closely for the pattern of soiling and also watch for any other changes, such as alteration of temperament, increased vigilance, avoidance or aggression. This is covered in the section on marking (*see* overleaf).

Treatment of Inappropriate Toileting

The details depend on an understanding of the underlying cause but there are some important common basic principles:

- Remove the cause.
- Re-establish toileting in the correct place.
- Deny access to previously soiled areas for a few weeks.
- Do not punish the cat as this is counter-productive and may lead to other, more serious problems.

Removal of the cause and re-establishing appropriate habits may mean moving the litter tray to a more private place, well away from noise and disturbance, using a different kind of litter tray (a cover, increased size or lower sides may help), different litter in order to re-establish the right habit (soft litters like sand, fine gravel and peat are very appealing to cats) or cleaning the tray more often. Avoid using strong-smelling disinfectants in litter trays unless they are thoroughly rinsed and dried afterwards.

Ensure there is one more litter tray than the number of cats in the house. Ensure there are no aversive stimuli in the outdoor environment or provide a tray for the cat who usually toilets outdoors.

It may well be necessary to confine the cat to a restricted area for a number of weeks, as the cat is more likely to use the litter tray if he has fewer other options around the house. In particular, shut doors into areas where the cat has regularly soiled. Remove the cat from confinement regularly to play and socialize but always replace in the confined area when you are not supervising or interacting with him. Within the area keep the litter tray as far away as possible from his food, water and bed. It can help to give praise, attention and a food reward after the cat finishes toileting.

It is vital to remove the smell from the soiled areas. Clean up any visible urine or faeces. Then use warm water and soak up deposits on to a paper towel. Next use biological products that are specially designed to break down the organic matter and neutralize the scent. Your vet should be able to advise you which one to use. Do not use products that merely disguise the scent with a strong perfume or are based on ammonium compounds, as these smell like urine to the cat. Remember that the cat's sense of smell is a thousand times more sensitive than ours, so effective cleaning is imperative.

When the cat gains access to the previously soiled areas again, try to change the cat's use of these. This may be done by either making the area less appealing, e.g. by placing plastic sheets or aluminium foil on the floor, or changing the association by placing food and water bowls or toys there. Each cat is an individual and you may have to experiment with this a bit before you find the right formula.

We have not explored every possibility here, so it is always best to discuss such problems with your vet first, and to gain reliable advice from the vet or behaviourist.

Some cats prefer a covered litter tray giving more privacy.

Marking

When a cat marks with urine, he or she will stand with the rear end directed towards an upright object, tail held vertically and quivering, and spray a stream of urine at the surface. Paddling of the back legs may also occur.

Most marking behaviour consists of urine spraying, but some cat will also deposit urine or faeces on horizontal surfaces. This can make the picture more confusing. If toileting on horizontal surfaces is used as for marking purposes, the deposit is usually left in a very obvious place, e.g. by a door. Conversely, inappropriate toileting can be random and often in a hidden location, e.g. behind or under furniture, which can help in distinguishing between the two types of house soiling.

Upright surfaces and novel objects are usually marked, and electrical items seem to be appealing, probably because when they are warm the urine smell is enhanced! Urine spraying is the normal form of urination in a small proportion of cats, i.e. these cats never squat. Cats may also use urine spraying when they find it painful to squat, e.g. due to arthritis or pain in the lower urinary tract.

Marking is more frequent in males than females, and is also much more common in entire (un-neutered) individuals of both sexes. It is more frequently found in cats in multi-cat households, with the incidence increasing in proportion to the density of the cat population. It is vital to confirm or refute any underlying medical cause in the case of the marking cat, as has already been stated.

Remember that scent marking is normal for cats in their wider territory, but that marking in the core territory is considered as a behaviour problem because it is unacceptable to humans and also because it may signify some underlying psychological disturbance in the cat, in particular stress.

Marking may be territorial, sexual (in the case of entire males and females), attention-seeking (more common in Orientals) or stress-related.

Territorial instincts are very strong in some individuals, and it can be difficult to prevent persistent territory marking. There may also be a significant overlap between territorial and stress-related marking, e.g. if the neighbours have a new cat. Neutering is advisable to prevent sexual marking in both sexes.

Cats that attention-seek by marking tend to do this in full view of the owners, often accompanied by other behaviours, such as hyperactivity, vocalization or disruptive behaviour.

Stress is the most common cause of marking behaviour in domestic cats. Certain individual cats are genetically programmed to cope badly with stressful situations or environments. If these cats are also poorly socialized as kittens and live in an environment that does not satisfy their needs, marking is one behaviour that may result.

The cat may mark in a random fashion or mark specific objects repeatedly. Marking of the owners is usually a sign of a very upset cat, whose owners are perhaps behaving in an unpredictable or threatening manner as far as the cat is concerned, e.g. by punishing the cat. Marking

This cat is marking a chair.

of the owner's bedding or clothes can signify that this is the only place the cat feels safe.

Common stressors for cats include the following:

- Cat-unfriendly environment, e.g. lack of choices to rest, escape, hide and feed, too much disturbance or noise, lack of stimulation.
- Changes in the environment, such as arrival of a new cat, new baby, visitors, building and decorating work, new furniture.
- Social unrest or conflict within a group of cats in the same household.
- Intimidation or attack from neighbouring cats or dogs.
- Building or road works outside.
- Inappropriate punishment.
- Too much attention from the owner, and at times which do not suit the cat.
- Too little attention from the owner.
- Changes of routine, e.g. Christmas.

Behaviours that can be caused by stress include:

- Indoor toileting and marking.
- Over-attachment.
- Under-attachment.
- Aggression.
- Excessive grooming and self-mutilation, compulsive disorders.

Medical conditions that can be caused by stress include:

- Lower urinary tract disease.
- Asthma.
- Inflammatory bowel syndrome.
- Chronic skin disease.

Treatment of Marking Behaviour

It is essential to try to establish the cause and, of course, to ensure your vet has ruled out medical problems first. Then the principles are to remove the cause, break the habit and do not punish the cat.

Removal of the scent of urine or faeces in the cat's environment is essential in all cases (*see* section on treatment of inappropriate toileting, page 189).

Sexual marking is treated by neutering, but the cat may also need to be denied access to marked areas for a number of weeks.

In the case of the attention-seeker, it will be necessary to look at the cat's whole life-style, how much stimulation and interaction he has with you or other pets and how to restructure this so that he does not need, or receive, attention from you in response to the unwanted behaviour. Attention-seekers may be bored or frustrated and lacking in adequate opportunities to exercise, play and investigate an interesting environment.

Territorial markers can be helped by looking closely at the environment and behaviour of other cats within and outside the home. It is important to prevent other cats in the area from entering your house and from spending time in your garden or looking through your windows. Your cat is likely to be stressed by these cats and closing curtains or blinds to reduce visual contact can help. The use of water pistols and sound aversion, such as a whistle or shaker can (made from an empty soft drink can with pebbles inside and the hole taped over), may help, but be careful not to scare your own cat. Avoid leaving food down in areas which may attract other cats.

Where it appears that stress is the underlying cause, you must look at everything you can do to encourage the cat to be more relaxed and feel less threatened. Look closely at the environment and facilities provided that make it cat-friendly or otherwise (*see* Chapter 2). A pheromone diffuser or spray, Feliway, can also help to enhance security of the cat's environment. Your vet should be able to advise on the correct use of these and may suggest other treatments, such as herbal remedies or medications that reduce anxiety. Remove any specific causes of stress or ensure the cat can remove itself from the stress-inducing situation. For example, if the cat is distressed by a new baby crying, let him retreat to another room with raised surfaces. If you have two cats that don't get on well, think of ways in which they can more easily avoid spending time together or consider re-homing one of them, for their own sakes.

If the cat is spraying because standing seems to be his preferred toileting position, ask your vet to check there is no pain causing this, and try using a covered litter tray or stand one tray vertically against another so that urine trickles down inside the cover.

AGGRESSION

Aggressive cats can pose a danger to humans or other pets, and some forms of aggression also indicate that the cat has an underlying health or welfare problem, so the problem must be treated seriously. Some common causes of aggression will be covered here but a full review is beyond the scope of this book. Owners with aggressive cats are advised to seek professional help; not only is a cat bite painful, but it can lead to infection and breakdown of the relationship between the cat and other cats or humans. Owners with young children or those with a deficient immune system must seek help immediately. If the aggressive cat is targeting another pet, the welfare of that animal must be protected.

The cat may growl, hiss or bite and once aroused will take at least 30 minutes to calm down. Meanwhile he is unpredictable and should be left alone until settled.

As with all behaviour problems, medical causes must first be ruled out by your vet.

Medical causes of aggression include:

- Irritability caused by liver or kidney disorders, or hormonal disease such as hyperthyroidism.
- Painful conditions caused by spinal disease or arthritis, dental disease, headache (may be related to high blood pressure or CNS tumour), trauma, abscesses and bite wounds, ear infection.
- Changes of temperament related to CNS disturbance or senile changes.

Treatment. The cause must be identified and treated. Meanwhile, precautions should be taken to avoid the situations in which the cat shows aggression, to prevent escalation of the problem. An example would be to stop grooming or handling a cat with arthritis of the spine or hips until the pain is adequately controlled. If

The use of two trays is helpful if a cat urinates standing up.

handling cannot be avoided, it must be done in such a way as to minimize pain.

If the aggression is not due to a medical cause, there are a number of possible non-medical types of aggression.

Play Aggression

This tends to develop in the kitten or young cat that may also have a strong hunting and predatory instinct. Some kittens appear to be genetically programmed to be more boisterous and aggressive in their play patterns than others, and if these individuals do not have the correct social interaction with humans or other cats, they may continue to bite in an uninhibited way as adults. Affected cats typically stalk, pounce and bite moving hands, feet or other parts of the body of humans or play aggressively with another cat. The other cat may be older, fearful or weaker. Hand-reared orphan kittens often have boisterous or aggressive play patterns.

Treatment
- Avoid punishment.
- Do not encourage kittens or cats to play with your hands or feet or allow biting.

- Encourage play with a variety of moving objects, such a balls, soft toys and windup objects.
- Give the cat more suitable activities, such as time outdoors climbing or harness-walking, if this is an indoor cat.
- Interrupt aggression using a shaker can. Dropping or sharply shaking the can at the time of aggression is an aversive stimulus.
- If the aggression is towards another cat, separate them except when closely supervised. Reward calm, non-aggressive behaviour using tasty food rewards and praise.
- In a single-cat household it can help to introduce another cat of similar age if the original cat is still young.

Fear Aggression

This may result when the cat feels threatened by a person, animal or other stimulus. Fearful behaviour patterns include hissing and growling, ears flat back, pupils widely dilated, body crouched down with tail tucked underneath. If a cat in a fearful posture is approached or handled, he may attack.

Fear aggression is influenced by a number of factors including genetic predisposition, early upbringing and socialization (e.g. comprehensive handling by a variety of genders and ages of people helps prevent it), certain stress factors in the environment, or aversive events, e.g. a cat may develop a fear of children in general if handled roughly by a child.

In general, treatment of fear aggression requires great care and patience and the outcome is not always favourable.

Treatment
- Avoid punishment.
- Identify the fear-eliciting stimulus and prevent close contact.
- Introduce a desensitization and counter-conditioning programme to gradually reduce the cat's fear of the stimulus. This involves controlled exposure to the stimulus. For example, if a cat is afraid of women, he may be placed in a large pen in the corner of a room, partially covered with a blanket initially. A woman may enter the room but not approach the pen or look at the cat. If the cat shows no fearful or aggressive behaviour, he can be rewarded with a tasty food treat. Day

A cat showing aggression.

by day the woman may move slightly closer to the pen before the reward is given, and eventually the cat may be allowed out, perhaps on a harness or on his owner's lap while treats are given. Other women need to be involved if the cat is to lose his general fear of women. This type of programme is best conducted under professional supervision.

- In the case of inter-cat aggression, do not allow the cats together unsupervised. This type of aggression can be very difficult to cure, and help from a behaviourist will be needed.
- Consider using a pheromone diffuser in the cat's environment to reduce anxiety.
- Certain herbal remedies or prescription medicines may be recommended in severe cases.

Petting-Induced Aggression

This is shown by certain cats when they are being stroked or on the owner's lap. These cats invite attention, perhaps by jumping up on a lap, but after a length of time bite the owner. This is particularly unpleasant because the owner is blissfully unaware that it is about to happen! It seems that some cats have a low tolerance of prolonged physical contact and, in fact, many cats tend to enjoy short, relatively frequent bouts of attention from the owner throughout the day. Unfortunately this does not always match the wishes of the owner, especially if they work all day and want undivided loving attention from the cat all evening. Even affectionate cats may have times when they want to be left alone.

Before biting, the cat may become rather tense, the ears may flatten down or he may flick his tail and become restless.

First, ensure there is no physical reason why the cat may resent being handled or petted (*see* medical causes of aggression on page 188).

Treatment
- Do not punish or force attention on the cat.
- Do not restrain or confine him.
- When giving attention, ensure it is for a shorter period than that which normally seems to provoke aggression.

- Before his aggression threshold is reached, gently move him away or move away from him, and reward him with a tasty food treat. A short play session is another type of reward, if the cat enjoys play more than food. It can also help to hand-feed from a bowl at the same time as stroking the cat.
- In the early stages it is best to ignore all attention-seeking from the cat and invite him to have contact with you when you want it. If he is not interested do not pursue the contact.

Redirected Aggression

This occurs when a cat is aggressive to a person or animal, but some other stimulus actually triggers it. For example, a cat may be watching a neighbour's cat through the window intruding on his lawn. He cannot attack the cat, but his aggression is aroused and he then attacks the next animal or person who touches him or moves near him. Unusual noises, smells, pain and unfamiliar environments may also trigger aggression in certain cats. It can happen at the veterinary surgery when the vet gives an injection and the cat bites the owner.

This type of aggression is often very severe, and significant, uninhibited biting occurs, as well as considerable distress to the victim. The cat is highly aroused, unpredictable and bite wounds can be deep and multiple. It is, therefore, recommended that professional help is sought in all such cases.

ATTACHMENT PROBLEMS

Owners become concerned if their cat is not behaving as they expect it to. To some extent this is because every cat is an individual and owners may have unrealistic expectations of their cat's behaviour, or may be expecting the cat to behave exactly like their previous pet. This is no more likely to happen than two children in the same family behaving in exactly the same way. As already stated, behaviour depends on a wide range of factors, including genetic traits, the kitten's early environment and socialization, the cat's current home environment, and behaviour of other pets and family members.

Object-related play —
kittens with balls.

Under-attachment is described as a lack of bonding between cat and owner, and there are varying degrees of this. For example, a farm cat who comes into the kitchen to feed and then lives the rest of the time outdoors and has very little contact with people, will have a weak bond with the human who feeds him, if any bond at all. If a new owner takes on such a cat it will be very difficult to establish a bond with him, he may not tolerate handling and the owner is likely to be dissatisfied if they were hoping for a lap cat to cuddle. However, he will probably be a great mouser! In this situation, a great deal of time and patience must be dedicated to building up his trust, and desensitizing and counter-conditioning him to the owner's presence and touch. In time the cat may tolerate short bouts of contact and affection, but may avoid all visitors and strangers. The bond is built up through the use of food; small frequent meals of highly palatable food are offered and the owner stands nearby initially but day by day begins to touch the cat while feeding. It is essential to go at whatever pace is comfortable for the cat, and forcing attention on him will be counter-productive. The use of a pheromone plug, Feliway, in the room and the pheromone wipe, Felifriend, on the owner's wrists may help.

Over-attachment is when the bond is so strong that the cat seems unable to cope with separation from the attachment figure. This can happen in the case of a hand-reared kitten, a cat with a single owner who spends all day with him, in anxious individuals or as part of an age-related syndrome (*see* overleaf). Affected individuals may constantly demand attention, may vocalize a great deal, whether the owner is present or absent, and try to follow the owner everywhere. Unfortunately when the cat cries around the owner, many people will assume he is hungry and will feed him every time, resulting in obesity and consequent health problems.

Interestingly, over-attachment behaviour can also be a human problem, with over-attached cat owners insisting on stroking, following and feeding their cats all the time. This can be a significant source of stress for the cat that could then begin to show signs associated with stress, such as excessive grooming, LUTD or even marking activity. Most cats prefer attention in short, frequent bouts and they are not always in the mood!

It is important to identify any stimulus that may be causing anxiety, or other factors that have led to over-attachment. Treatment then depends on removing any adverse factors in the environment and changing the way owner and cat interact. Short bouts of physical contact, small, measured feeds at specific times of day (or alternatively, if using an all-dry diet, provide half the ration in the morning and half in the evening, and allow the cat to help himself to small meals with no human interaction), and a change of emphasis to more play and less cuddling. Involving another person in the cat's care will also help, so the cat is not totally dependent on one individual. The owner–cat relationship should be fun and pleasant for both parties, and is generally much healthier as a result.

EXCESSIVE GROOMING, RIPPLING SKIN AND SELF-MUTILATION

Fastidious grooming is a habit of most normal, healthy cats but, on occasions, it can become a compulsive habit and the cat will groom himself so intensely and frequently that he spends most of his waking hours indulging in this activity. Affected cats may lose weight and develop secondary alopecia (hair loss) or skin inflammation in certain areas. Other cats may self-mutilate by biting certain parts of the body, such as the tail, and others may develop rippling or twitchy skin leading to agitation, intense grooming or hyperactivity.

There are many medical conditions that may cause irritation of the skin or even pain in areas below the skin, such as the spine or tail. These include flea allergic dermatitis, allergies, skin infections, spinal lesions, abscesses, tumour formation and arthritis. Your vet must examine and investigate these cases very carefully before assuming a non-medical cause.

Non-medical causes include stress, boredom, anxiety and frustration. As with the other conditions discussed, it is essential to identify the underlying cause of the behaviour and then try to remove the cause. The cat's environment and routine must be optimized, and management may also involve use of medication, especially in cases where the cat is either obviously distressed or the lesions are severe. Professional help should be sought.

AGE-RELATED CHANGES

Old age is likely to be accompanied by changes in behaviour, some of which are totally normal and to be expected. For example, older cats tend to sleep more and are generally less active. However, some behaviours are indicative of either sensory loss, physical disease or senile brain changes.

Sensory loss may include loss of hearing, vision, sense of smell and taste, all of which can affect the way the cat responds to its environment, owners and diet. For example, a deaf or blind cat may crave the owner's presence or be startled and even aggressive when touched or picked up.

There is a plethora of physical and medical conditions associated with old age (though not exclusively), which are covered in earlier chapters; these include kidney, heart and liver disease, hyperthyroidism, arthritis, diabetes, vestibular disease and CNS tumours, all of which can significantly alter the cat's behaviour. Regular veterinary examinations, preferably twice yearly, are advisable when your cat reaches the age of ten. Blood and urine tests may also be advised by your vet.

Senile brain changes can lead to restlessness and alterations of sleep patterns, anxiety, aggression, excessive vocalization, changes in interaction with people and other cats, breakdown of litter training and disorientation. However, a number of these behaviours may also be caused by medical conditions and sensory loss, so always consult your vet before making any assumptions. Often the cat has a combination of sensory, medical and senile problems, and it is important to take a multi-pronged approach to improve the cat's health and welfare.

If all medical and sensory conditions have been ruled out or effectively controlled first, there are a number of treatments that can help senile cats. In general, maintain an optimum, low-stress and controlled environment. Old, senile cats do not like surprises. Initiate regular, short sessions of play or interaction of some sort, talk to the cat and give regular physical contact, avoid giving attention on demand, ensure the cat has a warm, comfortable, safe place to rest. Feed frequent small, palatable meals and never punish the cat.

Anxiety. In addition to the ideas above, anxious individuals may benefit from pheromone diffusers in the environment, anxiolytic herbal remedies and occasionally may need prescription medicines.

Excessive vocalization and restlessness at night. The old, vocal cat is often also restless at night, thus managing to keep the whole household awake! In such cases it may be possible to alter diurnal rhythm by increasing stimulation and activity during the day. Avoid responding to vocalization in a positive way, e.g. by feeding or stroking. Ensure the cat has all his functional needs attended to, in terms of ready access to food and water, litter tray and a warm, secure bed. Cat igloos or placing the bed near a radiator overnight can help.

House soiling. This may occur because the senile cat is disorientated and is confused about where the litter tray is. Medical conditions, such as arthritis and other problems related to mobility, or diseases causing increased urination, defecation or incontinence are obviously potentially significant. As with house soiling in younger cats, stress factors can be significant and must be addressed.

Other behavioural-management ideas include provision of more litter trays, low sided and larger trays, more frequent cleaning, and the use of litter that is more attractive to the cat. Appropriate cleaning of soiled areas is also important, denying access to soiled areas for a few weeks and, if necessary, confinement to a smaller area to encourage ready access to and use of the litter tray.

Aggression. Older cats may become grumpy, especially with other pets, and aggression can also be a sign of anxiety or fear. One of the most common causes is the addition of another cat to the household, especially a very playful cat or kitten, whose agenda is very different from that of the resident old-timer. This must be managed according to guidelines for introducing a new cat in Chapter 4.

Chapter 20
First Aid – Accidents and Emergencies

First aid is the immediate emergency care given to a cat that has just suffered a serious injury or illness. It will usually be a sudden, unexpected emergency, and you may have to provide first aid prior to seeking veterinary help. The aims of first aid are threefold: to keep the cat alive; to prevent unnecessary suffering; and to prevent further injury.

Where a sudden, acute injury or illness has occurred and you are not fully certain of the best immediate action, the wisest course is to contact the vet immediately and follow her instructions. You may well be advised to take the cat to the practice immediately, but in some cases, there are immediate life-saving actions that you can and should take first. Unless you are sure

that what you are doing is in the cat's interest, then the most effective course of action will be to transport the cat safely and comfortably to the vet practice.

However, there are some emergency situations where the owner or finder has to act, and where first-aid action is appropriate and safe, they are included in this chapter. First-aid kits are available at most vets and pet shops, and any cat owner would be advised to have one of these in a safe but memorable place at home.

Priorities of successful first aid:

• Keep calm. If you panic, you will only waste valuable time and be unable to help effectively.

One way to carry an injured cat.

- Contact your local vet practice or the nearest one as soon as possible, as you may get advice that could save the cat's life.
- Avoid injury to yourself from a painful, distressed or injured cat, which may bite or scratch you because it is hurt. To avoid this, lift him gently but firmly by the scruff of the neck with one hand and support his rump with your other hand. Then cover him in a towel or blanket before picking him up. By limiting the cat's movement in this way you will also prevent further damage to him.
- Locate and stop any haemorrhage by pressure, as blood loss can lead to shock and death.
- Make sure the cat can breathe and that his windpipe is not obstructed. If he cannot breathe, brain damage or death can occur within five minutes.
- Let him lie in his most comfortable position.

It is a wise precaution to assemble a first-aid kit for your cat at home, or purchase one, in case you need to help him unexpectedly and urgently. A suggestion as to the contents, in addition to a cat box in which to transport him, would be as follows:

- Phone numbers:
  - your own vet or, if they are not on 24hr call,
  - the nearest emergency veterinary clinic.
- Thermometer (your cat's temperature should not rise above 103°F/39.4°C or fall below 100°F/37.8°C).
- Sterile lint and bandages.
- Adhesive tape.
- Tweezers.
- Petroleum jelly.
- Antiseptic lotion.
- Cotton balls or swabs.
- Splints.
- Towels.
- Torch.
- Scissors – blunt-ended.
- Thin-ended pliers.
- Plastic eyedropper or syringe.
- Sterile saline solution.
- Latex gloves.
- Nail clippers.

TRANSPORTING AN INJURED CAT

As mentioned in Chapter 4, every cat owner should have a cat-carrier basket or box for use in routine transport to the veterinarian or cattery, so hopefully this will be available in any emergency occurring at or near home. If not, a large zipper bag, picnic hamper or the like will suffice. Take care when moving injured cats, as it is very easy to make the situation worse. A cat can usually be lifted gently into a cat-carrier and then driven to the surgery. If a broken leg or spinal injury is suspected, it is often better not to try to splint or support it, but just to ensure the cat is lying comfortably in a blanket in the cat-carrier. If a broken spine is suspected, the cat must only be moved with great care and transported on a rigid board or even a road atlas if that is all that is available.

Drive slowly and carefully to the vet having telephoned first to ensure the vet will be there

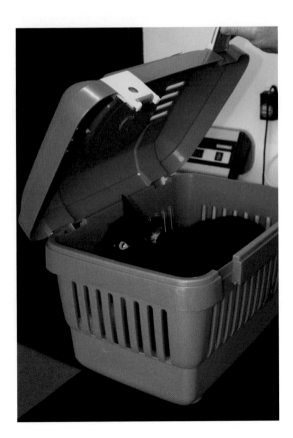

Top-opening cat-carrier.

and expecting you. Ensure the cat is not subjected to excessive sudden movements that will cause pain and may do more damage than a slightly longer drive would have done.

SOME PROBLEMS REQUIRING FIRST AID

Road Traffic Accident (RTA)

Cats are involved in road traffic accidents more commonly than dogs because they are rarely on a collar and lead, and venture quite a way on their own, crossing many roads in some cases. It may not always be immediately obvious that your cat has been in an accident, as the potential injuries can be so variable, so if he seems to be behaving oddly and looks a bit dishevelled, wet or muddy, suspect an RTA and look for grazes or oil marks on him. The claws may be frayed due to landing or tumbling on the road surface, and he will often be lame or unable to walk on his hind legs or to move his tail. He may even just creep home and hide away somewhere, not being spotted until some time after the accident.

Action. If he just has the odd graze and can walk well and doesn't seem unwell, gently bathe any sore areas in warm saline or dilute disinfectant to avoid infection, but then watch him carefully for a while to check that he doesn't deteriorate and that shock does not set in. If you are at all worried about his condition, contact your vet and transport him as described above. There are very few instances where the vet needs to come to you — cats are generally very easy to transport and the vet will have far better facilities and assistance at the surgery, meaning that your cat will receive better and quicker attention there.

Air-Gun Pellet Wound

If you suspect that your cat has been shot, clip the hair around the wound to make it easy to locate and gently apply a wad of warm, wet cotton wool to prevent any haemorrhage. Then contact your vet as soon as possible. The pellet may be located by your vet palpating the area or by X-ray — two views, one from the side and one from above, are required to locate the pellet (or indeed any 'foreign body' within the animal). The pellet may be removed or left in place, depending where it was lodged. Depending on where the cat was shot, this could be very serious and shock may ensue.

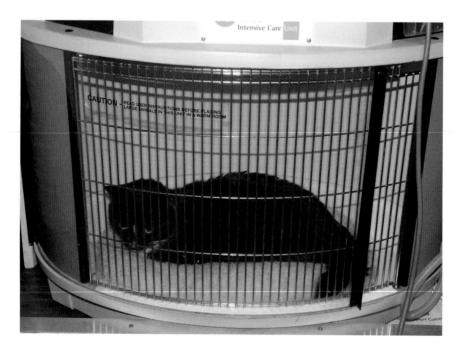

A road accident cat in an intensive care unit.

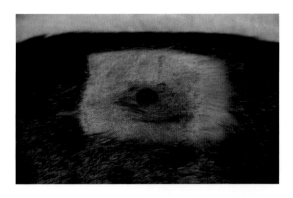

Air-gun pellet wound in the skin.

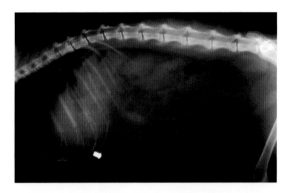

An X-ray of a cat hit by an air gun pellet.

Shock

Shock often follows a road traffic accident or other severe trauma, such as a dog attack or an air gun injury, and is a complicated and serious clinical syndrome. It leads to an inadequate blood supply to vital organs, and all the actions you undertake in first aid are to prevent or minimize this shock, which can and does cause death. Indeed, it is shock not a broken bone that is the major cause of death after a road accident, and the possibility of delayed shock means that most road accident victims should have a thorough examination and often a short stay in the surgery.

Signs of Shock
- Unconsciousness or extreme weakness.
- Pale gums.
- Skin feels cold as do extremities, such as ears.
- A rapid heart beat and weak pulse.
- Rapid shallow breathing.

Causes of Shock
Shock is usually caused by a massive blood loss, as a result of haemorrhage. This may be obvious if on the surface or from any of the cat's orifices, but may not be apparent if the bleeding is internal. Shock can also be caused by the large fluid loss caused by burns and scalds. Severe stress or trauma, such as the extensive injuries and pain following a road accident, can also lead to shock.

First-Aid Treatment of Shock
Ensure that the cat continues to breathe by clearing the airway and give mouth-to-mouth resuscitation if he seems to have stopped breathing. Cup his face in your hands and blow down the nostrils about every three seconds. If the heart appears to have stopped, try to give external massage by pressing the chest between your hands with the cat lying on his side, at the rate of sixty times per minute.

Control any haemorrhage, as any further blood loss may be critical. Keep the cat warm by wrapping him in a blanket or a coat, and lay him on his side with his head lower than the rest of his body to encourage flow of blood to the brain, and to ensure he does not breathe in any blood or saliva.

The Veterinary Surgeon's Approach
As the main effect of shock is to reduce the volume of circulating blood, the vet will correct this as a matter of priority by giving a transfusion of a plasma substitute, saline or even whole blood, if available and necessary. This is dripped slowly into a vein, usually in the cat's foreleg or jugular vein in the neck, in the surgery under supervision. As a transfusion may take hours to correct the shock, the cat would usually be hospitalized for some time for this procedure, during which time he must be monitored closely by a vet or veterinary nurse. In the hospital, once the drip is set up, the cat would be kept warm under an infra-red lamp or on an electric blanket, together with adequate bedding to prevent heat loss.

Burns and Scalds

This can happen when a cat walks on to a hot hob, knocks over a pan full of hot oil or

A relaxed cat with an intravenous drip in progress.

water, or boiling water is inadvertently spilt on to him. The skin is rapidly killed by high temperature, so immediate action is needed.

Action. Immediately cool the skin down using cold, running water, if possible, or cover the area gently with a cloth or towel soaked in cold water. Do not apply anything else to the burnt area. Contact the vet immediately and take the cat to the surgery.

Burns, however, can also be caused by friction, oil, tar and other corrosive chemicals.

Action. Chemical burns should be bathed gently with warm water to wash away any remains of the chemical. If the skin appears injured, then make arrangements to see your vet. It is essential that these chemicals are completely removed, even by clipping, if necessary, as cats groom themselves very thoroughly and will take the chemical into their mouths and may swallow some. This can lead to mouth or internal damage (*see* under Poisonings, page 205).

Electrocution

Kittens especially are very inquisitive and sometimes will investigate and chew through a live electric cable. This can cause severe electrical burns to the mouth and lips, as well as cardiac arrest and death.

Action. In all cases *switch off the electricity first or you may also be electrocuted*, or at least push him away from the electrical supply with a wooden broom or even a chair. If he is not breathing, try artificial respiration by gently pressing his chest but he should be taken to the vet as soon as possible.

Foreign Body in Mouth

Fish bones and other small bones, especially cooked chicken bones, can become wedged between the teeth or in the throat. This is very uncomfortable or painful for the cat that will usually begin to paw at his mouth, salivate excessively and move his jaw as if chewing.

Action. If you can see and reach the object with your fingers or with a pair of tweezers, it may be possible to remove it; but take care not to get bitten. A short piece of wood, such as a piece of doweling, placed across his mouth between the upper and lower jaws should enable you to remove the object safely. If you can see but cannot reach such a foreign body, or suspect one based on the above signs, call the vet immediately.

Fish Hooks

These can lodge inside the mouth or in the skin when cats eat fish left around with the fish hook still in it. Because the hook has a barb on the point, do not try to pull it out, as this will be impossible without tearing the cat's tissue, which will be very painful.

Action. If you can reach the hook, either push it on through the tissue, if possible, or cut the hook in two with pliers, pincers or a hacksaw, and then push the barbed end forwards and through. If you cannot remove the hook, take the cat to the vet. If fishing line leads into the mouth, do not pull it but leave it in place and take him to the vet. *Do not cut the line* as this will make it more difficult for the vet to trace and remove the hook.

Bee and Wasp Stings

These often occur in the summer, as inquisitive kittens and adult cats try to play with, or paw at, these insects. This means that most stings are in, or around, the mouth or front feet. The sting hurts, so the cat paws at his mouth or licks his foot, and a painful swelling usually appears.

Action. Wasps withdraw their sting and fly away. The sting is alkaline, so bathe the area with an acid such as vinegar. Bees, however, leave the sting in the cat, and then die. If you can locate it, remove the sting with tweezers. It looks like a dark short hair with a tiny bit of bee flesh on the free end. Bee stings are acid, so bathe with an alkaline such as bicarbonate of soda.

I remember which to use by VW (Vinegar Wasp) and BB (Bee Bicarbonate)!

Heat Stroke

Occurs in hot weather, or other hot situations, often in cats shut in cars or other small enclosed glass areas, such as greenhouses, and especially where there is not enough ventilation. It is an acute emergency: for instance, in a car with the windows all closed on a summer's day, where the outside temperature is, say, 21°C, the greenhouse effect rapidly increases the temperature inside the car to over 35°C or more. Within minutes the cat can be in severe distress, gasping for breath, wild eyed and, if not cooled down rapidly, can die.

Action. The cat's body temperature will be very high (43°C or more), so he must be immediately removed from the heat, placed in the shade and cooled in a cold bath or with a running hose-pipe. When he is no longer distressed, he should be moved to, and kept in, a cool place. As he will be somewhat dehydrated, water should be offered for him to drink as soon as he is capable. If he does not recover rapidly after this first-aid treatment, or if you would prefer a vet to be involved, contact your local surgery; but always try to cool him down first.

Drowning

Even though cats rarely enter water voluntarily, they can swim quite well, but they can become trapped, e.g. in a swimming pool, or be chased in by a dog and unable to get out. If they can't escape, they will become tired and may drown.

Action. If you think there is any chance that the cat is still alive, hold him upside down by his hind legs and gently swing him to and fro. This should enable any water in the lungs to run out, and the swinging motion can also act as a method of artificial respiration.

Fits and Convulsions

Convulsions occur out of the blue, when you are least expecting them, especially if it is the first one you have seen. The cat will usually go rigid, then start to twitch all over and be unable to stand. This may last for a few seconds, several minutes or even longer (*see* Chapter 14).

Action. It is important immediately to prevent him from damaging himself during the fit, so carefully wrap him in a blanket and hold him gently but firmly. When the fit is over, or if it seems to be lasting for more than a few minutes, contact your vet for advice.

Haemorrhage (Bleeding)

With surface wounds, stop or slow down the bleeding by applying pressure at the bleeding point with your thumb, or with a pressure bandage. This latter is probably the better method, if you have any material available. Place a pad of cotton wool, handkerchief or cloth against the wound and tightly bandage around it. If the bleeding still continues despite this, apply another dressing on top of the first. If the bleeding continues worryingly, a tourniquet may be useful on the legs or the tail. In this case, tie a narrow piece of cloth around the leg above the wound fairly tightly until the bleeding stops. Do not use string or elastic, as these would constrict the circulation too much. *Tourniquets should not be left on longer than fifteen minutes at a time.* If the bleeding is serious, or doesn't stop, contact your vet immediately.

For internal bleeding, keep the animal quiet and warm. Minimize any movement and seek veterinary assistance, as soon as possible.

Cuts, Bites and Deep Scratches

Minor injuries should be bathed in warm, saline solution or a dilute, household disinfectant, and more extensive ones should be then examined by a vet. Bite wounds from other cats are often deep, penetrating wounds, as they are caused by the long canine tooth. These should always be taken seriously, as they invariably lead to abscesses due to bacteria on the cat's tooth being taken through the skin into the deeper tissues. The small opening rapidly closes over with a blood clot, which traps the infection in and a painful abscess almost always results. You should always bathe such a wound to keep it open, but as such a high proportion of these wounds develop abscesses, I recommend that you take a bitten cat to the vet for antibiotic treatment.

Iliac Thrombosis / Heart Failure

This should be suspected if your cat suddenly becomes very distressed, cries loudly and continuously, and usually can't move. What has happened is that a part of a clot or thrombus on a heart valve has broken off, been carried down the main aorta and lodged where this divides into the two main, but smaller, arteries to the hind legs. The cat also cannot usually

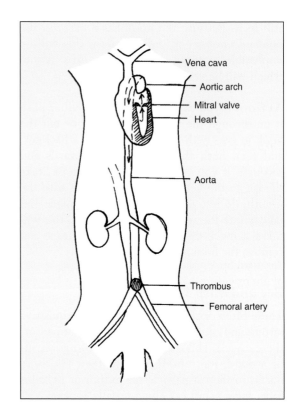

Fig 47 *Iliac thrombosis.*

move his hind legs and has no pulse in the affected leg(s). His breathing will be mouth breathing and panicky, and his gums and tongue will be pale or blue. It is a very painful and acute emergency.

Action. Ensure he can breathe and has a good air supply, gently lie him down on his side, or however he is most comfortable, in a cat-carrier and immediately take him to the surgery, having alerted them that you are on your way, regardless of the time of day or night. Your vet will examine him and decide on the best course of action. Surgery to remove the clot is only sometimes possible, especially as an affected cat also has a severe heart problem, which may not have been suspected before this emergency (*see also* page 96).

Nose Bleed (Epistaxis)

This may be caused by a knock or by violent

sneezing, or may be a sign of an underlying medical problem.

Action. Keep the cat quiet and, if possible, hold a small ice pack on his nose. Contact your vet if the bleeding persists.

Ruptured Eye

This is an acute emergency and usually happens after a cat or dog fight, or a road traffic accident. The cat will be in severe pain and keep his eye tightly closed, but fluid from inside the eye will leak out and down his face.

Action. Speed is essential, so gently place a pad of lint or cotton wool soaked in lukewarm water over his eye, hold it in place and immediately contact your local vet.

Poisonings

As cats are fastidious groomers, poisonings are more likely by licking poisonous chemicals off the coat, either obtained by accidentally contacting the chemical or by the owner using an unsuitable and dangerous parasite medication meant for other species. Cats rarely take in poisons by mouth voluntarily, but there are a few exceptions.

If you suspect any poisoning, when contacting the vet or taking your cat in, always take the suspected poison packet or container, or other details in with you, or inform the practice over the telephone. Veterinary surgeons have reference books with poison antidotes listed and they also have the knowledge and ability to telephone various Poison Information Centres for advice. Any case of suspected poisoning should be dealt with by a vet to give the cat the maximum chance of survival.

Insecticides

It is vitally important to only use insecticides specifically prepared for use on cats, as those meant for other animal species are often poisonous to cats. If amounts of this are swallowed by the cat when grooming, serious poisonings can occur. If you suspect you have used the wrong product, you should immediately wash the cat in mild soap and water, and rinse and dry him thoroughly. If odd behaviour or symptoms appear after you have applied such an insecticide, contact your vet immediately.

Tar, Paraffin and Oil

If such a substance gets on to a cat's coat, it is important to remove it immediately. Detergents, such as neat washing-up liquid or gel used to clean hands, can be used carefully to remove the excess oil or tar and prevent skin and internal damage. This should then be rinsed off with water. Should the cat have the opportunity to lick the offending substance off, the lips, tongue or throat are likely to become ulcerated, and the cat will suddenly begin to salivate profusely, and make vigorous licking or mouthing movements. Depending on the chemical, widespread internal damage can also then occur. If the cat is showing signs of mouth pain or vomiting, gently rinse the mouth out with cotton wool soaked in lukewarm water and call the vet.

Lily Poisoning

All species of plant in the lily family are toxic to cats and cause acute renal failure. Cats rarely chew lily plants but the pollen from some of the larger flowers can brush off on to the cat's coat and then be taken in while grooming.

Action. Brush or wash off the pollen. Prevention is best – ensure no heavily pollinated lily flowers are in a position where the cat could brush against them.

Slug Bait (Metaldehyde)

Cats seem to find these granules tasty and occasionally will eat enough slug bait to cause central nervous system disturbances. For this reason, slug bait should not be placed where pets can reach it. In addition, if slug bait must be used, any dead snails should immediately be disposed of to prevent the death of song thrushes from eating these poisoned snails.

Signs. The cat appears initially unco-ordinated but if enough has been eaten, this may progress to unconsciousness and fits.

Action. If your cat is fitting or showing any

Slug-bait pellets should never be placed loose on soil.

nervous signs, check and remove any slug bait from the cat's mouth and call the vet as soon as possible. There is no specific treatment for metaldehyde poisoning, but if the cat has just eaten the poison, your vet may be able to make him vomit to empty the stomach. To counteract the convulsions, your vet may have to heavily sedate the cat but this condition can be fatal.

Alphachloralose (Rat and Mouse Poison)
Cats will rarely eat this but may eat a mouse or rat that has been killed by this poison. It usually causes severe depression, but can sometimes cause excitation with fits. There is no specific antidote, but it is very important to keep the cat warm and the cat may recover. Your vet may have to give supportive treatment also.

Warfarin (Rat and Mouse Poison)
This commonly used poison causes death by internal haemorrhage, as it blocks the clotting mechanism of blood. If a cat eats some of the poisoned grain, or more likely eats a poisoned rat or mouse, the same can occur causing the cat to haemorrhage.

Symptoms. Affected cats will be weak and lethargic, have pale mucous membranes and often blood in their faeces or urine.

Treatment. Warfarin contains a substance that interferes with the normal clotting of blood by blocking the activity of the body's vitamin K, which helps blood to clot. Luckily the antidote to prevent this interference is an injection of doses of vitamin K, given in conjunction with intravenous fluids, using plasma or, ideally, a whole-blood transfusion in severe cases.

Action. If you suspect your cat may have taken in warfarin, contact your vet immediately, as there is this specific antidote, vitamin K, available, which will enable the blood to clot and prevent further haemorrhage. But, importantly, all rodent poisons should always be placed carefully where cats and dogs cannot reach them, such as in narrow pipes, or call in the experts to lay the poison.

Antifreeze
Antifreeze, used in cars over winter to stop the coolant freezing, is deadly to cats (and dogs), even in small doses. Some cats like the taste of antifreeze because it is somewhat sweet. Most antifreeze contains ethylene glycol, which is toxic to cats and dogs – just one teaspoon can kill a small cat.

Signs of poisoning can occur within a few hours of ingestion and include excessive thirst and urination, unco-ordination, vomiting, rapid heart and respiratory rate followed by coma and death.

Action. If you suspect your cat has drunk some antifreeze, he should be taken to a vet for emergency treatment, as soon as possible, to try to prevent internal damage, especially to the central nervous system and kidneys. There is no specific antidote but your vet can help with emetics to make the cat vomit, and intravenous fluids to try and flush the poison through the kidneys. The important thing to remember is *never* leave an open bottle of antifreeze around the house, garage or car, and immediately clean up any spillage.

Raisins, Grapes, Sultanas
These are poisonous to cats if somehow combined into their food. Be careful to ensure these are not left lying around and available to an inquisitive cat.

Chapter 21
The Old Cat

In line with what is happening with the human population, cats are also living longer and this is due to several factors. Advances in veterinary knowledge, in both diagnosis and treatment of ailments, a more nutritious diet and a greater importance of the cat as a pet, have all led to a larger proportion of older cats in the cat population. The care of the older cat is, therefore, an important aspect of both ownership and veterinary practice. Cats are no different from people in their requirements as they become older – a good diet, company, freedom from pain, creature comforts and a secure, calm environment.

Broadly speaking one year of a cat's life is equivalent to about six of a human. This is a reasonable rule of thumb for the middle-aged cat, but a more accurate comparison would be obtained using the table below.

Cat ages in years roughly compared with humans

Cat	Human
1 year	16
3 years	30
6 years	40
9 years	50
12 years	65
15 years	75
18 years	90
20 years	95

A healthy sixteen-year-old cat with owner.

This is still only a rough guide, as the ageing process varies between individual cats and, seemingly, some breeds, such as Siamese, tend to live longer. Cats commonly live to fifteen years of age now, a proportion to twenty and a very few have even lived to their mid-thirties!

There is no need to treat a cat any differently as old age approaches, certainly up to twelve years of age, provided he is not overweight and has been well-cared for throughout his life. It is recommended that cats have health examinations as kittens and then at least once a year, usually at the time of the vaccination booster. In this way any problem can be detected and treated early. When the cat reaches ten to twelve years old, a more frequent health check is advisable. The extent of these examinations will depend on the condition of the cat, the recommendation of the vet and the requirements of the owner.

A routine physical examination of an older cat would usually take your vet five to fifteen minutes to complete. This general assessment would probably include taking his temperature, checking his eyes, ears, mouth, skin and coat, listening to his chest, palpating his abdomen, and checking his bones and joints. If no obvious abnormality is detected, or behavioural change described by the owner, it should not be necessary to take the investigation further. If, however, your vet has reason to suspect the beginnings of a problem with one of his major organs, she may suggest taking a blood sample or an X-ray, which could reveal whether his liver, kidneys, thyroid or heart, for example, are functioning normally or beginning to fail. Appropriate action can then be taken to correct or minimize the problem, to give him a better chance of living longer.

I would suggest a six-monthly health check from the age of twelve years, increasing to quarterly health checks from the age of fifteen. If your cat suffers from a particular problem, then obviously your vet will advise you on the frequency of visits. In our practice we have some healthy old cats that come to see us merely once a year, but we need to see others with, say, thyroid or kidney problems much more frequently. A routine health check, even every two months in some cases, enables us to monitor their progress and amend their treatment or diet,

resulting in both healthier patients who live longer and owners who are less worried.

As mentioned earlier, provided your older cat shows no signs of illness, the most important considerations you will have, and can help with, as old age approaches are diet, fitness and bodily condition.

DIET

If your older cat is fit and well, and of a normal body weight, your aim should be to feed a diet that will maintain the function of his major organs and slow down, or prevent, the development of disease. If he already has the beginnings of, say, kidney, liver or any other old-age problem, then a particular special diet may well prolong his active happy life. Specific diets are available that cater for the needs of the healthy older cat in terms of fewer calories, quality protein and higher fibre, all of which help to keep the older organs functioning and prevent obesity as he becomes less active. These diets are highly palatable and digestible, and are accepted by most cats, provided you change the diet gradually over, say, a week or two. If you prefer to make up your cat's own diet, your vet or one of the nurses will be able to suggest an appropriate one for your particular cat. Whatever the diet you use, it should be an appropriate one and should be fed in amounts comparable to a normal diet. Water should, of course, be available at all times but nothing else should be added to the diet.

FITNESS AND MOBILITY

If your cat has kept fit throughout his life, and is of normal weight, there is no need to try to change his habits as he becomes older. It does become more important to ensure he is in at night, and not outside getting chilled or wet. Many cats will continue to enjoy spending some time outside, especially in the warmer months, until they reach a ripe old age and positively enjoy sleeping curled up in the sun. It is important, however, to notice and, indeed, keep a look out for any changes in his behaviour as he ages.

BODILY CONDITION

As your cat's body ages, all his organs and body systems age with it, and are not as efficient as they were. This includes his heart and circulation, lungs and, as mentioned above, his loco-motor system, especially the muscles and joints. With advancing age in an otherwise healthy cat these systems will be able to support and transport a cat of the correct weight but may fail if the cat is grossly overweight. Heart disease is not common in cats but hearts can fail, and joints can be badly stressed under the increased weight, thus crippling the cat. Arthritic changes are much more painful and significant in the overweight cat. Surveys show that some 60 per cent of our feline patients are overweight and it is not uncommon for us to be presented with a cat whose weight may be over 7kg (15lb) despite an adult cat average of 4–5kg (9–11lb) – a 75 per cent increase or even more. To put this in perspective, with the same percentage increase in weight, a human whose normal weight should be, say, ten stone (64kg) would weigh seventeen and a half stone (112kg) and be grossly overweight. It is the percentage difference that matters, not the apparently small (to us) difference in weight!

Obviously, a cat of normal weight will approach old age with a greater likelihood of reaching it. It follows, therefore, that you should diet your cat as he approaches old age, if you have let his weight gradually increase throughout his life. A strict diet to lose weight may not be forever, but once the weight loss has been achieved, the food intake should not return to the old regime but may possibly be increased almost to the previous level. The aim of such a diet is to reduce the calorie intake to about 60 per cent of normal, which will mean that the cat will have to convert his body fat to provide the energy he needs to live. A high-fibre diet should be fed so that the cat's appetite is satisfied and he does not feel hungry, but maintenance levels of essential nutrients, such as protein, vitamins and minerals, must be provided so that deficiencies do not occur. As mentioned earlier, your veterinary practice will be able to provide details of such diets available or of a suitable homemade dietary regime.

An overweight old cat.

SPECIFIC PROBLEMS OF OLD AGE

Arthritis

Older cats, like dogs and humans, do get arthritis, so if you notice he is limping, has difficulty in walking, climbing upstairs or jumping on to the chair or work top, he should be examined by the vet. Medications exist to help cats with arthritis. Along with medication, consider a ramp or steps, if he has a favourite safe refuge in the house.

Deafness

Hearing does become less acute in old age but, in general, deafness is not a common problem in the older cat. If you suspect he is hearing less well, he should be taken to the vet for a physical examination to ensure that his ears are not blocked by wax or polyps, or to check if there is a disease process occurring in any part of the ear. If none of these are present, the problem is likely to be senile deafness, for which nothing can be done. However, he may be able to hear sounds at the lower (bass) end of the scale better, so male voices or clapping may help. However, his other senses will develop, so he will adapt by greater use of these, such as touch, sight, feeling vibrations of people moving, smell and so on.

One early sign of deafness may be increased volume of his calling or meowing as he is less able to hear it. This can also be a sign of early dementia, so it's important that the vet examines him.

Blindness

For fuller information on blindness see Chapter 12. However it is worth mentioning Retinal detachment again here as it is a common cause of blindness in older cats where it often follows hypertension (raised blood pressure) due to kidney, heart or thyroid problems. It is very important for older cats, even though they may appear normal, to have their blood pressure measured by the veterinary practice, usually one of the veterinary nurses, from time to time.

Kidney Failure

This is a very common problem in the older cat and it can and does cause death. However, it can be managed to some degree if caught in the early stages, using various medications and a specific kidney diet. This condition is covered more fully in Chapter 15.

Hyperthyroidism

The thyroid glands can become over-active, especially in age, due to a tumour forming in them. Affected cats lose weight but still eat, their fur becomes poor and it is all too easy to put this down to old age. A blood test will easily diagnose this problem and treatment is available that controls the condition and returns the cat to normal appearance and function, sometimes for years. This condition is covered more fully in Chapter 18, The Endocrine System.

Tumours

Tumours can occur at any age but are more common in the older cat. Some, especially the benign (non-cancerous) ones, are operable but cancerous ones are rarely responsive to any form of treatment, and when they occur in an old cat that has had a long happy life, it may be kinder to put him to sleep.

EUTHANASIA

This is the medical term for the gentler expression of 'putting to sleep'. Most pet animals, including cats, do not die naturally – they are 'put to sleep' by the vet, hopefully in old age to save them from suffering unnecessary pain or discomfort. This is certainly an advantage that vets and their patients have over the medical profession, as animals that are terminally ill, incurably in pain or have lost essential body functions and have no happy active life to look forward to at all, can have their life painlessly and gently ended with dignity.

It is never easy to think about this final kind act for an old cat in advance but in my experience, despite owners being convinced they will not know when it is time, they actually do. Because your cat is such an important member of the family, when it comes to it, and he is so obviously not able to be a normal cat or enjoy life any more, despite the sadness of the impending loss, the mental or physical discomfort he is in makes you want to end this for him, so that he has a dignified end to a life that you have been privileged to share with him.

When the time comes, the reasons for choosing euthanasia are fairly clearcut and it is very important for you, the cat's owner, to understand that your vet can only euthanase your cat *with your consent*. You should never be afraid to take your cat to see your vet because you are worried that she may recommend euthanasia – we only ever carry this out when it is in the cat's interest. No vet likes to lose a patient and where treatment is available it will be given if you so wish, so for this reason you should not delay in contacting the surgery if you are at all worried, especially as old age comes on. Equally, however, if your vet feels that it may not yet be time to put the cat to sleep and recommends treatment instead, you can override this and request euthanasia. This situation does arise occasionally, and your vet has only two choices: either euthanase the cat as requested or politely refuse and refer you and your cat away to another vet. We cannot, without your consent, take the cat in and find it a new home instead of putting him to sleep. With such consent though, many vets can and do attempt to re-home, especially young cats, from time to time when this situation arises.

Although euthanasia is almost always performed for the benefit of the cat, it occasionally has to be carried out for the benefit of the owners.

Benefit of the Cat

To assess the situation and decide whether euthanasia is necessary or not, your vet will consider the basic needs of a cat and whether they are being fulfilled. She will ascertain whether the cat has:

- freedom from pain, distress and discomfort that cannot be controlled;
- ability to walk and balance fairly well;
- ability to eat and drink without vomiting;
- freedom from inoperable tumours that are painful;
- ability to breathe without difficulty or distress;
- ability to urinate and defecate without difficulty or incontinence;
- an owner who is able to cope physically and mentally with any nursing that may be needed.

If *any* of these basic needs are missing and *treatment is not possible*, then the cat may no longer be able to live a normal happy life and euthanasia should be gently carried out.

Benefit of the Owner

This category would include cats that are a real problem to the family and euthanasia is the only feasible answer. For example, we are presented from time to time with cats that urinate or defecate all over the house despite prolonged and serious attempts by owners or behaviourists to train them out of this habit. This causes both an aesthetic and hygiene problem and in most homes is impossible to live with. It would be wrong to re-home these cats and give another family the same problem – countryside homes, where such a cat could live its life outdoors, are few and far between! And of course cats may have to be put to sleep by charities just because there are too many cats for too few good homes

– the real answer to this is to prevent birth in the first place by neutering.

The Procedure

In the vast majority of cases, cats are not troubled by this kind and gentle procedure, in which a smooth, peaceful transition takes place from consciousness to unconsciousness over a few seconds following the injection into a vein of an anaesthetic overdose. This is the method employed by most veterinary surgeons with only a few exceptions, which will be mentioned later.

Whether you wish to be present or not is a decision for you, the individual owner. Some owners feel they must be there with their pet, while others cannot entertain the idea. In general, unless your vet advises otherwise, I would recommend that you stay with your cat for the procedure, rather than just leave him with the vet. The advantages are that your cat is usually happier and calmer with you there, you feel happier being there for him right at the end, and also you know exactly what happened and how peaceful it was.

The cat is gently held in a lying or sitting position by you or a veterinary nurse, who gently lifts one of his forelegs at the elbow. This paw is then held by the vet, while carefully clipping some hair away over the main vein, the cephalic vein, into which the injection will be given. This is the same situation as when taking a blood sample, for instance, and is very similar to that procedure in humans. The vet then usually applies surgical spirit to the skin to make the vein easier to locate, while the nurse applies gentle pressure across the elbow to hold up the blood flow and enlarge the vein enabling the vet to inject into it. This is called 'raising the vein'. The cat is normally completely at ease in this position, but if this in any way upsets the cat or is made difficult by the cat for the vet, a sedative may be given first.

The vet inserts the fine needle painlessly into the vein and injects an overdose of an anaesthetic solution prepared specially for this purpose. In most cases, the cat is completely unaware of the injection and the speed of action is so rapid that unconsciousness ensues within five to ten

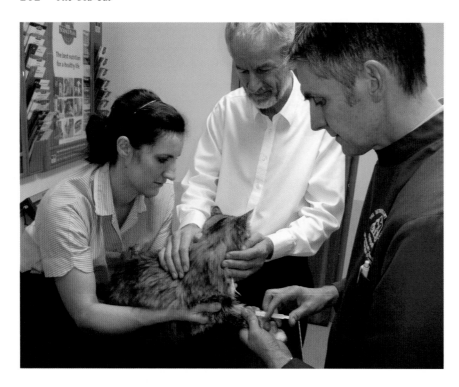

Euthanasia – a peaceful caring solution when the time comes.

seconds. The cat gently, but quickly, falls asleep on the table. Within two minutes or so, breathing ceases and shortly after this the heart stops. The transition is smooth and peaceful and there can be no kinder way of ending life.

As the heart stops and the cat passes away, quite often there is an odd shiver or twitch of a muscle or two, sometimes even the chest muscles, with the cat seeming to take a breath. This is referred to as the 'last gasp'. These are all nervous reflexes and can be a little disconcerting but cannot be avoided. The important thing to realize, however, is that the cat is totally unaware of this and at peace.

At Home or in the Surgery?

In my opinion, an owner has the right to decide where euthanasia should take place. It is the last thing we will do for the patient and it should be carried out where it will cause the least distress to him. If the cat is sat on the surgery table when the decision is reached, obviously it is not sensible to subject him to a further car journey or the owner to prolonged distress, if immediate euthanasia is necessary. If, however, the need is not immediate, when the time comes the owner

should not have to transport an infirm old cat to the surgery, if it would distress him. It should, however, be borne in mind that it may be easier for all concerned and, therefore, better for the cat, if this is carried out in the surgery where expert help is readily available, although of course a nurse can accompany the vet to the house, if necessary.

Disposal of the Body

Cremation and burial facilities can invariably be arranged through your vet or, of course, you are at liberty to bury this important member of your family in your own garden. The important thing to remember is to bury him with at least two feet of soil over him and preferably in a cardboard or wooden box. In many cases, you will probably not have had time to think about this next step and your vet should be able to hold on to his body for up to, say, twenty-four hours, while you take the time to discuss this with your family.

Afterwards

I would suggest that there are a few things that you should and should not do. You've lost an old friend, a member of your family, so:

- Do allow yourself to grieve. It is completely normal and natural, and you will feel all the better after it. Do expect this feeling to last for quite a while.
- Don't reproach yourself for having taken his life – if the decision was a carefully considered one on the vet's recommendation or with his agreement, you have made the correct choice.
- Don't blame yourself for having your cat put to sleep – there was no other choice except to let the cat suffer. Death is rarely something that could have been avoided by more attention from the owner.

- Don't blame the vet for being unable to cure the cat of an incurable complaint!
- Don't think it would be unfair on the old cat to contemplate taking on another cat when the time comes. It certainly wouldn't – unless you are going to compare him with the new one. Cats live on average twelve to sixteen years, we live seventy to ninety years, so it is obvious we all may have many more than one cat during our lifetime. None ever replace the one we lost, but they all have their own unique loveable character.

Useful Addresses

FAB
Feline Advisory Bureau,
Taeselbury,
High Street,
Tisbury,
Wiltshire SP3 6LD
www.fabcats.org

GCCF
Governing Council of the Cat Fancy,
5 King's Castle Business Park,
The Drove,
Bridgwater,
Somerset TA6 4AG
www.gccfcats.org

RCVS
Royal College of Veterinary Surgeons,
Belgravia House,
62–64 Horseferry Road,
London SW1P 2AF
www.rcvs.org.uk

BSAVA
British Small Animal Veterinary Association,
Woodrow House,
1 Telford Way,
Waterwells Business Park,
Quedgeley,
Gloucestershire GL2 2AB
www.bsava.com

BVA
British Veterinary Association,
7 Mansfield Street,
London W1G 9NQ
www.bva.co.uk

Association of Pet Behaviour Counsellors
www.apbc.org.uk

National Cat Club
www.nationalcatclub.co.uk

Pet Health Council
www.pethealthcouncil.co.uk

OTHER COUNTRIES

USA
VET ASSOC
American Veterinary Medical Association -
1931 North Meacham Road
Suite 100
Schaumburg
IL 60173-4360
USA
www.avma.org

Canada
VET ASSOC
Canadian Veterinary Medical Association -
339 Booth Street
Ottawa
Ontario
K1R 7K1
Canada
www.canadianveterinarians.net

South Africa
VET ASSOC
South African Veterinary Association -
P O Box 24033
Monument Park
Pretoria 0105
South Africa
www.sava.co.za

Australia
VET ASSOC
Australian Veterinary Association –
Unit 40
2A Herbert Street
St Leonards NSW 2065
Australia
www.ava.com.au

New Zealand
VET ASSOC
New Zealand Veterinary Association -
P O Box 11-212
Wellington
New Zealand
www.vets.org.nz

Glossary

Acne A skin disease, usually on the chin, caused when the hair follicles become clogged with black sebaceous material, forming comedones (blackheads).

Acute A disease of short duration; relatively severe.

Allergens An allergy-producing substance such as pollens, dust mite, and so on.

Allergy An exaggerated reaction by the immune system in response to contact with certain foreign substances.

Alopecia Hair loss.

Anabolic Applied to a substance that builds up tissue.

Anaemia A deficiency of haemoglobin, which carries oxygen inside red blood cells round the body. Anaemia can also be caused by a lack of iron in the body.

Analgesia Pain relief.

Anorexia Not eating.

Anthelmintic A medicine to kill internal worm parasites.

Antibiotic A chemotherapeutic agent with activity against microorganisms such as bacteria, and sometimes fungi and protozoa.

Antibody A protein formed within the body that neutralizes pathogens such as bacteria and viruses.

Antidote A remedy to counteract the effects of poison.

Anti-emetic A medicine which counteracts vomiting.

Antigen A substance that stimulates the production of an antibody.

Anuria Failure to produce urine.

Arthritis Inflammation of a joint.

Asthma An allergic respiratory disease.

Ataxia Inco-ordination.

Atopy An inhaled allergy, usually causing itchy skin.

Atrophy Partial or complete wasting away of a muscle or other part of the body.

Aural Of the ear.

Auriscope An instrument for examining the ear.

Aversive stimulus One that an animal will move away from.

Bacteria Single celled microorganisms. Pathogenic bacteria cause infections and are a major cause of disease

Bilateral On both sides.

Biopsy A small sample of tissue taken for diagnosis.

Breech A birthing difficulty where the kitten is coming out backwards, hips not legs first.

Calculus Either dental tartar or a urinary stone.

Calling A cat in oestrus and ready to mate is said to be calling.

Cancer A disease in which the cells show uncontrolled growth, invasion of adjacent tissues and, sometimes, metastasis via lymph or blood.

Cardiomyopathy Disease of the heart muscle.

Cartilage Connective tissue found in joints and elsewhere in the body.

Castration The neutering of the male by removing the testes.

Catabolic Applied to a substance that breaks down tissue.

Chemotherapy Treatment with drugs that kill cancer cells or make them less active.

Chronic A problem of longer duration, often persistent.

Chyle A milky fluid (*see* Lymph).

Cleft palate Where the centre of the upper roof of the mouth fails to join completely during development.

Coitus The act of mating.

Colitis Inflammation of the large bowel.

Colostrum The first milk produced after birth rich in antibodies.

Coma A deep state of unconsciousness from which a cat cannot be awakened.

Congenital A characteristic or problem acquired during development in the uterus and not through heredity.

Contrast medium A substance, such as barium or air, used in radiography to increase the contrast of an image.

Corticosteroid A steroid hormone produced in the adrenal gland.

Cryosurgery The application of extreme cold to destroy abnormal or diseased tissue.

Cryptorchidism Having only one or no testis descended into the scrotum.

CT (Computer Tomography) scan Imaging that combines special X-ray equipment with sophisticated computers to produce multiple images of the inside of the body.

Cyanotic Blue-coloured mucous membranes due to lack of oxygen in the blood.

Cystitis Inflammation of the bladder.

Defecation The elimination of faeces.

Dew claw The fifth claw, usually only found on the front feet of cats, which is equivalent to our thumb.

Diabetes insipidus A disease of the pituitary gland in the brain causing excess thirst.

Diabetes mellitus Sugar diabetes usually due to lack of insulin production in the pancreas.

Diaphragm The large thin muscle separating the chest and abdomen.

Dilate To widen or expand.

Diuretic A substance that increases the rate of urination and thus the fluid output from the body.

Domestic longhair A non-pedigree cat with long hair.

Domestic shorthair A non-pedigree cat with short hair.

Dysfunction Abnormal functioning.

Dyspnoea Difficulty in breathing.

Dystocia An abnormal or difficult birth – either due to the foetus or queen.

ECG An electrocardiogram measures the electrical impulses produced by the heart, which cause it to beat.

Eclampsia Calcium deficiency in a lactating queen causing seizures.

Ectoparasite A parasite of the outside of the body.

Embolus An object that moves from one part of the body in the blood causing a blockage of a blood vessel in another part of the body (embolism).

Emetic A medicine which causes vomiting.

Endocrine The secretion of a substance (a hormone) into the bloodstream.

Endoparasite An internal parasite.

Enteritis Inflammation of the intestines.

Epistaxis A nose bleed.

Euthanasia Gentle mercy killing to save an animal suffering.

Exocrine The secretion of a substance (often an enzyme) out through a duct.

Faeces The solid waste produced by the body.

Feline odontoclastic resorptive lesion (or FORL) A seemingly cat-specific disease, where the tooth enamel has been lost exposing the dentine.

FeLV Feline leukaemia virus.

Feral A domesticated cat living wild.

FIP Feline infectious peritonitis.

FIV Feline immunodeficiency virus.

Fracture A break in a bone.

Gangrene Death of tissue.

Gastritis Inflammation of the stomach.

Gestation The length of pregnancy – in cats usually about sixty-three days.

Gingivitis Inflammation of the gums.

Glaucoma An eye disease in which the normal fluid pressure inside the eyes slowly rises damaging the retina and therefore sight.

Glossitis Inflammation of the tongue.

Granuloma A type of inflammatory reaction resulting in a nodule of immune cells trying to destroy a foreign substance.

Haematoma A collection of blood outside the blood vessels, a blood blister.

Haemoglobin The iron-containing protein attached to red blood cells, which transports oxygen around the body.

Haemorrhage Bleeding, loss of blood.

Haemothorax Haemorrhage into the lung or chest filling the air spaces.

Hairball A mass of intertwined hair in the stomach or intestines swallowed usually during excessive grooming.

Hare lip Where the centre of the upper lip fails to join completely during development.

Hereditary A characteristic genetically transferred from parent to offspring.

Hormone A chemical substance produced in the body that controls and regulates the activity of certain cells or organs.

Hyper More than normal.

Hypertension High blood pressure.

Hypo Less than normal.

Idiopathic A disease arising spontaneously, or of unknown cause.

Imaging X-rays, ultrasound and other scanning and their interpretation.

Immune-mediated disease A condition resulting from abnormal activity of the immune system.

Incontinence The unconscious and uncontrolled leakage of urine from the urethra.

Incubation period The time between exposure to the disease and the onset of signs.

Insecticide A substance used to kill insects.

Intermediate host An animal that harbours a parasite for a short transition period, during which some developmental stage is completed before that host is eaten (usually) by the target species (*see* e.g. Tapeworms).

Intravenous fluid therapy The giving of liquid substances into a vein, usually slowly. Often called a drip.

Jaundice A yellowish discoloration of the skin, and mucous membranes caused by a bile salt in the blood.

Kilogram One thousand grams (2.2 pounds).

Lachrymal Of tears.

Larva A juvenile form of some species, such as an insect or parasitic worm.

Leucopaenia A lower than normal number of white blood cells in the blood.

Leukaemia An abnormal overproduction of white blood cells (leukocytes).

Lymph Lymph is a clear or white fluid made up of fluid from the intestines called chyle, which contains proteins and fats, and red and white blood cells. It circulates between the lymph nodes and eventually back into the bloodstream.

Marking Urine spraying deliberately to mark the cat's smell.

Metabolism The set of chemical reactions that occur in the body in order to maintain life.

Metastasis The process by which a cancer spreads to other parts of the body.

Microchip Small sensor injected under the skin to identify your cat.

Mite Tiny eight-legged parasitic member of the spider family.

Moggie A domestic mixed breed cat.

MRI Magnetic resonance imaging is a medical imaging technique used to visualize the structure and function of parts of the body.

Mucous membrane The lining of all body passages that communicate with the air, such as the respiratory and alimentary tracts.

Myelin Fatty substance forming the outer sheath around many nerve cells.

Myelography An X-ray of the spine and spinal cord using contrast medium.

Nasal Of the nose.

Nematode A roundworm.

Neonatal Newborn.

Neurone A nerve cell.

Nictitating membrane The third eyelid.

Nystagmus An involuntary side to side flicking movement of the eyes.

Obese A cat that is 25–30 per cent or more overweight. As a guide a normal average sized male cat may weigh about 4–5.5kg and a female about 3.5–4.5kg.

Obligate carnivore An animal such as a cat which requires animal protein to exist.

Ocular Of the eye.

Oedema Also known as dropsy, this is the abnormal accumulation of fluid under the skin, or in one of the body cavities.

Oestrogen Female sex hormone that stimulates oestrus.

Oestrus The period during the female's reproductive cycle when mating occurs.

Ophthalmic Of the eye.

Ophthalmoscope An instrument for examining the eye.

Oral Of the mouth.

Overshot A cat whose upper jaw is longer than the lower jaw.

Parasite An organism living on or in another (host) animal which is harmed to some degree.

Parasiticide A substance used to kill parasites.

Parturition Birth.

Pathogen A biological agent that causes disease or illness.

Pedigree cat A purebred cat whose ancestors are known and documented.

Periodontal disease A disease of the tissues that support the teeth.

Pharynx The throat, i.e. the area at the back of the mouth and nose and immediately before the larynx.

Pheromone A chemical that triggers a natural behavioural response in another member of the same species.

Pinna The ear flap.

Plasma The fluid part of the blood carrying the normal blood cells.

Pleura The membrane lining the inside of the chest.

Pneumothorax Leakage of air into the chest when a lung has been ruptured.

Polydactyl A cat with more than the usual number of claws.

Polydipsia Excessive thirst.

Polyoestrous Having several oestrus periods per year.

Polyp An abnormal growth of tissue from a mucous membrane.

Polyphagia Excessive appetite.

Polyuria Producing a more than normal amount of urine.

PRA Progressive retinal atrophy of the eye.

Prescription A form written by a vet to enable you to buy restricted medicines at a chemist; or can be used to mean the medicine itself.

Progesterone Female hormone which prepares the uterus for pregnancy.

Prognosis The expected course of a disease.

Pruritus Itchiness.

Puberty The age of sexual maturity.

Pupa The life stage of some insects undergoing metamorphosis (transformation).

Purulent Containing pus.

Pus Thick opaque usually yellowish-white fluid matter produced during pyogenic bacterial infections.

Pyogenic A bacterial infection which makes pus.

Pyometra A disease of the uterus which fills with pus.

Queen A breeding female cat.

Quick The sensitive nail-bed area of the claw.

Radiography The taking of X-rays.

Radiology The interpretation of X-rays.

Radiotherapy Treatment with 'radiation', usually X-rays, to treat illness, usually cancer.

Rhinitis Inflammation of the internal areas of the nose.

Ringworm A common skin complaint of the cat caused by a fungus.

Roundworm An internal parasite of the cat living in the intestine.

RTA Road traffic accident.

Saline A salt (sodium chloride) solution.

Sclera The white outer covering of the eyeball.

Semen Fluid from the prostate and seminal vesicle containing the sperm.

Serum The clear liquid that is left after blood has clotted.

Shock A life-threatening condition which ensues when the body is not getting enough blood flow.

Sign A characteristic of disease which is observed in the patient (*see* Symptom).

Socialization Providing the skills and habits necessary for acting and participating within normal family life.

Spay The neutering operation of the female, correct name ovariohysterectomy.

Stomatitis Inflammation of the mouth.

Strabismus A squint in an eye or eyes (cross-eyed).

Stud tail Excessive oil production by the dorsal tail gland of the cat.

Subcutaneous Under the skin.

Suture A surgical stitch.

Symptom Strictly speaking a change noticed and reported by the patient. Thus in veterinary medicine, the word sign is more correct as noticed and reported by the owner (*see* Sign). Both words are used in this book.

Taurine An amino acid essential for cats, found in meat and meat products; required for proper development and functioning of the retina and heart.

Testosterone Male hormone produced in the testes.

Therapeutic Having a healing effect.

Therapy Treatment.

Thrombus Is a clot that forms and causes a blockage within a blood vessel and is not carried from somewhere else (*see* Embolus).

Toileting Passing urine or faeces.

Tom An entire male cat.

Transport host An animal which harbours the parasite until the main host is reached but is not necessary for the parasite's life cycle to be completed.

Trauma Damage.

Tumour A swelling or lump formed by an abnormal growth of cells. Can be benign (no potential to spread) or malignant (ability to spread – cancer).

Ultrasound scan A painless test that uses sound waves to create images of organs and structures inside the body.

Undershot A cat whose lower jaw is longer than the upper jaw.

Unilateral On one side.

Uraemia The accumulation of nitrogenous waste products (urea) in the blood that are usually excreted in the urine.

Urea The organic chemical compound produced when the body metabolizes protein, and eliminated in the urine.

Urine The liquid waste product of the body filtered and secreted by the kidneys.

Vaccine A mild or killed form of a pathogen given to stimulate immunity against that disease.

Vasectomy The operation on a male to prevent fertilization but not mating.

Vector A carrier of disease from one animal to another, not being affected itself.

Vestibular Of the balance mechanism of the body.

Veterinary Health Advisors Veterinary nurses specifically trained in pet health, diets, weight, and general health information.

Veterinary Nurse A qualification recognized by the Royal College of Veterinary Surgeons.

Virus A sub-microscopic infectious agent that cannot grow or reproduce outside a body cell.

Vulva Entrance to the vagina.

Zoonosis Any disease transmissible between animals and man.

Index